Blood Will Out

Journal of the Royal Anthropological Institute Special Issue Book Series

The Journal of the Royal Anthropological Institute is the principal journal of the oldest anthropological organization in the world. It has attracted and inspired some of the world's greatest thinkers. International in scope, it presents accessible papers aimed at a broad anthropological readership. We are delighted to announce that their annual special issues are also repackaged and available to buy as books.

Volumes published so far:

Blood Will Out: Essays on Liquid Transfers and Flows, edited by Janet Carsten
Making Knowledge: Explorations of the Indissoluble Relation between Mind, Body and Environment, edited by Trevor H.J. Marchand
Islam, Politics, Anthropology, edited by Filippo Osella and Benjamin Soares
The Objects of Evidence: Anthropological Approaches to the Production of Knowledge, edited by Matthew Engelke
Wind, Life, Health: Anthropological and Historical Perspectives, edited by Elisabeth Hsu and Chris Low
Ethnobiology and the Science of Humankind, edited by Roy Ellen

BLOOD WILL OUT

ESSAYS ON LIQUID TRANSFERS AND FLOWS

EDITED BY JANET CARSTEN

Royal Anthropological
Institute

This edition first published 2013
Originally published as Volume 19, Special Issue May 2013 of *The Journal of the Royal Anthropological Society*
© 2013 Royal Anthropological Institute of Great Britain & Ireland

Registered Office
John Wiley & Sons Ltd, The Atrium, Southern Gate, Chichester, West Sussex, PO19 8SQ, United Kingdom

Editorial Offices
350 Main Street, Malden, MA 02148-5020, USA
9600 Garsington Road, Oxford, OX4 2DQ, UK
The Atrium, Southern Gate, Chichester, West Sussex, PO19 8SQ, UK

For details of our global editorial offices, for customer services, and for information about how to apply for permission to reuse the copyright material in this book please see our website at www.wiley.com/wiley-blackwell.

Library of Congress Cataloging-in-Publication Data

Blood will out : essays on liquid transfers and flows / edited by Janet Carsten.
      pages cm
   "Originally published as volume 19, special Issue May 2013 of The Journal of the Royal Anthropological Institute"–
   Includes bibliographical references and index.
   ISBN 978-1-118-65628-0 (pbk.)
   1. Blood–Symbolic aspects. 2. Blood–Social aspects. 3. Blood–History. I. Carsten, Janet, editor of compilation. II. Journal of the Royal Anthropological Institute. Special issue.
   GT498.B55B578 2013
   306.4–dc23

                         2013020970

A catalogue record for this book is available from the British Library.

Cover image: Cover image: Outside exhibition of portraits painted in blood of Indian martyrs for Independence, held in Delhi in 2009 (photo Jacob Copeman).
Cover design by Richard Boxall Design Associates.

Set in 10 on 12pt Minion by Toppan Best-set Premedia Limited
Printed in Singapore by Ho Printing Singapore Pte Ltd

1   2013

Contents

Notes on contributors

Bettina Bildhauer is a Reader in German at the University of St Andrews. She is the author of *Medieval blood* (University of Wales Press, 2006) and *Filming the Middle Ages* (Reaktion, 2011), and co-editor (with Robert Mills) of *The monstrous Middle Ages* (University of Wales Press, 2004) and (with Anke Bernau) *Medieval film* (Manchester University Press, 2009), as well as the author of several shorter pieces on medieval blood. *Department of German, University of St Andrews, St Andrews, Fife, UK.*

Fenella Cannell is Reader in Social Anthropology at the London School of Economics and Political Science. Her books include *Power and intimacy in the Christian Philippines* (Cambridge University Press, 1999) and *The Christianity of anthropology* (Duke University Press, 2006). Her current research is with American Latter-day Saints. *Department of Anthropology, London School of Economics, London, UK.*

Janet Carsten is Professor of Social and Cultural Anthropology at the University of Edinburgh. She is the author of *The heat of the hearth: kinship and community in a Malay fishing village* (Clarendon Press, 1997) and *After kinship* (Cambridge University Press, 2004); and editor of *Cultures of relatedness: new approaches to the study of kinship* (Cambridge University Press, 2000) and *Ghosts of memory: essays on remembrance and relatedness* (Blackwell, 2007). *Social Anthropology, School of Social and Political Science, University of Edinburgh, Edinburgh, UK.*

Jacob Copeman is a Lecturer in Social Anthropology at Edinburgh University. His publications include *Veins of devotion: blood donation and religious experience in North India* (Rutgers University Press, 2009/Routledge, 2012), *Blood donation, bioeconomy, culture* (ed., Sage, 2009) and *The guru in South Asia: new interdisciplinary perspectives* (co-ed. with Aya Ikegame, Routledge, 2012). *Social Anthropology, School of Social and Political Science, University of Edinburgh, Edinburgh, UK.*

Susan E. Lederer is the Robert Turell Professor of the History of Medicine and Bioethics at the University of Wisconsin School of Medicine and Public Health. Her books include *Flesh and blood: organ transplantation and blood transfusion in twentieth-century America* (Oxford University Press, 2008) and *Subjected to science: human experimentation in America before the Second World War* (Johns Hopkins University Press, 1995). *University of Wisconsin, School of Medicine and Public Health, Madison, WI, USA.*

Emily Martin is Professor of Anthropology at New York University. She is the author of *The woman in the body: a cultural analysis of reproduction* (Beacon Press, 1982 [1987]), *Flexible bodies: tracking immunity in American culture from the days of polio to the age of AIDS* (Beacon Press, 1994), and *Bipolar expeditions: mania and depression in American culture* (Princeton University Press, 2007). Her current work is on the history and ethnography of experimental psychology. *Department of Anthropology, New York University, New York, NY, USA.*

Maya Mayblin gained her Ph.D. in 2005 from the London School of Economics and Political Science. She is the author of *Gender, Catholicism, and morality in Brazil: virtuous husbands, powerful wives* (Palgrave Macmillan, 2010), and held a British Academy Post-Doctoral Fellowship at the University of Edinburgh, where she is Lecturer in Social Anthropology. *Social Anthropology, School of Social and Political Science, University of Edinburgh, Edinburgh, UK.*

Kath Weston is Professor of Anthropology and Women, Gender, and Sexuality at the University of Virginia. Her publications include *Families we choose* (Second edition, Columbia University Press, 1997), *Gender in real time* (Routledge, 2002), *Traveling light: on the road with America's poor* (Beacon Press, 2008), and 'Biosecuritization: the quest for synthetic blood and the taming of kinship' (in *Blood and kinship: matter for metaphor from ancient Rome to the present* (eds) C.H. Johnson, B. Jussen, D.W. Sabean & S. Teuscher, Berghahn, 2013). *Department of Anthropology, University of Virginia, Charlottesville, VA, USA.*

Nicholas Whitfield completed his Ph.D. in the Department of History and Philosophy of Science at the University of Cambridge. He is currently a Postdoctoral Fellow in the Department of Social Studies of Medicine, McGill University. *Department of Social Studies of Medicine, McGill University, Montreal QC, Canada.*

Acknowledgements

The workshop for which this book was first written was held at the University of Edinburgh in May 2010, and funded by the Leverhulme Trust as part of a Leverhulme Major Research Fellowship. I am grateful to all the contributors for their many inspirations and comments, to the Leverhulme Trust for making this work possible, and to Jonathan Spencer for his support, his comments, and for suggesting the title. I also thank Richard Fardon and the anonymous readers for *JRAI* for their very helpful comments on an earlier draft of the introduction. Julie Hartley provided initial help collecting materials; I am grateful to her, and to Joanna Wiseman and Evangelos Chrysagis for their editorial assistance.

Introduction: blood will out

JANET CARSTEN *University of Edinburgh*

Newspaper reports from Bangkok in March 2010 described a novel form of political demonstration. Thousands of demonstrators gathered to empty plastic containers of donated blood, collected from volunteers, on the fences and gateways to government headquarters. In a rite that seemed to combine elements of sacrifice and curse, and was also clearly a transformation of forms of civic participation in blood donation campaigns, the pouring away of blood became a vividly expressive act of political opposition to the perceived illegitimacy of the current regime (Associated Press 2010; see also Hugh-Jones 2011; Weston, this volume).

A little more than a year later, in April 2011, from a quite other part of the world, it was reported that, as prelude to Pope John Paul II's beatification, a phial of his blood would be displayed as an object of veneration by the Vatican: 'The Vatican said the blood, which had been stored in a Rome hospital, had been kept in a liquid state by an anti-coagulant that was added when it was taken from him' (Hooper 2011).

The entanglement of the medical and religious encapsulated by the papal phial was further underlined by the description of how this blood had been obtained, and its potential future destinations:

> The Vatican said doctors had taken a quantity of blood from the pontiff while he lay dying, which had been sent in four containers to the blood transfusion centre at the Bambino Gesu hospital in Rome. Two 'remained at the disposal' of his private secretary, Stanislaw Dziwisz, who was later made a cardinal and the archbishop of Krakow (Hooper 2011).

What is blood? This volume begins from the premise that the meanings attributed to blood are neither self-evident nor stable across (or even within) different cultural and historical locations. The many meanings of blood that are captured in the essays that follow vividly attest to its polyvalent qualities and its unusual capacity for accruing layers of symbolic resonance. Whether literally present in spaces of blood donation, as in the twentieth-century London or US contexts discussed here by Nicholas Whitfield and by Susan Lederer, respectively, or indicated through elaborated metaphor, as in

Blood: Will Out: Essays on Liquid Transfers and Flows, First Edition. Edited by Janet Carsten. © 2013 Royal Anthropological Institute of Great Britain & Ireland. Published 2013 by John Wiley & Sons Ltd.

Kath Weston's discussion of the deployment of sanguinary metaphors in depictions of the economy, blood has the capacity to flow in many directions. Analysing the meanings of blood in particular contexts illuminates its special qualities as bodily substance, material, and metaphor. But, taken together, these essays also attempt to answer another kind of question: can we have a theory of blood, and what would such a theory look like? If blood, like money, seems to be more or less ubiquitous, it departs from money in lacking a well-worked seam of sociological or anthropological theory with which it is associated. This initial puzzle suggests that, in assembling a volume on blood, we need to attend both to implicit theories of blood and to the several dispersed fields where they might be located.

The significance of blood, as the two opening vignettes make clear, is not limited to any of anthropology's classic domains: politics, religion, kinship, or even to their more recent offshoots, such as the body or medical anthropology. Rather, the interest in blood lies in its propensity to travel within, between, and beyond all of these. Its scope, in other words, requires a broad view, and returns us to the insights of foundational work on symbolism, such as that of Claude Lévi-Strauss (1969a [1962]) or Victor Turner (1967). While the former drew attention to the fact that 'some objects are good to think', the latter attended closely to the links between material properties and their emotional resonance in specific contexts. In demonstrating blood's recurring but divergent significance across cultural and historical contexts, the essays collected here articulate another theme familiar from classic studies of symbolism: a tension between the 'arbitrary' nature of the sign (Saussure 1960 [1916]) and the particular power of 'natural symbols' (Douglas 2003 [1970]).[1]

But what kind of thing is blood? Is it an unusual bodily material, a sub-category of corporeal substance, or is it part of some larger category whose significance is not constrained by bodily features? Is it part of the person and relationships, or an object that can be commodified (Baud 2011)? Or does its uniqueness stem, as Stephen Hugh-Jones (2011) argues, from the many spheres in which it participates, and the corollary that it is irreducible to the category either of commodity or of personhood? The connections between the essays collected here suggest that the meanings of blood are paradoxically both under- and over-determined. Seemingly open to endless symbolic elaboration, its significance appears from one perspective to be curiously open; but from another point of view, it is this very excess of potentiality that is overdetermined. Not only does blood have a remarkable range of meanings and associations in English (Carsten 2011), but many of these readily encompass their antinomies (Bynum 2007: 187). The essays in this volume demonstrate that blood may be associated with fungibility, or transformability, as well as essence; with truth and transcendence and also with lies and corruption; with contagion and violence but also with purity and harmony; and with vitality as well as death.

The contexts presented here are indeed wide-ranging: depictions of blood in German medieval religious and medical texts (Bildhauer); politically inspired portraiture executed literally in blood in contemporary India (Copeman); Mormon conceptions of blood in the United States (Cannell); transformations in ideas about blood donation in twentieth-century Britain and the United States (Whitfield; Lederer); practices concerned with the flow and fungibility of blood, food, and water in the body among peasants in Northeast Brazil (Mayblin); working practices in clinical pathology labs and blood banks in Malaysia (Carsten); the interpenetration of blood and finance in descriptions of trade and capitalism in the global economy (Weston); and up-to-date brain imaging for medical purposes in the United States in which blood seems strangely absent (Martin). In keeping with this diversity of contexts, the contributors approach their material in remarkably different ways. While several of the contributions are historically framed, relying on both documentary and visual material, others attend to contemporary narratives about blood, and are based on close observation of particular contexts or the interplay between spoken exegesis and visual images. Some of the discussions rely on a juxtaposition of such different kinds of evidence. We hope that the range of evidence and approaches offered within and between these essays will be an added enticement for readers to engage with our subject matter.

The obvious geographical, cultural, and historical discontinuities between the sites discussed here suggest that commonalities between them might be fortuitous or far-fetched. In fact, the essays demonstrate continuities in blood symbolism where we might not expect them – in the idea that blood reveals the truth, for example, which appears in the context of medieval medical and religious texts discussed by Bettina Bildhauer, in the exegesis on portraits painted in blood of Indian martyrs for Independence analysed by Jacob Copeman, in the history of twentieth-century blood-typing documented by Lederer, and in the Malaysian political rhetoric and practices of clinical pathology labs that I describe. But there are also discontinuities in contexts where we might perhaps expect to see similarities. For example, the two historical considerations of the twentieth-century development of blood donation and transfusion services considered here, that of Britain, discussed by Whitfield, and of the United States, by Lederer, reveal some very different underlying social anxieties – in the one case about class, and in the other about race, among other concerns.[2] To take another example, the two contemporary Christian settings – that of Latter-day Saints in the United States considered by Fenella Cannell, and rural Catholics in Northeast Brazil by Maya Mayblin – reveal strikingly divergent ideas about blood. The rather 'eviscerated' notions of blood articulated in the Mormon case may be linked to wider Protestant precepts and iconography, while Mayblin's analysis shows a remarkable 'fit' between the ideas about blood, water, and sacrifice that she elucidates and prevailing conditions of water scarcity in the local ecology. The contrast thus appears to speak to a complex interplay between historical forces and the development of Christianity in specific locations. But it also is suggestive of how symbolic registers may be elaborated (or reduced) in an implicitly contrastive logic that underlies and contributes to the historical differentiation of divergent branches of a world religion.

If discontinuities between the cases discussed here emerge as much as continuities, this might perhaps be regarded as an expected outcome of the close attention paid by the authors of these essays to the specific sites, locations, historical eras, and cultures they have studied. In this sense, the essays are separately and collectively intended as a contribution to an 'anthropology of blood'. In drawing together the themes that unite them in this introduction, however, I have endeavoured to foreground continuities where these emerge – perhaps partly because these seem more arresting in the face of the obvious dissimilarities between contexts. This disposition also reflects the starting-point for this collective endeavour, which was not only to grasp the cultural specificities of ideas about blood, but also to look for commonalities, and to understand their wider significance. Locating this discussion in a wider anthropological literature has also highlighted how, while there is much previous work that is relevant, there has been surprisingly little sustained attention given to placing this topic in a comparative frame.

In tracing the ways in which blood flows within and beyond the locations discussed in this collection, what emerges most clearly is the literal uncontainability of blood – its capacity to move between domains, including the religious, political, familial, financial, artistic, and medical, which in other contexts are often kept separate. Delineating the contours of this uncontainability of blood, and examining how it operates, brings to light further themes that illuminate blood's particular qualities. Some are closely tied to its material attributes and its bodily manifestations, others involve symbolic or meta-phoric elaboration, but often the distinctions between physical stuff and metaphorical allusion seem porous and difficult to disentangle. Some symbolic associations may refer to or resonate with others, and may also allude to physical or material qualities. A distinction between literal or material qualities and metaphorical ones is of course further undermined by the fact that, as the essays collected here show, what are claimed as the literal or material qualities of blood are themselves culturally and historically variable.[3] Tim Ingold's emphasis on the processual and relational properties of mate-rials seems apt here: 'To describe the properties of materials is to tell the stories of what happens to them as they flow, mix and mutate' (2011: 30).

In the discussion that follows, the themes of materiality, bodily connection, conta-gion, violence, transformability, and vitality are associated with apparently literal or physical attributes of blood. But they may also emerge in more symbolic or metaphori-cal ways. So, as in the example of the Thai political demonstrations or Pope John Paul II's blood with which I began, these themes segue into others that are less closely tied to blood's physical manifestations: ancestral connection, truth, morality, corruption, and transcendence. And this suggests that blood might be a productive medium through which to consider symbolic processes, metaphor, and naturalization (see Jackson 1983; Lakoff & Johnson 1980).

The main themes of the essays have already been mentioned: blood's multiple and sometimes contradictory registers; the relation between metaphor and materiality; blood's apparent capacity to encapsulate the truth; its association with vitality. All of the essays in different ways bring together practices or discourses that might more conventionally be analysed separately, including those concerning religion, medicine, politics, kinship, and economics, showing how images of blood or ideas and practices relating to blood run through these, sometimes providing continuities, but also often disjunctures, of register.

In keeping with blood's tendency to flow between and beyond specific sites, the structure of this introduction does not adhere to the bounded domains of classic anthropological texts. Through the medium of blood, we see how – as in real life – politics may merge with religion or medicine, and the lines between morality, kinship, religious ritual, and health practices may be difficult to discern. This necessitates paying close attention through these themes to the ways in which metaphors are deployed, as well as to blood's physical attributes, before tacking back to our starting-point. To explore what blood is, what a theory of it might look like, or the wider processes such a theory might illuminate, we need first to delineate some of blood's distinctive features.

The materiality of blood

Anthropological analysis does not always proceed from what is hidden or obscure. Sometimes it is the most obvious features of objects or relations that call for attention. Blood has a unique combination of material properties that make it distinctive within and outside the body. Colour and liquidity are the most striking of these, but their co-occurrence and association in the body with heat, and the propensity of blood to clot, turning from liquid to solid, may be equally important to its capacity for symbolic elaboration (see Carsten 2011; Fraser & Valentine 2006). Colour was of course central to Victor Turner's classic symbolic analysis, and his discussion underlines the significance of the connection between the striking visual features of blood and its emotional resonance (1967: 88-9).

Several of the authors in this volume connect blood's material properties to the way it is symbolically elaborated in particular contexts. Bildhauer's discussion of medieval texts, building on her earlier study (Bildhauer 2006), shows how both colour and heat together are central to its medical and miraculous properties. Here we are immediately confronted with the impossibility of separating these qualities from religious notions. Medieval concepts of blood, as Caroline Bynum (2007) has shown, are bound up with ideas about the sacred and, in particular, with the miraculous eternal vitality of Christ's blood, encapsulated in powerful relics. While Christ's blood in these ideas is seen as exceptional, the blood of humans, as discussed below, holds the body and soul together. Normally hidden in the body, when it becomes visible it gives access to the truth. Because of its living qualities, bleeding is a sign of crisis. Good blood is a sign of health, while either too much or too little blood in the body may cause sickness and require regulation through medical attention. Blood can thus secure life, but also be a source of danger through its lack of boundaries.

In an utterly different context – but one that is linked by the importance of Catholicism – Mayblin considers the significance of blood for peasants in the drought-ridden Northeast of Brazil. She shows how blood partakes in a 'fluid economy' where its liquid property is part of a wider system of ideas in which access to water for agriculture is paramount to survival, but which also connects to religious ideas about the significance of Christ's sacrifice. Here peasants understand themselves to be involved in their own sacrificial labour in the fields in which the water and nourishment they lose through the sweat and energy of hard work must be continually replenished. Crucially, water and food that are consumed are transformed in the body into blood. But when these villagers are unwell, their preferred form of cure is to administer sterile isotonic solution, *soro*, intravenously as a form of instant infusion that replenishes and strengthens the body. This especially pure form of liquid can be likened to the sacrificial water that gushes from Christ's side, as depicted in highly valued local religious imagery, and which is associated with the holy spirit and with life. *Soro* is understood to be particularly effective in replenishing blood that is continually depleted through everyday human sacrificial labour. Here water, food, and blood exist as transformations, or possible substitutions, of each other, and exhibit varying states of purity – a theme that is also present in Bildhauer's discussion of medieval texts, and to which I return below.

While material properties of blood are clearly central to both Bildhauer and Mayblin's analyses, they are also just one starting-point for grasping the medical and religious understandings delineated in their essays. In analogous ways, the colour and liquidity of blood might be seen to enable other practices discussed in this volume. The portraits of Indian martyrs for Independence described by Copeman that are literally (as well as metaphorically) painted in blood make use of its redness and liquid form – though interestingly, as neither quality persists outside the body, these have to be artificially enhanced. Here the interpenetration of metaphorical and literal meanings of blood is especially dense, and the emotional resonance of these pictures rests on the complex entanglement of historical, national, political, medical, and bodily perceptions of sacrifice (see also Copeman 2009*a*). If Copeman's essay offers a particularly vivid depiction of how different meanings of blood evoke and amplify each other, it also powerfully demonstrates the centrality of visual and material cues to these wider resonances.

But of course blood's physical properties cannot simply be thought of as the causal factor in what is obviously a very complex web of signification. Sometimes these properties actually limit the uses to which blood may be put. Thus in the twentieth-century development of blood collection for transfusion and of blood-typing, discussed by Lederer and by Whitfield for the United States and Britain, respectively, physiological barriers to the use of one person's blood in the body of another had to be overcome. Nevertheless, as both these essays demonstrate, the fact that transfusion might result in adverse bodily reaction was itself amenable to interpretation in social and racial terms. The history of premodern European ideas about the links between blood and heredity shows how elements in such thinking long pre-dated innovations in blood collection (de Miramon 2009; Nirenberg 2009). Such entanglements were both persistent and amenable to historical transformation in new circumstances (see, e.g., Foucault 1990 [1976]: 147).

Accounts of one of the earliest experiments in animal-to-human blood transfusion, conducted in 1667 under the auspices of the Royal Society, in which Arthur Coga was transfused with the blood of a sheep, indicate that the religious and moral connotations of blood were very apparent to participants. Coga's assertion (made in Latin) that 'sheep's blood has some symbolic power, like the blood of Christ, for Christ is the lamb of God', reportedly 'became a topic of London wit' (Schaffer 1998: 101). While the leap from scientific experiments on transfusion to Lamb of God was taken humourously, concerns about the moral and spiritual qualities of blood permeate contemporary discussions about such experiments (see Schaffer 1998). It appears likely that, as Mayblin suggests, the liquidity of blood encourages a heightened possibility of multiple associations envisioned in terms of flow within and between bodies. But the entanglements of scientific rationalism and religious imagery also underline that the material qualities of blood are only one plausible starting-point for understanding its symbolic salience.

Fungibility and substance

We are already confronted by the difficulty of containing an anthropological discussion of blood within any of its particular dimensions. Attention to its material qualities has merged with consideration of religious, political, racial, and other matters. But there is an interesting symmetry here in terms of understandings of blood within the body. The essays of Bildhauer and Mayblin underline how blood may be conceived as the transformation in the body of food that has been consumed. These are just two instances of a culturally more widespread phenomenon, partly associated with the spread of humoral medicine, and which can also encompass other bodily fluids, such as semen and breast milk, that are understood as transformations of blood (see, e.g., Carsten 1997; Good & delVechio Good 1992). Thus blood itself is not a stable entity, and its composition and quantity may be altered through adjustments to diet, blood-letting, or other means that are undertaken to achieve improvements to health and/or the proper balance of different humours.

Changes in the composition or quantity of blood in the body may be purposefully achieved but they may also be inadvertent, resulting from illness, accident, or misadventure or – as in the case of peasants in Northeast Brazil – from the sheer wear and tear of hard work. But one might say that processes of life itself and social exchange bring about such alterations. The consumption of food, breastfeeding, and sex are widely understood to have serious implications for health and well-being. Elaborate rules governing these practices in order to maintain purity or reduce the possibility of contagion, such as those of the caste system in India, are one expression of such ideas (see, e.g., Daniel 1984; Lambert 2000; Marriott 1976; Marriott & Inden 1977). The physical importance of blood within the body, and its role in supporting life, make it an apparently obvious focus for regimes of bodily vigilance through blood-letting or other means. One might see the widespread occurrence of menstrual taboos or the negative associations of menstruation as more or less over-determined both by the significance of blood and by the connection of menstruation with processes of fertility, sex, and gender (Knight 1991; Martin 1992 [1987]; this volume).

As well as being subject to transformation within the body, blood can of course also be thought to be a vector of connection between bodies or persons. This may be articulated as occurring through the transfer of semen or breast milk (both, as noted, perceived as transformed blood), through maternal feeding in the womb, or through habitual acts of commensality, which are perceived to produce blood of the same kind in the different bodies of those who share food. Here liquidity seems to be a key quality, and the symbolic resonance of bodily fluids may be enhanced by the fact that sexual intercourse, breastfeeding, and family meals are often occasions of heightened emotionality (Taylor 1992; Turner 1967). As historians and anthropologists have observed, the physical transformation understood in Christian ideas to be set in train by marital relations – in which husband and wife become 'one body' or 'one flesh' – had profound implications for ideas about marriage and marriageability in Europe (Johnson, Jussen, Sabean & Teuscher 2013; Kuper 2009). A parallel can be drawn here with a concern in Islamic contexts about the potential incestuous implications of breastfeeding in case of future marriage between those who have consumed milk from the same woman (Carsten 1995; Parkes 2004; 2005).

In many cultures, being 'of one blood' or the phrase 'blood relation' connotes kinship. While this connection might seem almost too obvious to be worth stating, and is certainly central to Euro-American ideas about relatedness (Schneider 1980 [1968]), anthropological renditions of exactly how the connection between blood and kinship is understood further afield have often been surprisingly imprecise or under-specified (Carsten 2011; Ingold 2007: 110-11).[4] And this seems to be partly a result of the implicit conflation of Euro-American indigenous ideas with anthropological analysis of the sort that David Schneider (1984) warned against. Somewhat bizarrely, however, considering the attention Schneider paid to sexual procreation in this regard, his own usage (and that of his informants) of blood and the 'blood relation' in *American kinship* was highly unspecified (Carsten 2004: 112), and this is the starting-point for Cannell's essay in this volume. As she elegantly documents, blood in US culture – or in the subculture that Mormonism represents – can have many meanings, and these cannot be assumed to be historically or culturally stable.

If materiality constitutes the first set of under-theorized aspects of blood to be considered here, then kinship can be seen as a second field in which blood is often invoked but more rarely analysed with much theoretical precision. Because of the continuities between kinship and wider ideas of social connection, this is a significant lapse that inhibits understanding of the ways in which rather abstract political ideologies that draw on kinship, such as nationalism, are rendered emotionally salient (Anderson 1991 [1983]; Carsten 2004: chap 6; Foucault 1990 [1976]; Robertson 2002; 2012). Before returning to the power of blood as political and religious symbol, I take up another apparently more physically circumscribed theme from the contributions in this volume – the importance of blood in medical contexts.

Donation

We have seen how the imagery of blood in kinship connection may blend ideas that have a literal referent, in terms of bodily fluids, with more symbolic or metaphorical usages. But metaphorical allusions to connections 'in the blood' apparently also occur in the absence of any obvious literal source. The donation and collection of blood for transfusion might then be expected to provide a rich and rather open set of opportunities for possible symbolic elaboration. Not surprisingly, anthropologists have recently turned to blood donation to explore its meanings and cultural significance (see Copeman 2009b). An emerging body of scholarship on blood donation in New Guinea (Street 2009), India (Copeman 2004; 2005; 2008; 2009a; 2009c), Brazil (Sanabria 2009), Sri Lanka (Simpson 2009), the United Kingdom (H. Busby 2006), and the Indian community in Houston, USA (Reddy 2007), amongst other locations, demonstrates the complex ways in which blood donation both draws on and expands local practices and idioms of gift-giving, the body, political, religious, or personal sacrifice, kinship connection, and ethics. One obvious point underlined by this work is the importance of considering blood donation not as an isolated phenomenon, but as a 'total social fact' – to co-opt an apt Maussian phrase.

Efforts to encourage blood donation in contexts of scarcity, as well as the declared motivations of donors, draw on ethical discourses from a combination of religion, politics, or kinship – as conventionally delineated by anthropologists. This suggests that an analysis of the symbolic mechanisms through which blood operates needs to place the medical contexts in which blood donation occurs within this much wider frame, and, conversely, that medical practices have the effect of multiplying the emotional and symbolic potential of blood (Copeman 2009a; 2009b; Hugh-Jones 2011). There is a parallel to be drawn here with organ donation, in which a shortage of available organs has been seen to jeopardize potentially the ethical management of transplantation. While attention has been focused on 'tissue economies' (Waldby & Mitchell 2006), issues of 'bioavailability' (Cohen 2005), or the trafficking of human organs (Scheper-Hughes 2000; 2004), it is also clear that such pressures are often ambivalently experienced, for example, through the medium of family ties (Das 2010; Fox & Swazey 1992; 2002 [1974]; Lock 2000; 2002; Sharp 1995; Simmons, Simmons & Marine 1987). Perhaps not surprisingly, the connections to donors and their families envisaged by organ *recipients* also have the potential to be elaborated in terms of kinship, and to be understood as transforming aspects of the person. This is particularly evident in cases of heart transplants, and is apparently associated with the heart's centrality to notions of the person and understandings of it as the seat of the emotions (Bound Alberti 2010; Lock 2002; Sharp 2006).

Blood donation seems generally to be apprehended in terms of more diffuse relations than those set in train by heart transplantation. Nevertheless, Copeman notes the strong link between the idea that donated blood has come 'from the heart' and the authenticity of the emotions flowing with donation. This is part of the efficacy of the blood portraits he describes. Blood donors I spoke to in both Malaysia and the United Kingdom often situated their acts of donation within a sequence of kinship experiences involving histories of family illness or parental acts of blood donation (see also Waldby 2002). And in Malaysia I was told of patients who spoke of the ways their bodies had been altered following blood transfusion in line with what they assumed had been the personal or ethnic characteristics of the source of the blood they had received.

Far from bracketing off these kinds of associations, in the conditions of scarcity that pertain to the availability of blood for medical uses, publicity for blood campaigns actually relies on the emotional resonance of family ties, ill-health, and often also of national sacrifice (Copeman 2009a; Simpson 2004; 2009). Historical accounts of the establishment of blood collection and transfusion services are of particular interest in showing the articulation of medical, political, familial, and other understandings of blood as they are reformulated for new purposes. The essays of Lederer and Whitfield in this volume speak to the complexity of these manoeuvres. The expansion, rationalization, and bureaucratization of blood banking in London during the Second World War together with new technologies of pooling and fractionating blood, described by Whitfield, necessarily distanced blood donors from recipients. This was accompanied, somewhat paradoxically, by a need to make potential recipients more vividly present to donors in order to maintain adequate supplies. New forms of propaganda featuring fictionalized stories about recipients were devised to meet this need. But how much specificity or distance was the right amount? While ideas of kinship and locality were deployed to maintain a sense of connection to recipients, Whitfield also shows how 'strategic anonymity' was a means to mitigate a shift from a system in which the danger of too much closeness between donor and recipient was recognized, to one where too great a distance posed a different kind of threat.[5]

During this period, in which existing class relations were perceived to be undergoing a thorough upheaval as a result of war conditions (as at least the British myth of this era would have it), it would seem that class distinctions between donors and recipients were downplayed. The stories used in publicity for blood donation are at once personalized and generic – they concern 'ordinary men and women', soldiers, sisters, and mothers – with features or faces made unspecific by the style of illustration. Here Jonathan Parry's acute observations about the gift (1986) – where it is only under the conditions of capitalism that there is a need to establish the fetishized category of the 'pure', disinterested gift – seem particularly apposite. Rhetorical allusions to a community bound by the gift of sacrifice for the nation express how the category of pure gift can be instantiated in blood donation. Richard Titmuss's emphasis on 'the gift relationship' (1997 [1970]) was thus, as Whitfield shows, an accurate reflection of a response to technological changes that had occurred some decades before his study.

In the US case discussed by Lederer, the development of blood-typing in the early to mid-twentieth century is interwoven with ideas about race together with religion and the Cold War. The scientific analysis of blood has the capacity to reveal the truth – as does blood in other cases discussed in this volume (see below). But what kind of truths are these? Here anxieties about the specificity of blood are accurately mapped onto social anxieties about racial mixing (see also Lederer 2008; Weston 2001), while class – a focus of British anxieties – remains a more submerged feature. Religion, as Lederer shows in this volume, may blend with or be separated from racial categories. Perhaps not surprisingly, her examples include discourses about the distinctiveness of Jewish blood, which was of course a theme in medieval and early modern European texts (Bildhauer 2006; this volume; Bynum 2007; Nirenberg 2009). But she also documents the active avoidance of interracial blood transfusion, an avoidance which apparently persisted in Mormon hospitals, even after the abandonment by the 1970s of separate blood supplies for white and black patients (Lederer 2008: 197).[6]

Lederer's exposition of the development of blood-typing and its capacity to blend with earlier associations of blood can be supplemented by more recent cases of anxiety about contagion, and scandals involving contaminated blood in China, France, the United States, the United Kingdom, and elsewhere associated with the HIV/AIDS pandemic (Anagnost 2006; Baud 2011; Chaveau 2011; Feldman & Bayer 1999; Laqueur 1999; Shao 2006; Shao & Scoggin 2009; Starr 1998). Thus while the donation of blood has the power to evoke community and kinship, and this may be reinforced by medical usages and scientific typologies, its 'symbolic overload' has clearly not been curtailed by scientific specification. The donation of blood is, for many who are not permitted to donate, an exclusionary rather than an inclusive act (Copeman 2009a; Seeman 1999; Strong 2009; Valentine 2005). The trope of 'bad blood', a 'euphemism' for syphilis in the United States, carries associations that merge race, ancestry, and sexual practice (Lederer 2008: 115-16, 148). And it is precisely because of the multiple connotations of blood, and the histories of these exclusions, that being refused permission to donate is as suffused with resonance as is the act of donation.

Religion-kinship-politics

Blood donation, as we have seen, has political, religious, economic, and familial significance. Each of the themes discussed here has segued into others; blood's capacity to flow in different directions renders its analysis peculiarly difficult to contain within any specified topic. The subheading 'religion-kinship-politics' is intended to gesture to this tendency, but also to serve as a reminder that these distinct domains are analytical artefacts as well as ideological features of modernity (see Cannell & McKinnon 2013; Yanagisako & Delaney 1995). While this ideology may predispose us to see the compartmentalization of realms of life, such as the clinical pathology labs described in my essay, or forms of Christian worship evoked by Cannell and by Mayblin, as obvious or self-evident, attending to the manner in which blood flows within and between such domains highlights their artefactual nature. My essay shows how, as the blood sample travels around the clearly delimited space of the lab, it accrues and sheds different kinds of attributes which enfold moral, ethical, and kinship ascriptions that hold within and beyond the lab's boundaries. Although these boundaries are actively guarded and maintained, they are, inevitably, also porous. 'Blood flows' thus illuminate not only blood itself, but also the work that domaining does – and the limits of domaining.

In this section and those that follow, I turn from the more physical attributes of blood to its looser, symbolic associations. A central paradox here concerns stability. Understandings of blood in the body, explored here by Bildhauer, Mayblin, and others, often emphasize its fungibility and its transformative potential. And Christ's blood is in Christianity attributed with transformative powers to a miraculous degree (Bildhauer, this volume; Bynum 2007). The ritual of Holy Communion, or Eucharist, for many Christians, involves a literal transubstantiation of communion wine into the blood of Christ (Feeley-Harnik 1981; Mayblin, this volume). The phial of Pope John Paul II's blood referred to at the beginning of this introduction clearly partakes of a long history of miraculous and transforming blood. But blood in Euro-American ideas of ancestry and descent is also generally understood to stand for permanence and fixity (Schneider 1980 [1968]). Weston (1995: 103) has commented on this tension in the meanings attributed to 'biological connection' and 'blood ties' in notions of kinship in the United States and Europe – where, in spite of its obvious association with the changing processes of life, biology is taken to stand for permanence. Blood may also be a potent symbol of disconnection and erasure in ideologies of kinship and ideas about family connection. Thus studies of adoption in Europe, the United States, and elsewhere show the importance of idioms of blood in articulating these disconnections, and also their permanent consequences (see Carsten 2000; Kim 2010).

In Cannell's contribution to this volume, different US Mormon understandings of blood are carefully teased apart. Significantly, the Mormon version of the ritual of Communion with which Cannell opens her essay involves a severely pared down reference to the Communion wine and its transformative potential. Here the symbolism of wine and blood is indicated by paper cups of water, and this can be associated with the Mormon proscription of alcohol as well as a wider history of Puritan practices and beliefs. But it also reflects an emphasis on the resurrected body of Christ, Cannell argues, and on redemption rather than the suffering body. One might say that Christ's blood has, like the Communion wine, been 'bleached' in the visual conventions of Mormon aesthetics – where the dazzling whiteness of favoured statues of Christ makes a stark contrast with, for example, the visceral prominence of red blood in the medieval images discussed in Bildhauer's essay (see also Bynum 2007) or Spanish seventeenth-century religious statuary (Bray 2009).

An emphasis on whiteness, light, and simplicity does not, however, inhibit a remarkable proliferation of Mormon ideas about blood. Here the blood of ancestry is highly elaborated: the injunction to trace family genealogy coexists with the revelation to teenagers of their biblical ascription to one of the twelve tribes of Israel in a ritual of Patriarchal Blessing. These two modes of ancestry reflect the joint importance of choice and destiny that is characteristic of Mormon eschatology. The reflections of Cannell's informants on possible interpretations of a particular ancestral ascription highlight the potentially troubling inferences of race and the ideas of permanence with which inheritance is invested. Here one senses that ideas about biblical descent are potentially in conflict with their personal and ethical implications for contemporary adherents. For some, there is unease about the connotations of these ideas – the manner in which personal agency, which is also a central Mormon tenet, may be constrained by the permanence of ancestry and ideas about race. Cannell suggests both that ideas about race are today less exclusionary than they were in the past (in line with more mainstream US ideology), and that the ambiguities surrounding blood, inheritance, and individual agency reinforce for adherents the mystery and sacredness of kinship that is central to Mormon beliefs.

Although Cannell's informants did not speak about these matters, it is significant that, as noted above, Mormon hospitals in the United States have a history of exclusionary practices of blood transfusion in which Mormons were reluctant to take African American blood (Lederer 2008: 197; this volume). This vivid exemplification of the manner in which literal and symbolic aspects of blood may flow into each other is also evident in Copeman's essay. As we have seen, the starting-point for Copeman's central protagonists seems uncompromisingly literal: portraits of Indian martyrs to Independence are painted in blood in order to evoke a strong emotional response in those who view them. Here, in a seemingly similar set of strategies to those of the Thai demonstrators described in my opening vignette, blood must be physically present to induce a reaction. But as Copeman shows, literalness also has a kind of evanescent quality: blood's colour fades; it is not necessarily clear how central the medium is to the message that viewers of these portraits perceive. In any case, blood's presence in both these cases is intended to invoke further layers of symbolic association – to the blood of martyrdom and sacrifice (see Castelli 2011; Copeman 2009a). It also serves as a reminder, or a threat, of further acts of violence and sacrifice that may be demanded in the name of the nation in the future. Here not only have religious, medical, corporeal, and political messages converged through the medium of blood, but temporal dimensions of what blood invokes in the past, present, and future have been merged so that the past is made viscerally present. Blood's literal presence is required, it seems, in order to make evident that its materiality is superseded by a plethora of higher symbolic meanings.

The truth of blood

What kind of stuff is blood? One answer given by the essays in this collection, perhaps unexpectedly, is that it is the stuff of truth. The capacity of blood to 'reveal the truth' – morally, personally, politically, and medically – is a striking theme uniting many of the contexts considered here. This emerges very clearly in Bildhauer's discussion of medieval texts, where blood that becomes visible has a unique capacity to reveal the inner state of the person, his or her moral purity or corruption, as well as his or her health. These ideas would seem to draw partly on biblical notions as well as on humoral medicine. Blood in Leviticus (17: 1-15) is described, as in the texts considered by Bildhauer, as both the animating life-force and the bearer of the soul. For this reason its consumption is proscribed in Leviticus.[7] But we have also seen that blood's truth-bearing capacities are reflected in the twentieth-century scientific development of blood-typing in the United States considered by Lederer. Here it is particular kinds of scientific, racial, personal, and moral truth that are revealed. In a parallel case, Jennifer Robertson (2002; 2012) has shown how the elaboration of discourses around blood-typing in Japan encompasses ideas about horoscopes, personality, blood donation, match-making, eugenics, and the nation. The possibility of finding true love through matching blood types, for example, or the importance of eating correctly for one's blood type, shows how the nature of these truths is continually under revision depending on the social and political context as well as the state of scientific discoveries.

In the context of clinical pathology labs and blood banks in Malaysia, discussed in my essay, the truths that blood is required to establish might be assumed to be straightforwardly medical. These are sites of diagnostic testing in which the blood sample is the most common medium for analysis. But here we see how, as bodily samples travel around the lab, they may be attributed meanings by the staff that conflate medical, personal, familial, and moral qualities. Samples and their accompanying documentation are thus liable to accrue layers of significance that might be thought quite outside the processes and purposes of laboratory analysis. Meanwhile, in the radically different context of Malaysian public politics, the heavily contested blood sample of the *de facto* leader of the opposition, Anwar Ibrahim, arrested in 2008 under a charge of sodomy, was claimed by the government as an icon of truth, and apparently required in order to reveal his moral state. But to an increasingly incredulous Malaysian public, it seemed that this blatantly political manoeuvre might backfire – to reveal instead political corruption in high places. In this somewhat bizarre conjunction of routine laboratory testing and theatrical politics, the truths that blood may reveal are far from stable; they have the capacity to uncover further truths, and also to destabilize moral and political certainties.

The truth-bearing quality of blood appears, then, to give it special efficacy, as is evident in Copeman's case of Indian blood portraits. Donating blood for the purpose of retouching these paintings, like other acts of donation, attests to the truth of the donor's commitment. But here the 'symbolic overload' of blood, its capacity to be read in so many ways, suggests that any one truth already implies all the other truths that may be embodied in blood. And this may connect to the way in which blood seems in many contexts to be perceived as a kind of essence – of the person, and of his or her bodily and spiritual health, disease, or corruption – as is clear, for example, in the cases discussed by Bildhauer and by Mayblin.

But there is a caveat here because we should beware of essentializing blood, or of an overly reductive approach to the different cultural and historical locations considered in this volume. As Fenella Cannell and Emily Martin show in their essays, blood may be many things even within one closely connected set of contexts. Martin's arresting example of contemporary medical images in which the brain appears without blood reminds us that, even within a quite narrow frame of medical understandings, blood has many meanings. If the blood-brain barrier discussed in her essay is physiologically important in limiting the uptake of pharmaceuticals by the brain, it can also be contrasted with images of a brain suffused with blood, and in which leakages or embolisms are a potential cause of death. While the brain can be visualized as devoid of blood but with millions of neurones firing to light up fMRI scans, Martin suggests that the cerebro-spinal fluid can also be seen as a purer form of blood, dealing with the higher cognitive functions of thought and control associated with the brain. And placing this understanding of the cerebro-spinal fluid alongside Martin's earlier insights about gender and medical representations of the body in *The woman in the body* (1992 [1987]), as she does here, provides a revealing contrast. Whereas menstrual blood and menopause were shown in that work to be associated with chaos, waste, pollution, and decay, and of course with women, blood's function here is one of nourishing the brain, and essentially maternal. But cerebro-spinal fluid is imagined as a highly refined and more male form of blood. Martin shows how this hierarchical differentiation of blood in the body is linked to purity and to gender imagery in a way that reveals striking parallels with the cases discussed by Bildhauer and by Mayblin. But she also makes clear that understandings of blood remain open to new truths of scientific discovery – for example, the prioritization of cognition – while still retaining their salience.

Vitality and flow; containment and stoppage; metaphor and naturalization

I suggested above that blood's apparently unique capacity among bodily substances to reveal the truth could be linked to its strong association with life itself. The idea that blood embodies the life-force is evident in the proscriptions of Leviticus, in Bildhauer's consideration of medieval texts, and in the practices of the Brazilian peasants considered by Mayblin, but it also occurs outside Judaeo-Christian contexts. Conducting village fieldwork in Malaysia in the 1980s, I was told that, at the time of death, 'the soul leaves the body and all the blood flows out' – even if this was not visible to the human eye. If a person died in the house, everything in the house, especially the food, became soaked with blood. Therefore food could not be cooked or consumed in a house where a death had occurred until after the funeral had taken place (Carsten 1997: 124).

Vitality in these ideas is apparently linked to the flow and liquidity of blood – to its mobility. Excessive bleeding is one obvious cause and sign of death – in this sense blood's truth-bearing capacity is incontrovertible. Images of both containment and of permeability occur in several of the contributions here. Outpourings of blood – whether induced through purposeful acts of violence or incurred by accident – are signs of danger. And, as Martin notes, stoppages of blood, clots and embolisms, are equally hazardous. But the flow of blood – or life – may also be perceived as religious sacrifice – as in practices discussed by Bildhauer and by Mayblin. In Christian contexts, such pouring out of blood may be linked to Christ's sacrifice for humanity, and the flow of blood can be a means to achieve transcendence (see Bynum 2007). Transcendence may also be sought through political acts of violence such as those considered by Copeman, or more explicit acts of martyrdom (Castelli 2011) that are also invoked in the idiom of sacrifice. The antinomies which blood encompasses here – involving life and death, movement and stoppage, health and disease, violence and peace, the sacred and the profane – make clear how its polyvalent associations extend in an extraordinary multiplicity of directions.

But even this plethora of resonances does not exhaust the symbolic idioms in which blood participates. Whereas Martin's essay, which closes this volume, draws attention to the spaces where blood does not flow, and to stoppages and blockages, Weston's opening contribution is concerned with the flow of lifeblood in the financial body. Her essay lays out with wonderful precision the layered resonances of different somatic models and understandings of blood to which contemporary descriptions of the economy refer. Images of 'lifeblood', 'circulation', 'flow', 'liquidity', or 'haemorrhaging' in the financial system resonate with understandings of blood in the body. While the circulatory model discovered by William Harvey in the early seventeenth century is predominant here, Weston shows how older notions that predate Harvey's model may also be called upon, involving, for example, ideas about stagnation of the economy and the blood-letting that is necessary to deal with it. As well as demonstrating the pervasiveness of sanguinary images in depictions of the financial system, and laying out an archaeology of somatic models, Weston's essay confronts the central problem of this volume: the issue of metaphor.

How should we understand the widespread occurrence of metaphors of blood, and what is their significance? Together with other contributors in this volume, Weston places the term 'resonance' alongside metaphor, but she also includes other figures of speech and literary device in her analysis, such as analogy, allegory, and synecdoche. The multiple resonances of blood, she suggests, which are evident in all the cases described here, enable a kind of ricochet effect, in which resonances referred to through linguistic means pile in on each other, but without requiring the primacy of one particular set of references or idioms to be specified or even suggested. Thus in the case she describes, the 'naturalness' of the organic analogy in finance is so deeply and historically embedded in patterns of language as to pass without question, and indeed one effect is to obscure the fragilities, instabilities, and inequalities of the financial system itself.[8] While one might object that this implies a Whorfian model of the world in which language determines thought and action, this conclusion is actually too simplistic. The significance of the bodily processes that are engaged here, the very materiality of blood, implies that there is no crude way in which one could ascribe primacy in these processes either to the physicality of blood or to linguistic devices. Rather, the power of metaphors and images of blood rests with the constant tacking back and forth, or resonance, among the different evocations that are described in these essays.

Here it is worth drawing attention to the importance of visual imagery that is vividly exemplified in several contributions to this volume. The depictions of medieval blood cited by Bildhauer, the blood portraits described by Copeman, or the exhortations to donate blood in wartime Britain noted by Whitfield make clear that the resonances of blood are captured visually as much as through language. While blood's visible qualities are important to its emotional resonance, and neither of these has to be expressed in words, it is also clear that what anthropologists may assume to be metaphorical or symbolic allusions to blood may actually be experienced in a more literal manner. Mayblin observes that a crucial quality of blood is that it can function as both metaphor and metonym – and this is central to theological debates about the Christian Eucharist (see Bynum 2007). The importance of Holy Communion to many Christians, including her informants, is that it literally makes the blood of Christ present. In this sense, the link between Christ's sacrifice and their own daily sacrifice of labour is tangible. In Copeman's essay on the blood portraits of Indian Independence martyrs, the real presence of blood is shown to be in such complex play with its multiple symbolic resonance in acts of sacrifice for the nation that its materiality might seem almost surplus to requirements. In fact, however, his analysis shows how what he calls the 'iconic' and the 'aniconic' aspects of the portraits (the representation of the martyrs and the physical presence of the artist in their blood) is a crucial part of the mimetic efficacy they seek to inspire. Weston, drawing attention to this interplay of signification in multiple directions, emphasizses 'both the generative possibilities of blood and its ability to pre-empt debate as it naturalizes social processes and perfuses multiple domains'.

Metaphorical and material aspects of blood are thus in constant communication with each other (see Fraser & Valentine 2006; Laqueur 1999). With reference to Thai demonstrators' use of blood as political protest, the suffusion of blood imagery in depictions of the economy, as well as the blood portraits discussed by Copeman, Weston adopts the term 'meta-materiality' to convey that what is invoked goes beyond both metaphor and the material – but also, and simultaneously, relies on both the material and the metaphorical to generate further resonances and further naturalizations.[9]

The significance of this meta-materiality is highlighted if we juxtapose Weston's material with Martin's images of a 'bloodless brain' where descriptions of brain physiology are shown to be deeply entangled with metaphorical allusions of blood. Depictions of the human brain analysed by Martin are suffused with layers of resonance to a hierarchical and gendered body. They thus also evoke an earlier anthropological literature on the way perceptions of nature itself provide material for metaphor-making (see, e.g., E. Leach 1976; Lévi-Strauss 1966 [1962]; 1969b [1949]; MacCormack 1980; MacCormack & Strathern 1980; Ortner 1974; Wagner 1975). Thus not only do images of blood have a naturalizing power, but depictions of nature itself can both partake of the 'meta-materiality' of blood and also contribute to it. And this further reinforces Weston's point about the ricocheting effects between different resonances of blood.

The political corollaries of these processes are worth pausing over. Laying out a theory of metaphor from the perspective of cognitive science, Dedre Gentner, Brian Bowdle, Phillip Wolff, and Consuelo Boronat (2001) place metaphors and analogy in a single frame. Distinguishing conventional metaphors from novel ones, they introduce the idea of 'the career of metaphor' (2001: 227). Eventually, they argue, metaphors become so conventionalized that the sense of metaphoricity disappears and one of polysemy remains. These authors note that 'the term *metaphor* can also apply to systems of extended meanings that are so familiar as to be almost invisible' (2001: 240, italics in original) – though, importantly, this does not imply any lack of affective power. Blood might be a case in point. The more entangled its multiple resonances and metaphorical allusions become (both historically and between domains that are in other contexts actively kept separate), the more difficult it is to prise them apart, or to subject arguments and assumptions into which they are enfolded to political or analytic questioning.

Conclusion: genes and vampires; multiple temporalities of blood

Martin's depiction of hierarchies of blood in the body that can be linked not only to ideas about purity and gender, but also to scientific discoveries, is worth probing further. It suggests – as does Weston's depiction of the different somatic models folded into imagery of the financial system – that blood is capable of simultaneously conveying multiple temporalities. We have seen that this idea is also present in Copeman's analysis of blood portraits of Indian martyrs for Independence, where past, present, and possible futures converge through the material medium of blood.

In fact, the possibility of such different temporalities being present in blood is indicated in other contributions to this volume. The technological advances in blood-typing and transfusion medicine that are probed by Lederer and Whitfield do not necessarily entail the abandonment of older ideas about transfers of blood but must accommodate and coexist with these – partly to ensure the maintenance of the available supply of blood. Cannell's exposition of different ideas about blood and ancestry among US Latter-day Saints, similarly, shows a remarkable coexistence and persistence of ideas that can be traced to different historical periods, but also the potential for the balance between these to change. And in Mayblin's evocation of the enthusiasm with which peasants in Northeast Brazil have incorporated intravenous rehydration fluids into pre-existing ideas about the body and religious sacrifice (thus speeding up or short-cutting the transformative potential of sacrifice), or in my depiction of the way blood samples in clinical pathology labs in Malaysia may accrue layers of moral, kinship, and ethical meaning, we see a similar layering of the multiple historicities of blood.

How should we understand the significance of this capacity of blood to absorb and carry references to different historical eras? One part of its importance is its very implicitness – such references are evoked without words; they amplify the symbolic range of blood, and the aptitude of such resonances for naturalization. As Copeman's example makes clear, the enhanced emotional purchase of such symbolic evocations is crucial to their political salience. Two contrasting extrapolations of blood's symbolic potential may illuminate these processes further. The first concerns new developments in genetic medicine. While advances in genetic medicine might be expected to undermine and reformulate older Euro-American ideas about kinship, inheritance, and personhood – encouraging a move to more fixed ideas of genetic essentialism (Finkler 2000; 2001) – it appears that this has only been the case to a quite limited degree. Instead, genetic understandings of disease are likely to be reinterpreted and folded back into older, familial idioms of blood and family ties (Lock 2005). As Sarah Franklin (2013) succinctly states, 'blood is thicker than genes'. Far from being displaced, it has the capacity and the resilience to absorb and acquire new meanings (see also Bestard 2009; Čepaitienė 2009; Edwards 2009; Franklin 2003; Porqueres i Gené & Wilgaux 2009; Rapp 1999).

Understanding of inheritance in terms of genetics is mainly associated with twentieth-century scientific advances. Vampire spirits, in contrast, have a rather longer and more widespread cultural presence, recorded in the literature on Greece (du Boulay 1982; 1984), colonial Africa (White 2000), and Malaysia (Carsten 1997), amongst other places. Like genes, vampires are associated in the popular imagination with blood. But instead of flowing in it, as it were, they remove human blood in order illicitly to obtain life after death. Vampires' need for the animating powers of blood thus expresses some of the antinomies we have already encountered in blood: nourishment and depredation, peace and violence, life and death. Whereas the symbolic capacity of genes seems to be heavily constrained by their lack of historical depth, vampires apparently call upon a longer historical trajectory to enrich the salience of their current manifestations. Their emergence in Europe is in fact a feature of modernity, associated with the Enlightenment, and with the spread of new scientific technologies (Luckhurst 2011). One might see the extraordinary contemporary efflorescence of vampire stories in Euro-American fictional genres partly as a reflection of recent health-related panics about contaminated blood, as well as anxiety over illicit economic and political depredations, but one could also see it as the latest manifestation of a more historically embedded set of concerns about essences and boundaries of the person, truth, moral worth, relatedness, and the religious and eschatological implications of these (Bildhauer this volume; Luckhurst 2011: xxvii-viii). Blood's capacity to dissolve different temporalities, to absorb and convey multiple historicities, renders it uniquely capable of taking on new messages and enfolding them within pre-existing cultural scripts.

The question 'what is blood?' posed at the beginning of this introduction might seem, by virtue of its cultural and historical specificity, to be unanswerable. But we have seen that, alongside the multiplicity of contrasts, distinctions, elaborations, and resonances, there are some remarkable continuities: blood, in many of the contexts encountered here, is life and truth, and it also encompasses the very opposite of these. Its over-determined polyvalence and plasticity can be linked to its importance as bodily substance, its material qualities, and its changeable and transformative propensities.

I have suggested two further questions for consideration: Can we have a theory of blood? And what might such a theory help illuminate? In attempting to answer these questions, I referred at the beginning of this essay to a contrast between blood and money. Whereas there is a long history of social science writing on money, the anthropology of blood has tended to be dispersed across many sub-fields, and its theoretical significance has on the whole remained rather implicit. But there is another point to this analogy, which we can now reclaim. Money, like blood, flows between domains – indeed that has been seen as its very purpose – and like blood too, it is often vested with transformative and generative powers (Bloch & Parry 1989). The symbolic potential of money partly rests on these capacities. Significantly, however, as Weston's essay beautifully shows, financial systems and markets may themselves be envisaged in the idiom of blood. If money partakes of the symbolic potential of blood, this implies a hierarchy of symbols, and that there is perhaps something about blood that endows it with a greater symbolic power. The essays in this collection suggest that this is linked to its material presence and physical qualities, its association with life itself, its extraordinary range of resonances, and the way these may be both literally made present or symbolically evoked in order to generate further associations. Indeed, we have seen that depictions of nature may both partake of and contribute to the meta-materiality of blood. Blood, in other words, has a naturalizing capacity which it may lend to money. The potent metaphor of blood banking illustrates, as Weston notes, the two-way traffic of such processes: the naturalization that blood enables can be extended to money, and thence reimported into the realm of technologized blood donation and circulation (see also Weston 2001).

The qualities of blood depicted here and its range of resonances are associated with a heightened propensity to evoke emotional responses. We have seen how blood has the potential to carry multiple historicities, and to dissolve the distinctions between past, present, and future. As the opening vignettes of the blood used by Thai political demonstrators or the blood of Pope John Paul II exemplify, the more such resonances pile in on each other, the more they have a self-replicating and over-determined power to propel further meanings. Life and death; nurturance and violence; connection and exclusion; kinship and sacrifice – the associations can multiply, flowing between apparently incommensurate domains in a quite uncontainable manner. Not least, they may be purposefully evoked in the rhetoric of familial, racial, ethnic, or national exclusion, and as calls to violent action. Partly because they can enfold long and layered histories in a quite implicit way, these idioms apparently have an exceptional emotional force. The essays in this volume suggest many reasons why it is important to understand or elucidate what one might call a theory of blood.

NOTES

[1] I am grateful to an anonymous reviewer for *JRAI* for suggesting this formulation.

[2] See Krementsov (2011) for a fascinating counterpoint on the 'socialist' history of blood transfusion in the Soviet Union.

[3] I thank Richard Fardon for this clarification and for pointing out that materiality can itself be a symbolic value.

[4] For a longer and more general review of the anthropology of bodily substance and the connections between substance and relatedness, see Carsten (2011). That the existence of such connections should not be assumed has been emphasized by Bamford (2004; 2007; 2009). See also Carsten (2001); Edwards (2000); J. Leach (2003); Sahlins (2011a; 2011b); Thomas (1999).

[5] There is a striking echo here of discussions of marriage and affinity in the anthropological literature in cases where finding a spouse who is neither too close nor too distant is a paramount concern (see, e.g., C. Busby 1997; Carsten 1997, chap. 7).

[6] On the entanglements of blood, race, kinship, and heredity, see also Dauksas (2007); Foucault (1990 [1976]: 147-50); Porqueres i Gené (2007); Stoler (1992; 1997); Wade (1993; 2002; 2007); Williams (1995). As this work shows, it is not necessarily the case even in European ideas that blood connotes immutable essence rather than being subject to change through various environmental influences.

[7] I am grateful to Jessica Spencer for drawing the relevant verses of Leviticus to my attention.

[8] But it is worth noting Marx's depiction of the nature of capital 'that, vampire-like, only lives by sucking living labour, and lives the more, the more labour it sucks' (1977 [1867]: 224).

[9] Fraser and Valentine (2006) also discuss the co-production of the symbolic and material aspects of blood and its 'agentive' properties, while Laqueur (1999: 6) has commented on the significance of the 'hyper-material quality' of blood – the fact that it is 'relentlessly material' as well as being overburdened with meaning.

REFERENCES

ANAGNOST, A. 2006. Strange circulations: the blood economy in rural China. *Economy and Society* **35**, 509-29.

ANDERSON, B. 1991 [1983]. *Imagined communities: reflections on the origin and spread of nationalism* (Second edition). London: Verso.

ASSOCIATED PRESS 2010. Thai protesters pour human blood on gates of government headquarters. *Guardian*, 16 March (available on-line: *http://www.guardian.co.uk/world/2010/mar/16/thailand-protesters-blood-government*, accessed 10 January 2013).

BAMFORD, S. 2004. Conceiving relatedness: non-substantial relations among the Kamea of Papua New Guinea. *Journal of the Royal Anthropological Institute* (N.S.) **10**, 287-306.

——— 2007. *Biology unmoored: Melanesian reflections on life and biotechnology*. Berkeley: University of California Press.

——— 2009. 'Family trees' among the Kamea of Papua New Guinea: a non-genealogical approach to imagining relatedness. In *Kinship and beyond: a genealogical model reconsidered* (eds) S. Bamford & J. Leach, 159-74. New York: Berghahn.

BAUD, J.-P. 2011. La nature juridique du sang. *Terrain* **56**, 90-105.

BESTARD, J. 2009. Knowing and relating: kinship, assisted reproductive technologies and the new genetics. In *European kinship in the age of biotechnology* (eds) J. Edwards & C. Salazar, 1-18. New York: Berghahn.

BILDHAUER, B. 2006. *Medieval blood*. Cardiff: University of Wales Press.

BLOCH, M. & J. PARRY 1989. Introduction: money and the morality of exchange. In *Money and the morality of exchange* (eds) J. Parry & M. Bloch, 1-32. Cambridge: University Press.

BOUND ALBERTI, F. 2010. *Matters of the heart: history, medicine, and emotion*. Oxford: University Press.

BRAY, X. 2009. *The sacred made real: Spanish painting and sculpture, 1600-1700*. London: National Gallery.

BUSBY, C. 1997. Of marriage and marriageability: gender and Dravidian kinship. *Journal of the Royal Anthropological Institute* (N.S) **3**, 21-42.

BUSBY, H. 2006. Biobanks, bioethics and concepts of donated blood in the UK. *Sociology of Health and Illness* **28**, 850-65.

BYNUM, C.W. 2007. *Wonderful blood: theology and practice in late medieval northern Germany and beyond*. Philadelphia: University of Pennsylvania Press.

CANNELL, F. & S. McKINNON 2013. The re-enchantment of kinship? In *Vital relations: modernity and the persistent life of kinship* (eds) F. Cannell & S. McKinnon, 3-38. Santa Fe, N.M.: SAR Press.

CARSTEN, J. 1995. The substance of kinship and the heat of the hearth: feeding, personhood and relatedness among Malays of Pulau Langkawi. *American Ethnologist* **22**, 223-41.

——— 1997. *The heat of the hearth: the process of kinship in a Malay fishing community*. Oxford: Clarendon Press.

——— 2000. 'Knowing where you've come from': ruptures and continuities of time and kinship in narratives of adoption reunions. *Journal of the Royal Anthropological Institute* (N.S.) **6**, 687-703.

——— 2001. Substantivism, anti-substantivism, and anti-anti-substantivism. In *Relative values: reconfiguring kinship studies* (eds) S. Franklin & S. McKinnon, 29-53. Durham, N.C.: Duke University Press.

——— 2004. *After kinship*. Cambridge: University Press.

——— 2011. Substance and relationality: blood in contexts. *Annual Review of Anthropology* **40**, 19-35.

CASTELLI, E.A. 2011. Verser notre sang, non celui des autres: rituel et résistance en temps de guerre (USA). *Terrain* **56**, 22-41.

ČEPAITIENĖ, A. 2009. Imagining assisted reproductive technologies: family, kinship and 'local thinking' in Lithuania. In *European kinship in the age of biotechnology* (eds) J. Edwards & C. Salazar, 29-44. Oxford: Berghahn.

CHAVEAU, S. 2011. Du don à l'industrie: la transfusion sanguine en France depuis les années 1940. *Terrain* **56**, 74-89.

COHEN, L. 2005. Operability, bioavailability, and exception. In *Global assemblages: technology, politics and ethics as anthropological problems* (eds) A. Ong & S. Collier, 79-90. Oxford: Blackwell.

COPEMAN, J. 2004. Blood will have blood: a study in Indian political ritual. *Social Analysis* **48: 3**, 126-48.

——— 2005. Veinglory: exploring processes of blood transfer between persons. *Journal of the Royal Anthropological Institute* (N.S.) **11**, 465-85.

——— 2008. Violence, non-violence, and blood donation in India. *Journal of the Royal Anthropological Institute* (N.S.) **14**, 278-96.

——— 2009*a*. *Veins of devotion: blood donation and religious experience in North India*. New Brunswick, N.J.: Rutgers University Press.

——— 2009*b*. Introduction: blood donation, bioeconomy, culture. *Body & Society* **15: 2**, 1-28.

——— 2009*c*. Gathering points: blood donation and the scenography of 'National Integration' in India. *Body & Society* **15: 2**, 71-99.

DANIEL, E.V. 1984. *Fluid signs: being a person the Tamil way*. Berkeley: University of California Press.

DAS, V. 2010. The life of humans and the life of roaming spirits. In *Rethinking the human* (eds) M. Molina & D. Swearer, 31-50. Cambridge, Mass.: Harvard University Press.

DAUKSAS, D. 2007. The transmission of ethnicity: family and state – a Lithuanian perspective. *In Race, ethnicity and nation: perspectives from kinship and genetics* (ed.) P. Wade, 145-68. Oxford: Berghahn.

DE MIRAMON, C. 2009. Noble dogs, noble blood: the invention of the concept of race in the late Middle Ages. In *The origins of racism in the West* (eds) M. Eliav-Feldon, B. Isaac & J. Ziegler, 200-16. Cambridge: University Press.

DOUGLAS, M. 2003 [1970]. *Natural symbols*. Oxford: Routledge.

DU BOULAY, J. 1982. The Greek vampire: a study of cyclic symbolism in marriage and death. *Man* (N.S.) **17**, 219-38.

——— 1984. The blood: symbolic relationships between descent, marriage, incest prohibitions and spiritual kinship in Greece. *Man* (N.S.) **19**, 533-56.

EDWARDS, J. 2000. *Born and bred: idioms of kinship and new reproductive technologies in England*. Oxford: University Press.

——— 2009. Introduction: the matter in kinship. In *European kinship in the age of biotechnology* (eds) J. Edwards & C. Salazar, 1-18. Oxford: Berghahn.

FEELEY-HARNIK, G. 1981. *The Lord's table: Eucharist and Passover in early Christianity*. Philadelphia: University of Pennsylvania Press.

FELDMAN, E.A. & R. BAYER (eds) 1999. *Blood feuds: AIDS, blood, and the politics of medical disaster*. Oxford: University Press.

FINKLER, K. 2000. *Experiencing the new genetics: family and kinship on the medical frontier*. Philadelphia: University Press.

——— 2001. The kin in the gene: the medicalization of family and kinship in American society. *Current Anthropology* **42**, 235-63.

FOUCAULT, M. 1990 [1976]. *The history of sexuality*, vol. 1: *An introduction* (trans. R. Hurley). Harmondsworth: Penguin.

FOX, R. & J. SWAZEY 1992. *Spare parts: organ replacement in American society*. Oxford: University Press.

——— & ——— 2002 [1974]. *The courage to fail: a social view of organ transplants and dialysis*. Chicago: University Press.

FRANKLIN, S. 2003. Rethinking nature-culture: anthropology and the new genetics. *Anthropological Theory* **3**: 1, 65-85.

——— 2013. From blood to genes? Rethinking consanguinity in the context of geneticization. In *Blood and kinship: matter for metaphor from ancient Rome to the present* (eds) C.H. Johnson, B. Jussen, D.W. Sabean & S. Teuscher, 285-306. Oxford: Berghahn.

FRASER, S. & K. VALENTINE 2006. 'Making blood flow': materializing blood in body modification practice and blood-borne virus prevention. *Body & Society* **12**: 1, 97-119.

GENTNER, D., B. BOWDLE, P. WOLFF & C. BORONAT 2001. Metaphor is like analogy. In *The analogical mind: perspectives from cognitive science* (eds.) D. Gentner, K.J. Holyoak & B.N. Kokinov, 199-253. Cambridge, Mass.: MIT Press.

GOOD, B.J. & M.-J. DELVECHIO GOOD 1992. The comparative study of Greco-Islamic medicine: the integration of medical knowledge into local symbolic contexts. In *Paths to Asian medical knowledge* (eds) C. Leslie & A. Young, 257-71. Berkeley: University of California Press.

HOOPER, J. 2011. Pope John Paul's blood to go on display at Vatican. *Guardian*, 26 April (available on-line: *http://www.guardian.co.uk/world/2011/apr/26/pope-john-paul-blood-vatican*, accessed 10 January 2013).

HUGH-JONES, S. 2011. Analyses de sang. *Terrain* **56**, 4-21.

INGOLD, T. 2007. *Lines: a brief history*. Oxford: Routledge.

——— 2011. *Being alive: essays on movement, knowledge and description*. Oxford: Routledge.

JACKSON, M. 1983. Thinking through the body: an essay on understanding metaphor. *Social Analysis* **14**, 127-49.

JOHNSON, C.H., B. JUSSEN, D.W. SABEAN & S. TEUSCHER (eds) 2013. *Blood and kinship: matter for metaphor from ancient Rome to the present*. Oxford: Berghahn.

KIM, E. 2010. *Adopted territory: transnational Korean adoptees and the politics of belonging*. Durham, N.C.: Duke University Press.

KNIGHT, C. 1991. *Blood relations: menstruation and the origin of culture*. New Haven: Yale University Press.

KREMENTSOV, N. 2011. *A Martian stranded on earth: Alexander Bogdanov, blood transfusions, and proletarian science*. Chicago: University Press.

Kuper, A. 2009. *Incest and influence: the private life of bourgeois England.* Cambridge, Mass.: Harvard University Press.

Lakoff, G. & M. Johnson 1980. *Metaphors we live by.* Chicago: University Press.

Lambert, H. 2000. Sentiment and substance in North Indian forms of relatedness. In *Cultures of relatedness: new approaches to the study of kinship* (ed.) J. Carsten, 73-89. Cambridge: University Press.

Laqueur, T. 1999. Pint for pint [review of D. Starr, *Blood: an epic history of medicine and commerce*]. *London Review of Books*, 14 October, 3-7 (available on-line: *http://www.lrb.co.uk/v21/n20/thomas-laqueur/pint-for-pint*, accessed 10 January 2013).

Leach, E. 1976. *Culture and communication.* Cambridge: University Press.

Leach, J. 2003. *Creative land: place and procreation on the Rai Coast of Papua New Guinea.* New York: Berghahn.

Lederer, S.E. 2008. *Flesh and blood: organ transplantation and blood transfusion in twentieth-century America.* Oxford: University Press.

Lévi-Strauss, C. 1966 [1962]. *The savage mind* (trans. J. Weightman & D. Weightman). Chicago: University Press.

——— 1969a [1962]. *Totemism* (trans. R. Needham). Harmondsworth: Penguin.

——— 1969b [1949]. *The elementary structures of kinship* (trans. J.H. Bell, J.R. von Sturmer & R. Needham). Boston: Beacon.

Lock, M. 2000. The quest for human organs and the violence of zeal. In *Violence and subjectivity* (eds) V. Das, A. Kleinman, M. Ramphele & P. Reynolds, 271-95. Berkeley: University of California Press.

——— 2002. *Twice dead: organ transplants and the reinvention of death.* Berkeley: University of California Press.

——— 2005. Eclipse of the gene and the return of divination. *Current Anthropology* **46** (Supplement, Dec.), 47-70.

Luckhurst, R. 2011. Introduction. In *Dracula*, B. Stoker, vii-xxxii. Oxford: University Press.

MacCormack, C. 1980. Nature, culture and gender: a critique. In *Nature, culture and gender* (eds) C. MacCormack & M. Strathern, 1-24. Cambridge: University Press.

——— & M. Strathern (eds) 1980. *Nature, culture and gender.* Cambridge: University Press.

Marriott, M. 1976. Hindu transactions: diversity without dualism. In *Transactions in meaning* (ed.) B. Kapferer, 109-42. Philadelphia, Pa: ISHI Publications.

——— & R. Inden 1977. Towards an ethnosociology of South Asian caste systems. In *The new wind: changing identities in South Asia* (ed.) K. David, 227-38. The Hague: Mouton.

Martin, E. 1992 [1987]. *The woman in the body: a cultural analysis of reproduction.* Boston: Beacon.

Marx, K. 1977 [1867]. *Capital: a critique of political economy*, vol. 1 (ed. F. Engels; trans. S. Moore & E. Aveling). London: Lawrence & Wishart.

Nirenberg, D. 2009. Was there race before modernity? The example of 'Jewish' blood in late medieval Spain. In *The origins of racism in the West* (eds) M. Eliav-Feldon, B. Isaac & J. Ziegler, 232-65. Cambridge: University Press.

Ortner, S. 1974. Is female to male as nature is to culture? In *Woman, culture and society* (eds) M.Z. Rosaldo & L. Lamphere, 67-88. Stanford: University Press.

Parkes, P. 2004. Fosterage, kinship and legend: when milk was thicker than blood? *Comparative Studies in Society and History* **46**, 587-615.

——— 2005. Milk kinship in Islam: substance, structure, history. *Social Anthropology* **13**, 307-29.

Parry, J. 1986. *The gift*, the Indian gift and the 'Indian gift'. *Man* (N.S.) **21**, 453-73.

Porqueres i Gené, E. 2007. Kinship language and the dynamics of race: the Basque case. In *Race, ethnicity and nation: perspectives from kinship and genetics* (ed.) P. Wade, 125-44. Oxford: Berghahn.

——— & J. Wilgaux 2009. Incest, embodiment, genes and kinship. In *European kinship in the age of biotechnology* (eds) J. Edwards & C. Salazar, 112-27. Oxford: Berghahn.

Rapp, R. 1999. *Testing women, testing the fetus: the social impact of amniocentesis in America.* London: Routledge.

Reddy, D. 2007. Good gifts for the common good: blood and bioethics in the market of genetic research. *Cultural Anthropology* **22**, 429-72.

Robertson, J. 2002. Blood talks: eugenic modernity and the creation of new Japanese. *History and Anthropology* **13**, 191-216.

——— 2012. Hemato-nationalism: the past, present, and future of 'Japanese' blood. *Medical Anthropology* **31**, 93-112.

Sahlins, M. 2011a. What kinship is (part one). *Journal of the Royal Anthropological Institute* (N.S.) **17**, 2-19.

——— 2011b. What kinship is (part two). *Journal of the Royal Anthropological Institute* (N.S.) **17**, 227-42.

SANABRIA, E. 2009. Alleviative bleeding: bloodletting, menstruation and the politics of ignorance in a Brazilian blood donation centre. *Body & Society* **15: 2**, 123-44.

SAUSSURE, F. DE 1960 [1916]. *Course in general linguistics* (trans. W. Baskin). London: Peter Owen.

SCHAFFER, S. 1998. Regeneration: the body of natural philosophers in restoration England. In *Science incarnate: historical embodiments of natural knowledge* (eds) C. Lawrence & S. Shapin, 83-120. Chicago: University Press.

SCHEPER-HUGHES, N. 2000. The global traffic in human organs. *Current Anthropology* **41**, 191-224.

——— 2004. Parts unknown: undercover ethnography of the organs trafficking underworld. *Ethnography* **5**, 29-73.

SCHNEIDER, D.M. 1980 [1968]. *American kinship: a cultural account.* Chicago: University Press.

——— 1984. *A critique of the study of kinship.* Ann Arbor: University of Michigan Press.

SEEMAN, D. 1999. 'One people, one blood': public health, political violence, and HIV in an Ethiopian-Israeli setting. *Culture, Medicine and Psychiatry* **23**, 159-95.

SHAO, J. 2006. Fluid labor and blood money: the economy of HIV/AIDS in rural central China. *Cultural Anthropology* **21**, 535-69.

——— & M. SCOGGIN 2009. Solidarity and distinction in blood: contamination, morality and variability. *Body & Society* **15: 2**, 29-50.

SHARP, L. 1995. Organ transplantation as a transformative experience: anthropological insights into the restructuring of the self. *Medical Anthropology Quarterly* **9**, 357-89.

——— 2006. *Strange harvest: organ transplants, denatured bodies, and the transformed self.* Berkeley: University of California Press.

SIMMONS, R.G., R.L. SIMMONS & S.K. MARINE 1987. *Gift of life: the effect of organ transplantation on individual, family, and societal dynamics.* New Brunswick, N.J.: Transaction.

SIMPSON, B. 2004. Impossible gifts: bodies, Buddhism and bioethics in contemporary Sri Lanka. *Journal of the Royal Anthropological Institute* (N.S.) **4**, 839-59.

——— 2009. Please give a drop of blood: blood donation, conflict and the haemato-global assemblage in contemporary Sri Lanka. *Body & Society* **15: 2**, 101-22.

STARR, D. 1998. *Blood: an epic history of medicine and commerce.* London: Warner.

STOLER, A. 1992. Sexual affronts and racial frontiers: European identities and the cultural politics of exclusions in colonial Southeast Asia. *Comparative Studies in Society and History* **34**, 514-51.

——— 1997. On political and psychological essentialisms. *Ethos* **25**, 101-6.

STREET, A. 2009. Failed recipients: extracting blood in a Papua New Guinea hospital. *Body & Society* **15: 2**, 193-216.

STRONG, T. 2009. Vital publics of pure blood. *Body & Society* **15: 2**, 169-91.

TAYLOR, C. 1992. *Milk, honey and money: changing concepts in Rwandan healing.* Washington, D.C.: Smithsonian Institution Press.

THOMAS, P. 1999. No substance, no kinship? Procreation, performativity and Temanambondro parent-child relations. In *Conceiving persons: ethnographies of procreation, fertility and growth* (eds) P. Loizos & P. Heady, 19-45. London: Athlone Press.

TITMUSS, R. 1997 [1970]. *The gift relationship: from human blood to social policy* (eds A. Oakley & J. Ashton, rev. edition). New York: The New Press.

TURNER, V. 1967. *The forest of symbols: aspects of Ndembu ritual.* New York: Cornell University Press.

VALENTINE, K. 2005. Citizenship, identity, blood donation. *Body & Society* **11: 2**, 113-28.

WADE, P. 1993. 'Race', nature and culture. *Man* (N.S.) **28**, 1-18.

——— 2002. *Race, nature and culture: an anthropological perspective.* London: Pluto.

——— (ed.) 2007. *Race, ethnicity and nation: perspectives from kinship and genetics.* Oxford: Berghahn.

WAGNER, R. 1975. *The invention of culture.* Englewood Cliffs, N.J.: Prentice-Hall.

WALDBY, C. 2002. Biomedicine, tissue transfer and intercorporeality. *Feminist Theory* **3**, 239-54.

——— & R. MITCHELL 2006. *Tissue economies: blood, organs and cell lines in late capitalism.* Durham, N.C.: Duke University Press.

WESTON, K. 1995. Forever is a long time: romancing the real in gay kinship ideologies. In *Naturalizing power: essays in feminist cultural analysis* (eds) S. Yanagisako & C. Delaney, 87-110. New York: Routledge.

——— 2001. Kinship, controversy, and the sharing of substance: the race/class politics of blood transfusion. In *Relative values: reconfiguring kinship studies* (eds) S. Franklin & S. McKinnon, 147-74. Durham, N.C.: Duke University Press.

White, L. 2000. *Speaking with vampires: rumor and history in colonial Africa*. Berkeley: University of California Press.

Williams, B.F. 1995. Classification systems revisited: kinship, caste, race, and nationality as the flow of blood and the spread of rights. In *Naturalizing power: essays in feminist cultural analysis* (eds) S. Yanagisako & C. Delaney, 201-38. London: Routledge.

Yanagisako, S. & C. Delaney 1995. Naturalizing power. In *Naturalizing power: essays in feminist cultural analysis* (eds) S. Yanagisako & C. Delaney, 1-22. London: Routledge.

1

Lifeblood, liquidity, and cash transfusions: beyond metaphor in the cultural study of finance

KATH WESTON *University of Virginia*

When the then newly elected President of the United States, Barack Obama, delivered his first address to Congress in 2009, blood was very much on his mind. The nation he proposed to lead was in the midst of one of the worst economic crises in its history and no one knew how or when things would improve. 'You can rely on the continued operation of our financial system', Obama promised his listeners, who might have paused to wonder why so much unsolicited reassurance should have been forthcoming. 'That is not the source of concern', he explained.

> The concern is that if we do not re-start lending in this country, our recovery will be choked off before it even begins. You see, *the flow of credit is the lifeblood of our economy*. The ability to get a loan is how you finance the purchase of everything from a home to a car to a college education; how stores stock their shelves, farms buy equipment, and businesses make payroll. But credit has stopped flowing the way it should (Obama 2009, my emphasis).

As indeed it had, if the mechanisms set up to measure 'liquidity' and 'cash flow' offered any guide.

'Lifeblood', 'liquidity', and 'flow' are just three in a series of linked somatic metaphors used to evoke visions of a thriving economy in contemporary global financial commentary. Together, they position blood (recast as money, cash, or credit) and its unimpeded circulation as integral to the health of a body economic. Although cultural studies of finance have turned to metaphor for inspiration in recent years, blood has received surprisingly little notice in these studies, despite the prominence of blood-related metaphors in current discussions of business practice. Instead, other sorts of biological tropes have held analysts' attention, from the 'animal spirits' of John Maynard Keynes to the 'glut' of savings in Asia and the 'toxicity' associated with irredeemable debt.

References to blood have surfaced repeatedly not only in presidential addresses, but also in press coverage of financial developments, advertisements for commodities, and how-to manuals directed at entrepreneurs. Sometimes these metaphors allude to blood

Blood: Will Out: Essays on Liquid Transfers and Flows, First Edition. Edited by Janet Carsten. © 2013 Royal Anthropological Institute of Great Britain & Ireland. Published 2013 by John Wiley & Sons Ltd.

directly, as with the notion of credit as lifeblood; sometimes they operate more obliquely, as is the case with financial liquidity, which finds its counterpart in assays of blood volume. Although such allusions might appear in twenty-first-century contexts, they are filtered through scientifically constituted, historically specific, sometimes contradictory conceptions of the workings of human bodies and the remedies prescribed to restore those bodies to health. During the Great Financial Crisis of 2008, for example, calls to administer 'cash transfusions' to insurance companies and investment banks became routine. Some scholars, such as Philip Mirowski (1989; 2009), have gone so far as to argue that the application of biological metaphors to economics is now on the ascendant. In the process, Mirowski contends, they may be overtaking metaphors derived from physics – such as force and the conservation of energy – that once infused neoclassical economics.

The essay that follows begins by examining contemporary symbolic resonances between blood and finance, but goes on to argue that the imagery associated with blood/money coursing through a 'healthy economy' is neither new nor strictly metaphorical. William Harvey published his treatise on the circulation of the blood, *Exercitatio anatomica de motu cordis et sanguinis in animalibus* (Anatomical disputation on the motion of the heart and blood in animals), in 1628 at a time when colonization of the Americas and the expansion of international trade had begun to reshape the English economy. This novel understanding of the physiology of blood circulation gave rise to economic analogues in which trade and finance appeared to be ordered by systemic and cyclical principles, with capital flowing through conduits, sometimes like water but more often like blood, with economies expanding and contracting to the diastolic and systolic rhythms of the heart. David McNally (2011: 26-7) traces the growing interest in anatomy during this period back to the colonial ventures of the previous century, which witnessed a newfound 'joy in partitioning and mapping' that applied equally well to land claims and the dissection of bodies. The result, he argues, was a 'semantic inflation' of the term 'anatomy' to encompass topics that ranged from melancholy, botany, and wit to the political economy of Ireland. Charles Webster has noted in passing the elaboration of 'suggestive analogies between dynamic conceptions that emerged in the two fields of economics and physiology at the time of Harvey's work on circulation' (1979: 27). By the early modern period, notions of circulation that linked blood to capital coexisted more or less uneasily with medieval conceptions of embodiment that still vie for the attention of policy-makers today, as evidenced for instance in the notion of economic stagnation, which invokes a previous regime of bodily regulation premised on humours.

Critiques of the organic analogy in government (the body politic) and in social theory (structural functionalism) are well known, but their implications for the study of economics and finance are just beginning to be explored. A more nuanced, historicized, culturally located reading of biological tropes promises to move cultural studies of finance beyond the explication of an endless succession of metaphors, towards interpretations that take account of other literary devices, including analogy, allegory, and synecdoche, while restoring the interplay of blood, liquidity, and circulation back into its political-economic-scientific contexts.

Finance as blood sport: lifeblood, liquidity, bloodbaths, pressure, flow

Leaf through an English-language business magazine or scan a financial blog and you might easily come away with the impression that finance is a blood sport. Financial managers are advised to pay attention to liquidity in order to 'ensure the life's blood of your organization' (Fisher 2009). An Internet post on 'Do-It-Yourself Retailing' describes the Cash Turnover Ratio as 'an excellent way to examine your store's blood pressure' (Aiken 2005). After the New York Stock Exchange acquires a number of Supplementary Liquidity Providers (deemed essential enough to the operations of the exchange to be dignified with the abbreviation 'SLP'), the headline reads, 'NYSE to get new blood' (Zendrian 2009). A music video adopts the voice of an auditor to castigate 'zombie bankers' with 'wallets full of blood' for their part in producing an economic collapse in Ireland (homoludo 2009). When *Forbes* describes similar events from a shareholder's perspective, it proclaims that 'market blood baths' are the things that really 'make investors squirm' (Myers 2009).

In global media coverage, accounts frequently shift towards the rhetoric of flows, but the substance that ought to be flowing in order to secure international trade and investment is still, more often than not, capital figured as blood. In an op-ed in *The Economic Times* on India's neoliberal embrace of less regulated markets, for example, Jim Quigley (2009), the CEO of Deloitte Touche Tohmatsu, avers, 'Because the free flow of capital is the life-blood of sustainable economic growth and expanding prosperity, the world community at large – especially the G20 nations – needs to continue to facilitate and safeguard the flow of capital across borders'. Moving from metaphor to analogy, Eduardo Cavallo and Alejandro Izquierdo (2009), in a discussion of Latin America's response to the credit crunch, describe credit flows as

> the blood of the world's economic system. When a human artery becomes clogged and the blood flow is interrupted, the consequences can be dire unless the flow is restored promptly. Similarly, a sudden stop in capital flows that blocks the normal supply of international credit to countries can inflict serious damage on the affected economies unless decisive action is taken.

Even computer modelling tools have been known to treat the flow of capital and the flow of blood as interchangeable for purposes of assessment. The Partition Decoupling Method, for example, can be used to track movements in the equities markets, the fantastic voyage of blood through the brain, or the flow of a politician's votes over the course of a career. According to Daniel Rockmore, one of the researchers who developed the tool, '[I]t is this idea of flow, be it capital, oxygenated blood, or political orientation, that we are capturing' (Science Daily 2008).

This series, if not quite set, of linked metaphors – lifeblood, liquidity, bloodbaths, blood pressure, flow, but also (as we shall see) circulation, transfusion, purging, and stagnation – yields more than a metaphorical understanding of the operations of finance. The smooth passage from metaphor to analogy in Cavallo and Izquierdo's commentary on Latin American finance offers a clue as to how this comes about. A particular piece of analysis or description might begin with a trope such as lifeblood, which, in its application to capital, credit, and cash flow, is so pervasive as to have become a cliché. From bodily fluids and anatomy it is literally a textbook operation to move on to physiology, so that the workings of the economy come to be evaluated in terms of a blood/capital supply that courses through the body economic at optimal pressure. Maghawri Shalabi, an economic researcher, is credited with recasting the relationship in the form of a structuralist syllogism: 'liquidity to the economy, what blood is to the heart' (Politics in Depth 2000). Interrupt the flow in any significant way and you get what neurologist James Park (2011) has termed a 'body economy' in 'septic shock'.

Nor does analogy exhaust the array of literary devices employed to illustrate the atlas of this globalized, financialized body. Synecdoche, for example, which political economists of the nineteenth century such as Marx deployed very effectively, can also come into play. Cash flow, just one among many standardized indicators used to value corporate assets, stands in for liquidity, which in turn stands in for that always desirable but ultimately nebulous condition called economic 'strength'.

Notice, too, the cultural and historical specificity of these metaphors, analogies, and instances of synecdoche as they resonate with readers for whom an economy nourished by blood has become naturalized. Lifeblood is not plain old blood, but blood conceived in medieval European fashion as the seat of vitality (Bildhauer, this volume; Bynum 2007). The idea of blood as nourishment itself significantly predates the scientific investigations of William Harvey, whose work in the seventeenth century revolutionized European understandings of what blood is and does. This body economic is also worlds and eras away from the idealized Chinese body explored by Shigehisa Kuriyama (2002), with its multiple pulses, its evaluation of health through colour, and its channels for winds that refuse to reveal themselves to the crude devices of dissection.

Kuriyama skillfully demonstrates how medical protocols for diagnosis that share certain categories can evoke fundamentally different notions of the body linked to different medical regimes. The 'pulse' of classical Chinese medicine was not at all the 'pulse' detected by the doctor of ancient Greek medicine. How, then, to understand the appearance of sanguinary discourse in financial commentary outside Europe and North America? One way, already familiar from studies of diaspora and globalization, would be to speak of categories that travel. There is certainly evidence of that: the trope of an economic system in cardiac arrest, for example, appears to have gained global currency after 2008 thanks to the 'circulation' of an already world-travelling publication, the *Financial Times*.[1] Yet knowledge of a point of departure does not explain much about the multiple valences, significations, and categorization practices that accrue to wandering tropes, as Vincanne Adams (2001) has shown in her work on the creative ambiguities fostered by Tibetan medicine's engagement with 'Western' science.

When authors as diversely located as Mohamed Arif (1998; writing about Malaysia's experience during the 1997-8 Asian Financial Crisis), Anders Petterson (2008; assessing the impact of the 2008 economic collapse on Indian art), and Spengler (2011; explaining volatility in equities markets in a column for the *Asia Times*) employ the tropes of 'cardiac arrest' and 'lifeblood' to make their points, there is something travelling, something shared, but also something likely to carry different meanings for readers in places where antibiotics coexist with regimes of bodily care that do not trace their lineage through European science. When the Bangladeshi Prime Minister, Sheikh Hasina, castigated microfinance for 'sucking the blood of the poor', the resonances beg to be explored, not assumed.[2] The same might be said for missives penned betwixt and between, such as the one from the Seoul-born, Washington D.C.-residing anonymous author of the blog 'Ask a Korean!' (2011), which hazarded that during the Asian Financial Crisis of 1997-8 'the State of Korea's reserves may have been the cholesterol in the blood vessels that caused the heart attack, but there were other factors that caused the overeating and unhealthy lifestyle that got it to the high level of cholesterol in the first place'. Likewise, when economist Ricardo J. Caballero (2010) titled his lecture to the International Monetary Fund 'Sudden financial arrest' and included 'defibrillation' in his list of keywords, who could know without asking what a roomful of cosmopolitan listeners from across the globe heard, found convincing or unconvincing, and why? Although this essay focuses on the history of European science in an attempt to understand how a circulatory conception of blood became naturalized in economic discourse, subsequent investigations would do well to attend to subtle shifts of meaning and practice as these tropes travel, rather than simply the mobility of the categories themselves.

From descriptions of an economy nourished by blood, periodically appraised in terms of vigour and well-being, it is but a short step to medicalized prescription. The latter part of this essay explores how a politics of blood can underwrite a diagnostic regime that is dedicated to ensuring an economy's 'health', in ways that end up promoting certain economic policies and interventions over others. First, however, I want to examine the historical introduction of the concept of circulation into this metaphorical mix. In the contemporary world of finance, the circulation of blood/cash/credit operates not simply as an organizing trope that condenses the meanings carried by the series of linked metaphors explored above, although it is that. Like other master tropes, this one has not so much succeeded as layered itself over the earlier conceptions it proposed to replace. The physiological connotations of circulation set metaphors such as lifeblood, liquidity, and flow in motion in such a way that they have come to appear merely descriptive of financial transactions, rather than based on an analogy with bodily processes or, heaven forbid, a characterization of affairs that is politicized and open to change.

Dissecting the physiology of capital circulation: The legacies of William Harvey

It has become a truism that capital circulates. What else would it do? When conditions are right, it is supposed to circulate freely and smoothly, returning to its owner bearing profits and awaiting reinvestment. Capital pours across borders, sometimes surging, sometimes streaming, occasionally flooding markets. In times of financial crisis, capital stagnates, refusing to make its appointed rounds, while policy-makers set about the bloody business of determining how to treat an economy that, by this measure alone, must surely be ailing. Scholarly accounts, like popular accounts, tend to feature circuits and flows of capital, not symmetries of capital, not metaphors derived from quantum spin or photosynthesis or optics, not even the theatrical metaphors once applied to trade and anatomical dissection in Renaissance England.

There was a time, of course, when to speak of circulation was to court charges of heresy. Contemporary schoolchildren who read about William Harvey's 'discovery' of the circulation of blood in the seventeenth century often wonder what all the fuss was about. According to Geoffrey Keynes, the brother of John Maynard Keynes and one of Harvey's few biographers, 'We have Aubrey's statement, attributed to Harvey himself, that after his book was published "he fell mightily in his Practize and that 'twas believed by the vulgar that he was crack-brained; and all the Physitians were against his Opinion and envyed him" ' (1966: 178). In his treatise on circulation, Harvey anticipated just this result, writing,

> But what remains to be said upon the quantity and source of the blood which thus passes, is of a character so novel and unheard-of that I not only fear injury to myself from the envy of a few, but I tremble lest I have mankind at large for my enemies, so much doth wont and custom become a second nature (Harvey 1889 [1628]: 47-8).

Why, people today might wonder, would Harvey have had to take such care in publishing the results of his experiments? Why should he have worried about the reactions of the College of Physicians or religious authorities? They do well to wonder, because they live in a time/place in which the circulation of blood in bodies and in capital markets has become as naturalized as Galen's proclamations about bodily humours once were. It is hard for them to conceive of a mammalian organism, or an economy, that would operate otherwise. When they entertain such a thought, it is generally construed in terms of some personalized ignorance about the way things really work, an ignorance already historically laid to rest by European science.

Harvey's *Exercitatio anatomica de motu cordis et sanguinis in animalibus* is widely credited as the publication that 'dispelled forever' the view of human physiology that had come down from Aristotle through Galen, with relatively minor modifications by Harvey's teachers at the University of Padua, a leading Renaissance institution for the study of anatomy (see Shackelford 2003: 43). Historians of science have also heralded *De motu cordis* as a pathbreaking work in terms of its recourse to observation and experimentation – that is, to scientific method – in making its arguments (see French 2006; McMullen 1998; Power 2007 [1897]). Before Harvey put forward the notion of what science today considers a unified cardiovascular system, the function of the veins and the connection of lungs to the heart were certainly subject to debate, but the terms of debate did not allow for a circular path by which blood made its way back to the heart, only to set out again on another journey through the body.

The medical curriculum to which Harvey would have been exposed during his early studies at Cambridge still relied on the four humours – blood, choler, phlegm, and melancholy – and still used Aristotle's works to demarcate its fields of study. Greek classics and Galen's treatises were leavened with translations of a few Arabic works, such as Ibn Sina's (Avicenna's) *Al-qanun fi'l-tibb* (The canon of medicine).[3] Public dissections that he witnessed at Cambridge and later at Padua would have offered Harvey the opportunity to observe anatomical structures in detail, although, as Lorraine Daston (1992) astutely points out, observing does not always mean seeing, and the conventions of seeing must also be learned, if only in order later to be overturned.[4] Vesalius' heirs on the faculty at Padua were themselves engaged in unravelling the mysteries of heart, lungs, and blood vessels, particularly the valves, which Fabricius called *ostiolum* ('little doors').

Most of Harvey's teachers and peers thought that veins existed to carry the blood to the body's extremities and provide them with nourishment. The idea that blood might return to the heart via a closed circuit had scarcely been entertained. It is in this context that *De motu cordis* ushered in its paradigm shift:

> I frequently and seriously bethought me, and long revolved in my mind, what might be the quantity of blood which was transmitted, in how short a time its passage might be effected, and the like. But not finding it possible that this could be supplied by the juices of the ingested aliment without the veins on the one hand becoming drained, and the arteries on the other getting ruptured through the excessive charge of blood, unless the blood should somehow find its way from the arteries into the veins, and so return to the right side of the heart; I began to think whether there might not be A MOTION, AS IT WERE, IN A CIRCLE. Now this I afterwards found to be true ... (Harvey 1889 [1628]: 48).

At the same time, Harvey was eager to dispatch beliefs about the action of the arteries and the heart that he perceived to be contradicted by reason and evidence. Why, he asked, would veins be larger near the heart than the liver if they truly originated in the liver? He repeated Galen's experiment of incising the trachea of a dog while it was still alive, using a bellows to fill its lungs, without discovering any trace of air travelling through the heart or the 'great vessels'. He concluded that arteries did not, as Galen maintained, contain air or *pneuma*. Neither could the interventricular septum be observed allowing blood to seep from one ventricle of the heart to another, as was commonly believed. What's more, based on Harvey's calculations, blood did not traverse the lungs solely to nourish them, since the volume of blood supplied to the lungs was so great as to render that old conviction improbable.

Last but not least, Harvey attempted to duplicate another of Galen's demonstrations, the ligature experiment, which he used to excellent effect to illustrate the process by which he inferred circulation (see Fig. 1.1). Application of pressure to a vein in the arm established the directionality of blood flow, with blood backing up at the site nearest the heart where the vein was pinched and failing to refill where the vessel was pinched farther down. Likewise, tying off a large vein near the heart and opening an artery resulted in arteries emptied of blood but veins fully engorged because blood could not travel 'backward'. By opening in one direction only, the valves in the veins helped establish a unidirectional flow. What more did physicians need to confirm that

> the blood in the animal body is impelled in a circle, and is in a state of ceaseless motion; that this is the act or function which the heart performs by means of its pulse; and that it is the sole and only end of the motion and contraction of the heart (Harvey 1889 [1628]: 71)?

Arteries and veins carried the same blood, not qualitatively different substances. Although the optical equipment of the day could not detect the presence of capillaries, Harvey was convinced a material connection was there, waiting to be discerned with a more sensitive apparatus.

It took time for circulation to become a commonplace in everyday European descriptions of how the world works and a centrepiece in studies of political economy. When it comes to travelling in circles, people in medieval and even Renaissance

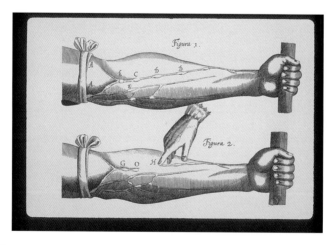

Figure 1.1. Illustration of the ligature experiment from Harvey's *De motu cordis*, 1628. (Photo: Richard Sennett.)

England were more familiar with the idea of circumambulation, in which they made a circuit of veneration within a church or cathedral. A scholar such as Patrick Geary (1986) who has written about the 'commodification' and 'circulation' of medieval relics consequently uses circulation as a contemporary analytic category rather than as a concept that also had symbolic resonance during the period under study.

Although initially received with scepticism, the concept of a body vivified by circulation did eventually enter popular discourse, until it came to be received less as theoretical assessment than as realist description. Still, it would be a mistake to seek to ground modern understandings of the movements of capital in modern understandings of the physiology of blood flow: that is, to treat financial circulation as an analogy elaborated upon a corporeal base. The analogy runs both ways, from the circulation of blood to the circulation of capital and from the circulation of capital to the circulation of blood, as they produce more complex discursive forms such as analogy. In this regard it is worth noting that Harvey was born into a farming and business family. His father had prospered with the expansion of international trade in the Mediterranean region during the late sixteenth century, and three of his brothers were members of the Grocers, Levant, and East India Companies, respectively (Shackelford 2003; Webster 1979). Categories such as 'redistribution' and 'exchange' that are embedded in Harvey's accounts of the relationship of blood to the organs were already circulating, as it were, with the bales and barrels shipped by late Renaissance merchants.

By the nineteenth century, references to circulation had become common whenever people tried to explain economic relations. Whether or not individual references to circulation referenced blood was not the point. Resonance, not reference, was the key. In a world where blood was known to circulate, any reference to circulation offered *matériel* for organic analogies that, in turn, could generate new modes of apprehension and political possibility while implicitly foreclosing others. Adam Smith felt comfortable attributing inequality to European policies that restricted 'the free circulation of labor and stock, both from employment to employment and from place to place' (1970 [1776]: Bk I, chap. 10). Marx's general formula for capital focused on the circulation of commodities: C-M-C (commodities transformed into money transformed back into commodities) and M-C-M (money used to purchase commodities in order to generate money) (Marx 1992 [1867]: chap. 4). The question for capitalist modernity was never *whether* capital or labour or goods circulated, but *how*, and how best to grasp the political implications of their travels.

Organic economic analogies: Mixing more than metaphors

In the aftermath of the Great Financial Crisis of 2008, John Mauldin (2010), a financial analyst, declared, 'The Federal Reserve and the central banks in general are running a grand experiment on the economic body, without the benefit of anesthesia'. Corporations that received government assistance during the crisis were said to go on 'life support', while banks judged 'too big to fail' were subjected to 'stress tests' like any cardiac patient and urged to write 'living wills' that would allow their affairs to unwind in an orderly manner should they become insolvent. Paul Volcker, the head of the US Economic Recovery Advisory Board and one-time chair of the Federal Reserve, took the analogy a step further when he proposed to institute a legal distinction between banks, which would be eligible to go on life support during an emergency, and non-bank financial corporations, which would instead become candidates for 'euthanasia' (Freeland & Guerrera 2010).

Commentators frequently portrayed the crisis itself as an episode of blood loss, and not just in North American media outlets. Sun Lijian, a professor of economics and finance at Fudan University, posted an entry on his blog about the effects of US Federal Reserve policy on the Chinese economy (Sun 2009). Referring to his post entitled 'Controlling blood loss is more important than receiving a blood transfusion', he depicted the Federal Reserve's purchase of mortgage-backed securities as a 'large-scale "blood transfusion" plan' designed to ameliorate the worst effects of the bleeding, in tandem with efforts to 'create new blood flow' through looser monetary policies. Without an uninterrupted, freely circulating, high-volume, liquid flow of capital and credit, the financial system seemingly could not recover.

Sometimes the organs that brought organic analogies to life were only tacitly evoked. While analysts often spoke of liquidity being 'pumped' into the system, for instance, they only occasionally identified the pump. In Harvey's account of circulation, the pump, of course, is the heart, whose regular rhythms of contraction and release keep blood moving through a circuit. What happens when that heart/pump falters? In an attempt to describe the situation after the US government took over the mammoth insurance corporation AIG on 17 September 2008, Nouriel Roubini put it this way: 'It was scary, how the entire system froze up. Every part of the financial system, every part of the credit system. Nobody could borrow money. It was like a cardiac arrest of the global financial system' (in F. Ferguson 2010). After the 2007 bank runs on Northern Rock in Britain, a team of social scientists at Cambridge even worked their way backwards through the analogy, asking whether a banking panic really could 'break your heart', and concluding that elevated male mortality rates from heart disease tend to accompany systemic banking crises (Stuckler, Meissner & King 2008).

In the contemporary world of finance, central banks serve as a kind of artificial heart, intervening to re-establish flow when circulation falters, and not always successfully. Three years after 'the financial system had a heart attack' following the collapse of the investment bank Lehman Brothers, opined financial writer Anthony Hilton (2011), an infirm global economy still had to 'get its strength back', despite the best efforts of the world's financial overseers. James Park (2011) extended the analogy a bit further, depicting the US Federal Reserve Bank's 'newly conjured solvent' of liquidity, designed to restore blood/credit flow, as 'trapped on the balance sheets of banks, away from the vasculature'.

In many cases, the organic analogy of circulation in finance to circulation in bodies is predicated on a second-order mechanical analogy. With only two cadavers allotted annually for dissection in the operating theatre of the University of Oxford, where Harvey later taught, the innards of a water pump were more familiar to Harvey's readers than the innards of a corpse. At one point *De motu cordis* even compares the contraction of chambers within the heart to the operation of a firearm, when a tug on the trigger, the sparking of the flint, and the ignition of the powder appear to coincide.

On the slippage between organic and mechanical analogy, here is Roubini again, writing with coauthor Stephen Mihm, about the limited powers wielded by the Federal Reserve Bank in the United States: 'The Fed could pump plenty of water or liquidity into the banks, but it could not make them lend' (Roubini & Mihm 2010: 145). A little further down, on the same page of their book *Crisis economics* and without any sense of mismatch or incongruity, they transition smoothly from this water-based hydraulic metaphor to a blood-based organic analogy: 'Measurements like the TED spread are a bit like blood pressure readings: they reflect the underlying health of the economy's circulatory system. They reveal how readily money flows through the economy, or how "liquid" markets are at a given moment.[5] One type of liquidity flows into another.

Organic analogies shape more than an economic body in distress. Transfusion may signify one type of emergency intervention, pumping to make up for blood loss and restore blood pressure another, but circulation represents a utopian default state in which capital (and sometimes labour) makes its rounds without obstruction and returns to its investor bearing profit. Ideally, capital flows in a cycle, with leading and trailing indicators of its current position along a circular trajectory.[6] Business, too, cycles around an endless ring of expansion and contraction, in a rhythm that corresponds to the diastolic and systolic cadence of the heart. During systole, the heart pushes blood through the veins much as the economy contracts, expelling uncompetitive businesses while nourishing the enterprises that remain. During diastole, the economy recharges, filling up with capital as credit expands, much as the heart gathers blood before going on to the next beat. Too much credit and 'hemodilution or inflation' can occur, unless, as James Park (2011) puts it, more 'special factors that make blood, the essence of life', are produced. By 'special factors', Park has in mind haematopoietic stem cells, the manufacturers of lymphocytes and erythrocytes in a human body and, by extension, 'the entrepreneurs who develop new products, build factories, and sell services for new markets'.

Like political organic analogies, economic organic analogies are somatic, but they tend to take as their object mammalian and more specifically human bodies. The liquid in liquidity (streaming cash or credit) is figured as blood, not sap. This despite the plant-based etymology of soma, which once referred to an intoxicating vegetable juice used in Vedic rituals. This despite frequent comparisons of the flow of 'life-giving' sap in plants to the flow of blood in animals. It is a reminder that other types of analogy, equally organic, are possible, even within the terms of what counts as an animate organism for Europeans, Americans, or members of a transnational business class educated according to the conventions of former colonial powers.

The particular resonance of blood for economic argument draws upon centuries of culturally inflected debate in Europe about royalty and relics, the blood of Christ and the blood of the experimentally transfused lamb.[7] Signification can also run in the other direction, of course, from blood to economics rather than economics to blood. Perhaps the most notable example would be the configuration of institutionalized blood donation services in the twentieth century as blood 'banking'.[8] This back-and-forth movement illustrates both the generative possibilities of blood and its ability to pre-empt debate as it naturalizes social processes and perfuses multiple domains.

Critiques of the organic analogy in political theory emphasize the misleading consequences of attributing the integrated, self-regulating, self-sustaining qualities of a biological life-form to institutions and social relations that can be none of these. The problem is not simply that an economy is not a body, that it cannot stretch or strategize or even perspire as it confronts ever-shifting financial challenges. In the realm of finance, organic analogies implicitly do the work of 'the economy' until that economy appears as a unified force located over and above us, a force subject to manipulation, perhaps, but with a life-course that it seems fruitless to question, much less to oppose outright. At best, the physical condition of 'the economy' can be scrutinized like that of any ailing patient and appropriate remedies prescribed. Rendered invisible are the ways in which capitalism reproduces inequalities, the ceaseless negotiations, the conflicts over land seizures and resource allocation, the push to incorporate every possible transaction into a market, the stubborn persistence of reciprocity and the narrowing of possibilities to give back.

The bloody politics of financial intervention

By taking financial transactions into the realm of health, disease, and diagnosis, analogies that rely upon what Catherine Gallagher (2008) has called 'somaeconomics' incorporate culturally and historically specific conceptions of bodies into prescriptions for a speedy recovery. At this point the metaphors begin to mix. When Adam Smith identifies an obstruction to the circulation of stock, he has inherited a world in which the circulatory system is scientifically established and blockages are understood to threaten the body as a whole. When Sun Lijian identifies an economy in a state of blood loss, the prescription for transfusions by central banks also invokes the paradigm shift ushered in by William Harvey, a body for which blood volume matters and circulation must rapidly re-establish itself in order to ward off death (see Lederer 2008). In contrast, when financial analysts identify the trouble as 'stagnation', they invoke an earlier medical regime in which physicians advocated bleeding to restore the sick to health.[9]

Different somatic models lead to different sorts of policy interventions. To characterize a financial crisis as a heart attack can make 'emergency' interventions seem sensible, if not requisite, in their scale and timing. To say that an economy 'haemorrhages jobs' is generally to advocate staunching the flow. The model here again is Harvey's: blood that has forsaken its return path to the heart is blood that brings the organism that much closer to crisis. This modern apprehension of blood as a fluid that moves through bodies via a series of closed conduits under pressure introduces an idiom of containment, what Bildhauer (in this volume) calls the 'popularity of seeing oneself as a container of blood, pierced at one's peril' (p. S73). As Martin (in this volume) points out, an emphasis on containment downplays permeability: that is, the ways in which substances such as nutrients, hormones, and oxygen carried by the blood eventually pass through the walls of the vessels. There is some evidence that jobs are not simply 'lost' or 'haemorrhaged' in times of crisis but instead filter into the underground economy in ways that augment informal sectors which themselves rely on unrecorded transactions (Mallet & Dinmore 2011; M.E. Smith 1990). The circulatory system analogy makes it harder to perceive such phenomena and to frame policy recommendations accordingly.

A rather different remedy has emerged with the call to treat financial panics and recessions as opportunities to 'purge' the economy of uncompetitive businesses.[10] Depletion, it seems, can be salutary for the type of body conceived centuries earlier by Galen.[11] In Galenic medicine, excess blood and stagnant blood posed a threat to health. Doctors attempted to balance humours through blood-letting to achieve *eucrasia* rather than to re-establish adequate pressure and circulation. No need to 'pump liquidity' into bodies or businesses conceived along these lines.

Sometimes contemporary financial commentary takes an earlier somatic model as its point of departure, only to dismiss the course of treatment it would seem to indicate. Consider the recommendation by the financier George Soros (2010) to institute currency boards in order to fix the exchange rate in such a way that a nation's money supply could never exceed its foreign reserves. During the type of financial panic in which banks withdraw credit and investors rapidly move capital out of a country, the board would sell foreign reserves, which would lower the domestic money supply accordingly. Paul Davidson, an economist, explained his opposition to the proposal this way: 'A currency board solution ... is equivalent to the blood letting [*sic*] prescribed by 17th century doctors to cure a fever. Enough blood loss can, of course, always reduce the fever but often at a terrible cost to the body of the patient' (1998: 13). Joseph Stiglitz took a similar view of the European austerity schemes developed to address sovereign debt problems attendant on the 2008 credit crisis. 'It reminds me of medieval medicine', he explained.

> It is like blood-letting, where you took blood out of a patient because the theory was that there were bad humours. And very often, when you took the blood out, the patient got sicker. The response then was more blood-letting until the patient very nearly died. What is happening in Europe is a mutual suicide pact (cited in Moore 2012).

In such critiques as these, the Galenic therapy figures as a discredited remedy, the sort that might be efficacious in alleviating symptoms but only by injuring the economy it promises to revive. Although the debate here turns on the trope of blood-letting, its appeal is to readers who already know about the circulatory system, readers who regard blood-letting as a misguided and outmoded treatment for a body now known to work differently.

Regardless of the somatic model or the medical regime brought into play following a diagnosis of economic ill-health, it is noteworthy that financial commentary seldom traffics in corpses, funerals, or cadavers. The body of the economy-as-patient is always alive, though perhaps just hanging on. It is a body awaiting a cure, and so, of course, its policy physicians. Whether they be proper doctors or empiricks (a term for quacks popular in Renaissance England), only time and profits will tell.

Meta-materiality: Beyond metaphor in the study of finance

All this takes us well beyond metaphor. On the one hand, metaphors connected to the physiology of blood, whether ancient, medieval, or modern, have provided the scaffolding for elaborate analogies, synecdoches, and a panoply of other literary devices whose significance for the study of finance has yet to be explored. On the other hand, there is something at play in these accounts that exceeds the literary, or at least lends rhetoric a certain fateful materiality. Some bodies appear blooded, their internal fluids stagnant, pressurized, or smoothly circulating, as the case may be. Others emerge from economic relations thoroughly bloodied, the signifier of their encounters with finance oozing through the skin for all the world to see.

One of the most famous adages in which blood figures in the history of European finance is attributed to Baron Rothschild, a member of the British nobility and scion of the Rothschild banking family. According to Daniel Myers, writing for *Forbes*, Rothschild is widely credited 'with saying that "the time to buy is when there's blood in the streets" '. Rothschild made a fortune buying into the Panic of 1871, when the Paris Commune seized the reins of government and had most investors running for cover. But that's not the whole story. The full adage admonishes, 'Buy when there's blood in the streets, even if the blood is your own' (cited in Myers 2009). According to economic historian Niall Ferguson (2000), the quotation itself is likely apocryphal. Yet it is still meaningful that various permutations of this quotation continue to move across the globe, ranging from 'buy when there's blood running on Wall Street' to 'when there's blood in the streets, buy property'. There are echoes of the French Revolution here, the crowds crying out for bread and blood, only one of which they received in the quantities demanded.

In a material sense the baron probably spilled more tears than blood as he scrambled to recoup his initial losses. But the crimson backdrop alluded to by the investors who succeeded him is something else again: it is the backdrop of social unrest, when weapons coax blood out of bodies, the hermetic seal of the skin no match for rough justice. This is not lifeblood as the circulating seat of economic vitality, the nourishing movement of capital, but lifeblood whose violent passage into the world circulates as a symbol of the depredations, loss, and discontent that accompany the expansion of market economies.

In this discourse the blood shed in pursuit of conquest waters the earth, a gruesome rain that allows profits to grow. There is blood in the water on Wall Street when derivatives sellers successfully ply their trade (Portnoy 2009). Cowry shells, used as currency to tally the sale of human flesh, turn monstrous, feasting on the bodies of Africans thrown overboard during the Middle Passage (Baucom 2005). The blood of the slaves who survive contributes to the fortunes of that self-same Rothschild family (Hoyos 2009). Blood escapes the bodies that could not, and becomes integral to the generation of wealth.

During the Great Financial Crisis of the early twenty-first century, commentators noted two related phenomena, although they did not pause to connect them. In the United States, sales of blood, eggs, hair, and sperm were up – way up – at centres that collected them. Meanwhile, in Thailand, protesters used their own blood in a variety of creative ways to register political demands linked to economic tensions.

In the first case, the blood bank at Stanford University, which recognized financial pressure as an incentive to part with bodily fluids, even began to offer career counsel-ling to prospective clients. 'It was definitely like: Give blood, get your resume critiqued', one donor explained (cited in Kimball 2009). In this case blood at its most material provided a barometer of economic conditions, setting up an indexical rather than an analogous relationship between the corporeal and the financial. From a trader's per-spective, the blood bank index could almost be considered a type of economic indica-tor, like the ones that track housing starts, trucking shipments, or the FTSE.

In the second instance, labourers and farmers in Thailand took to the streets to demand a new government, the latest economic meltdown shadowed for many by memories of the 1997-8 Asian financial crisis, when the baht suddenly dropped in value. Their tactic of spattering human blood on government offices and drenching their clothes with blood earned them the sobriquet 'Red Shirts'. The point, they said, was to dramatize the sacrifices they were willing to make for democracy. Like the Indian nationalist painters discussed by Copeman (in this volume) who used physical blood to create their art, like the peace activists who poured their own blood over draft files in the United States during the Vietnam War, the Thai protesters advanced what Copeman calls a 'sanguinary politics', in which blood signifies both the excesses of the regime under protest and the willingness of the demonstrators to sacrifice for their cause.[12] But to signify as sacrifice, a certain understanding of how bodies work, heal, and die must already be in place. (Recall that medieval European body, which figured less as hermetic container than as a creature prone to imbalance or excess, and which was wont to benefit rather than suffer from moderate applications of the knife.) While the Red Shirts were busy organizing mass blood donation events that observers praised for their hygiene (see Fig. 1.2), the President of the Board of Governors of the Stock Exchange of Thailand, Patareeya Benjapolchai, felt compelled to issue reassuring public statements about the rapidity with which she expected everything to 'return to normal' (Ahuja 2010).

Blood as economic indicator, blood as political gambit, blood as business as usual. In each case the symbolism is of great significance for financial analysis, but the meanings do not run simply through metaphor, nor can they be taken literally. At play is a kind of

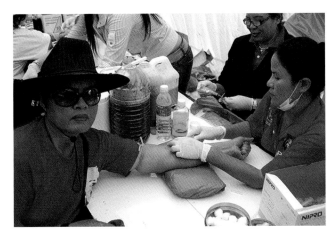

Figure 1.2. Donating blood for the Red Shirt campaign in Thailand. (Photo: Newley Purnell.)

meta-materiality in which the use of symbolically charged materials such as blood sets up a resonance that draws attention to power differentials and insists that people look again. It is the very physicality of the blood that allows it to signify so forcefully as protest, as sacrifice (Copeman, this volume), as revelatory of truth (Carsten, this volume), as a commodified substance in a time of economic distress (Lederer and Whitfield, this volume), as a reminder of costs and cruelties obscured by abstracted economic relations. Meta-materiality is no metaphysics. The sellers of blood during the Great Financial Crisis who could not afford breakfast had to ward off fainting episodes once their bodies were down a pint. They knew well that cash gained through the commodification of blood can represent a loss for the body, and the consequences of that loss are none too lyrical.

Meta-materiality goes beyond metaphor to enlist the material, beyond the material to figure substance through metaphor, analogy, and whatever other historically situated heuristic devices people find available. In Bangkok the protesters did not soak their shirts in a substance reminiscent of blood; it *was* blood, and that made all the difference. What's more, it was their own. But because these bodies were not the ones sold to, or the ones railed against, the blood the protesters shed was symbolically incompatible with the blood that others had the luxury to retain. Theirs was never the economic body of financial management, with its policy prescriptions for monetarist intervention or restraint by central banks imaged through modern or medieval somatic conceptions, as the case may be. The meta-material character of the Red Shirts' protest matters, the conditions under which those breathing, bleeding bodies raised their voices matter, because different somatic relations open up different possibilities for engagement.

William Harvey wrote another book after *De motu cordis* that is much less celebrated, when it is read at all. *Exercitationes de generatione animalium* (Disputations on the generation of animals) puzzles over the origins and development of life itself. Even Harvey's most sympathetic critics have regarded this book as a throwback, an excursion into mysticism (or even senility) that contrasts sharply with the prescience of his work on cardiovascular circulation. Certainly no one, today or in Harvey's day, would consult *De generatione* for a definitive explanation of embryology.[13] Yet this book has much to say, albeit obliquely and at the remove of centuries, about the discursive connection between the *circulation* of money and the *generation* of wealth. Renaissance debates about biological generation, like Renaissance debates about circulation, have made their way unheralded into accounts of finance. Where does wealth come from? Why does capital beget more capital? What makes a family fortune grow? Who can legitimately claim the spoils? How do fractional reserve banking and derivatives create credit out of thin air? The early modern controversies once associated with circulation and generation are with us still. They have simply been displaced.

NOTES

Many thanks to everyone who participated in the Edinburgh workshop on 'The Multiple Meanings and Symbolic Resonance of Blood' for their intellectual generosity and insightful comments on an early draft of this chapter. Janet Carsten provided the perfect blend of editorial acumen and wit, as well as much-needed encouragement and hospitality when the after-effects of the Eyjafjallajökull volcano detoured my workshop flight. A previous version of the essay was also presented in the Department of Social Anthropology's seminar series at the University of Aberdeen, where James Leach, Marysia Zalewski, and their colleagues provided excellent critical feedback. Geeta Patel deserves special thanks for getting me to push my thinking that last little bit past where I thought I could go.

[1] A conjecture based upon mention of the *Financial Times* (without citation) in association with the repetition of the 'cardiac arrest' trope in a range of global media outlets, both print- and Internet-based. One possible source published in the *FT* early in the unfolding crisis is an op-ed titled 'Only new thinking will save the global economy', in which Mohamed El-Erian (2008) argued that indices of economic and financial relationships at that time exhibited 'characteristics of cardiac arrest'.

[2] For a discussion of the political context for Hasina's statement, see Sobhan (2012).

[3] Keynes (1966: 16) takes the brevity of Harvey's sojourn at Padua, in association with the sophistication of his later researches, as a sign that Harvey had learned more during his time at Cambridge than previously thought.

[4] See Daston's (1992) discussion of shifting pedagogies and conventions of observation in the history of European science, particularly those associated with the rise of what she calls aperspectival objectivism.

[5] The TED spread represents the difference between the interest rate banks charge for the loans they make to one another and the interest rate on the short-term US Treasury debt known as T-bills. The 'T' in TED stands for T-bills, the 'ED' for eurodollar futures contracts.

[6] For an exposition of the relationship between capital flow cycles and the perceived interruption of sovereign debt crises, see Reinhart & Rogoff (2009).

[7] An allusion, of course, to the first well-documented attempt at human blood transfusion, in which Jean-Baptiste Denys injected the blood of a lamb into a young boy in mid-seventeenth-century France, but also to John Leacock's forgotten interspecies transfusion experiments in early nineteenth-century Edinburgh, which he performed on dogs, cats, and sheep (see Schmidt & Leacock 2002). For a fine discussion of sedimented meanings in European conceptions of blood, see Bynum (2007).

[8] See Weston (2002) and Lederer and Whitfield in this volume. I am grateful to Janet Carsten for making the connection in this context.

[9] Keeping in mind that Harvey himself saw no tension between an understanding of blood as a substance that circulated through the body under pressure and the practice of phlebotomy, which he likely employed in his ministrations as a physician and correlated with observed recoveries of patients (see Davis 1971). Whether or not the theory of circulation should have any effect on the treatment of disease was a topic hotly debated throughout the latter part of the seventeenth century. Blood-letting became discredited in the hands of Harvey's successors, who invoked the circulation doctrine to argue the dangers and ineffectiveness of bleeding patients.

[10] 'Purging' as a way to restore the body economic to health is advice popularly associated with financial commentators who subscribe to tenets of the Austrian School of Economics (see Mansharamani 2011: 40-1).

[11] See Bildhauer in this volume for examples from medieval Europe of how occasional blood loss could be conceived as a means of safeguarding the body, so long as those losses were properly regulated.

[12] On the featured use of blood during draft board protests against the Vietnam War, see Berrigan with Wilcox (1996).

[13] But see also Cobb (2006: 29), whose revisionist reading situates Harvey's *De generatione* as problematic in its conclusions but none the less a work that 'placed the question of generation at the heart of scientific debate', sparking a succession of inquiries into where living things come from.

REFERENCES

ADAMS, V. 2001. The sacred in the scientific: ambiguous practices of science in Tibetan medicine. *Cultural Anthropology* **16**, 542-75.

AHUJA, A. 2010. Protesters splash blood outside Thai PM's office. Reuters, 16 March (available on-line: *http://www.reuters.com/article/2010/03/16/us-thailand-politics-idUSTRE62D03320100316*, accessed 11 January 2013).

AIKEN, B. 2005. Cash turnover: an excellent way to examine your store's blood pressure. *Do-It-Yourself Retailing*, 1 September (available on-line: *http://www.highbeam.com/doc/1G1-18904743.html*, accessed 11 January 2013).

ARIF, M. 1998. The Malaysian economic experience and its relevance for the OIC member countries. *Islamic Economic Studies* **6: 1**, 1-41.

ASK A KOREAN! 2011. IMF bailout of Korea during East Asian financial crisis (Part II). 19 July (available on-line: *http://askakorean.blogspot.co.uk/2011/07/imf-bailout-of-korea-during-east-asian.html*, accessed 11 January 2013).

BAUCOM, I. 2005. *Specters of the Atlantic: finance capital, slavery, and the philosophy of history*. Durham, N.C.: Duke University Press.

BERRIGAN, P. & F.A. WILCOX 1996. *Fighting the lamb's war: skirmishes with the American empire*. Monroe, Me: Common Courage Press.

BYNUM, C.W. 2007. *Wonderful blood: theology and practice in late medieval northern Germany and beyond*. Philadelphia: University of Pennsylvania Press.

CABALLERO, R.J. 2010. Sudden financial arrest. Lecture delivered at the International Monetary Fund's 10th Jacques Polack Annual Research Conference, 8 November (available on-line: *http://economics.mit.edu/files/6010*, accessed 11 January 2013).

CAVALLO, E. & A. IZQUIERDO 2009. Dealing with an international credit crunch: lessons from Latin America. 3 April (available on-line: *http://www.economonitor.com/blog/2009/04/dealing-with-an-international-credit-crunch-lessons-from-latin-america/*, accessed 11 January 2013).

COBB, M. 2006. *Generation: the seventeenth-century scientists who unraveled the secrets of sex, life, and growth*. London: Bloomsbury.

DASTON, L. 1992. Objectivity and the escape from perspective. *Social Studies of Science* **22**, 597-618.

DAVIDSON, P. 1998. The case for regulating international capital flows. Paper presented at the Social Market Foundation Seminar on Regulation of Capital Movements, London, 17 November (available on-line: *http://econ.bus.utk.edu/publications/davidsonpapers/reg2.pdf*, accessed 11 January 2013).

DAVIS, A.B. 1971. Some implications of the circulation theory for disease theory and treatment in the seventeenth century. *Journal of the History of Medicine* **26**, 28-39.

EL-ERIAN, M. 2008. Only new thinking will save the global economy. *Financial Times*, 3 December.

FERGUSON, F. (dir.) 2010. *Inside job*. Documentary film distributed by Sony Pictures.

FERGUSON, N. 2000. *The House of Rothschild, the world's banker, 1849-1999*, vol. 2. New York: Penguin.

FISHER, W.A., III 2009. Liquidity – ensure the life's blood of your organization (available on-line: *http://www.focusedfr.com/uploads/LIQUIDITY-_April_2009.docx*, accessed 11 January 2013).

FREELAND, C. & F. GUERRERA 2010. Goldman faces stark choice on 'Volcker Rule'. *Financial Times*, 12 February, 1.

FRENCH, R. 2006. *William Harvey's natural philosophy*. Cambridge: University Press.

GALLAGHER, C. 2008. *The body economic: life, death, and sensation in political economy and the Victorian novel*. Princeton: University Press.

GEARY, P. 1986. Sacred commodities: the circulation of medieval relics. In *The social life of things* (ed.) A. Appadurai, 169-91. Cambridge: University Press.

HARVEY, W. 1889 [1628]. *On the motion of the heart and blood in animals*. London: George Bell and Sons.

HILTON, A. 2011. Reminder of how weak financial system still is. *London Evening Standard*, 7 October (available on-line: *http://www.standard.co.uk/business/reminder-of-how-weak-financial-system-still-is-6451395.html*, accessed 11 January 2013).

HOMOLUDO 2009. Irish fact or science fiction? Wallets full of blood: zombie banker blues. 8 May (available on-line: *http://www.olwill.com/?p=170*, accessed 11 January 2013).

HOYOS, C. 2009. Rothschild and Freshfields founders had links to slavery, papers reveal. *Financial Times*, 27-8 June, 1, 4.

KEYNES, G. 1966. *The life of William Harvey*. Oxford: Clarendon Press.

KIMBALL, H. 2009. Cash poor? Hit the blood bank – and get career advice. Newser.com, 21 February (available on-line: *http://www.newser.com/story/51452/cash-poor-hit-the-blood-bank-and-get-career-advice.html*, accessed 11 January 2013).

KURIYAMA, S. 2002. *The expressiveness of the body and the divergence of Greek and Chinese medicine.* New York: Zone.

LEDERER, S.E. 2008. *Flesh and blood: organ transplantation and blood transfusion in twentieth-century America.* Oxford: University Press.

MCMULLEN, E.T. 1998. *William Harvey and the use of purpose in the scientific revolution.* Lanham, Md: University Press of America.

MCNALLY, D. 2011. *Monsters of the market: zombies, vampires, and global capitalism.* Leiden: Brill.

MALLET, V. & G. DINMORE 2011. Negative effects: a hidden economy ranging from sweatshops to professionals. *Financial Times,* 9 June, 11.

MANSHARAMANI, V. 2011. *Boombustology: spotting financial bubbles before they burst.* Hoboken, N.J.: Wiley.

MARX, K. 1992 [1867]. *Capital,* vol. 1. New York: Penguin.

MAULDIN, J. 2010. The implications of velocity. John Mauldin's Weekly E-Letter, 13 March (available on-line: *http://www.mauldineconomics.com/frontlinethoughts/the-implications-of-velocity-mwo031210,* accessed 11 January 2013).

MIROWSKI, P. 1989. *More heat than light: economics as social physics, physics as nature's economics.* Cambridge: University Press.

——— 2009. Desperately seeking biological warrants: the role of recent metaphors in trying to understand economic crisis. Paper delivered at the After the Crash, Beyond Liquidity conference, University of Virginia, October.

MOORE, M. 2012. Stiglitz says European austerity plans are a 'suicide pact'. *The Telegraph,* 29 April (available on-line: *http://www.telegraph.co.uk/finance/financialcrisis/9019819/Stiglitz-says-European-austerity-plans-are-a-suicide-pact.html,* accessed 11 January 2013).

MYERS, D. 2009. Buy when there's blood in the streets. Forbes.com, 23 February (available on-line: *http://www.forbes.com/2009/02/23/contrarian-markets-boeing-personal-finance_investopedia.html,* accessed 11 January 2013).

OBAMA, B. 2009. Remarks of President Barack Obama – as prepared for delivery address to joint session of Congress, 24 February (available on-line: *http://www.whitehouse.gov/the_press_office/remarks-of-president-barack-obama-address-to-joint-session-of-congress/,* accessed 11 January 2013).

PARK, J. 2011. The financial crisis: of blood and fungibility. *Financial Times,* 11 May (available on-line: *http://blogs.ft.com/economistsforum/2011/05/the-financial-crisis-of-blood-and-fungibility/,* accessed 11 January 2013).

PETTERSON, A. 2008. Re-assessment of the Indian art market. Indian Art News, 31 October (available on-line: *http://www.indianartnews.com/2008/10/italy-based-artist-kammie-soni-in-india.html?m=1,* accessed 11 January 2013).

POLITICS IN DEPTH TEAM 2000. Egypt: generating cash liquidity (available on-line: *http://www.onislam.net/english/politics/africa/418510.html,* accessed 11 January 2013).

PORTNOY, F. 2009. *F.I.A.S.C.O.: blood in the water on Wall Street.* New York: Norton.

POWER, D. 2007 [1897]. *William Harvey: masters of medicine.* Whitefish, Mont.: Kessinger Publishing.

QUIGLEY, J. 2009. The shift is on! Cross-border capital flows and the dynamic ascendancy of India. *The Economic Times,* 17 November.

REINHART, C.M. & K.S. ROGOFF 2009. *This time is different: eight centuries of financial folly.* Princeton: University Press.

ROUBINI, N. & S. MIHM 2010. *Crisis economics: a crash course in the future of finance.* New York: Penguin.

SCHMIDT, P.J. & A.G. LEACOCK 2002. Forgotten transfusion history: John Leacock of Barbados. *British Medical Journal* **325,** 1485-7.

SCIENCE DAILY 2008. Computational tool to untangle complex data developed. 18 December (available on-line: *http://www.sciencedaily.com/releases/2008/12/081216131022.htm,* accessed 11 January 2013).

SHACKELFORD, J. 2003. *William Harvey and the mechanics of the heart.* Oxford: University Press.

SMITH, A. 1970 [1776]. *The wealth of nations.* New York: Penguin.

SMITH, M.E. (ed.) 1990. *Perspectives on the informal economy.* Lanham, Md: University Press of America.

SOBHAN, Z. 2012. Olive branch or poison pill? *Sunday Guardian,* 29 April (available on-line: *http://www.sunday-guardian.com/analysis/olive-branch-or-poison-pill,* accessed 11 January 2013).

SOROS, G. 2010. America must face up to the dangers of derivatives. *Financial Times,* 23 April, 9.

SPENGLER 2011. Zombinomics and volatility. *Asia Times,* 14 June (available on-line: *http://www.atimes.com/atimes/Global_Economy/MF14Dj05.html,* accessed 11 January 2013).

STUCKLER, D., C.M. MEISSNER & L.P. KING 2008. Can a bank crisis break your heart? *Globalization and Health* **4: 1,** 1-4.

SUN, L. 2009. US Federal Reserve decisions will severely affect the Chinese economy (*http://chinanewswrap.com*, accessed 1 May 2010, no longer available on-line).

WEBSTER, C. 1979. William Harvey and the crisis of medicine in Jacobean England. In *William Harvey and his age: the professional and social context of the discovery of circulation* (ed.) J.J. Bylebyl, 1-27. Baltimore: Johns Hopkins University Press.

WESTON, K. 2002. Kinship, controversy, and the sharing of substance: the race/class politics of blood transfusion. In *Relative values: reconfiguring kinship studies* (eds) S. Franklin & S. McKinnon, 147-74. Durham, N.C.: Duke University Press.

ZENDRIAN, A. 2009. NYSE to get new blood (available on-line: *http://www.iinews.com/site/rss/WSL110308.pdf*, accessed 11 January 2013).

2

The way blood flows: the sacrificial value of intravenous drip use in Northeast Brazil

MAYA MAYBLIN *University of Edinburgh*

My mouth is dried up like baked clay ... you have brought me down to the dust of death.

Psalm 22:16

It was clinic day at the health post in the village of Santa Lucia; it happened every fifteen days. The brick building designated as the health post consisted of a single, rectangular room. Towards one end a faded cotton curtain separated the waiting area from the visiting doctor, Dr Renato,[1] who sat behind a laminate table. In a corner of this consultation area was a cupboard holding two cardboard boxes: one containing plasters, bandages, and antibacterial solutions; the other containing intravenous tubes, hypodermic needles, and packets of *soro* – sterile isotonic fluid. The clinic had barely begun but already the waiting area was full with patients. There were two assistants working with Dr Renato that morning: Rita, the nurse, and Lia, a general assistant-cum-receptionist. Both women lived in the village, and between them and Dida, the health post cleaner, the clinic was kept clean and in good working order. It was Dida who held the keys to the building and she who, every fifteen days, would leave home early in the morning to unlock the door and prepare the space for the doctor's arrival.

During fieldwork I was a regular attendee at the village clinic. Conversing with people in the waiting room was a good way to pass the hours. On this particular occasion I was greeted, somewhat unusually, by the sight of Lia, sitting at the receptionist's desk, and being hooked up to an isotonic drip. Rita, the nurse, was adjusting the drip stand beside her. Once she had made sure that the administering tube was not tangled, and that Lia's arm was comfortably connected up, she retreated behind the curtain to assist Dr Renato. Lia passed the rest of the clinic in the role of receptionist, as normal. When she was required to stand up and move around, she simply trundled the drip stand along with her. I later learned that Lia had arrived at work that morning feeling 'weak' (*fraca*). Dr Renato had checked her over and, unable to detect any illness, had suggested she take the morning off to rest. Lia, however, had refused, and after some discussion it was agreed that she could receive a litre of simple isotonic fluid in the clinic, while at work, to 'strengthen' her.

Blood: Will Out: Essays on Liquid Transfers and Flows, First Edition. Edited by Janet Carsten. © 2013 Royal Anthropological Institute of Great Britain & Ireland. Published 2013 by John Wiley & Sons Ltd.

This chapter is about blood and the blood-like substances that make up the fluid economy of an area historically parched by drought. It seeks to locate blood within a culturally and climatically specific network of essential fluids that must flow in particular directions. My reflections are based on data collected between 2002 and 2010. Santa Lucia is a rural village located in the semi-arid interior of the Northeast Brazilian state of Pernambuco. Its inhabitants are predominantly Catholic, and survive through a mixture of semi-subsistence agriculture, livestock rearing, and itinerant wage-labour in nearby towns and the manioc flourmills that dot the region. As described in the opening vignette, my initial interest in Santa Lucian notions of blood was sparked not by blood itself, but by what I came to perceive as a local fascination with receiving *soro*. Here I explore what might have motivated this fascination by focusing, firstly, upon the symbolic interchangeability of blood with rain, tears, *soro,* and other fluid-like substances in the local context; and, secondly, upon the direction in the way such liquids tend to flow.

Curiously enough, Lia was not the only one to whom nurse Rita had administered a drip that week. A few days prior to this she had been called to the house of Edileusa, whose elderly mother, Dona Leonor, had taken a bad turn. According to Edileusa, Dona Leonor had become suddenly quiet and turned 'white as tapioca', as though all the blood had left her body.[2] Dr Renato was absent from the village, but Rita telephoned him and the advice she received was to fix Dona Leonor up to an isotonic drip. Edileusa explained to me that Dona Leonor, like all elderly people, had blood that was weak (*fraco*) and drying up (*secando*). The drip had fortified her. She had gone to sleep with the first drop and woken up an hour or so later, refreshed and alert. On another occasion Lulu, a mother of two, complained of feeling 'weak/soft' (*mole*). On this occasion, too, there was no readily diagnosable reason for Lulu's 'weakness'. Nurse Rita was sent for, blood pressure was checked, and a phone call to Dr Renato was made. Following the phone call Lulu received a litre of *soro* in her own front room. Various neighbours – mostly women and children – slipped in and out of the room as Lulu received this treatment.

During fieldwork I both witnessed and heard speak of several other occasions in which *soro* was administered to people at home. Upon being called to a house, the first thing nurse Rita would do was check the afflicted person's blood pressure. Further tests and questions might follow and very often the visit would be rounded off with a course of intravenously administered isotonic fluid. If the patient in question had a known medical condition and medicine was available for it, this could be added to the bag of fluid. Where rehydrative fluid was not absolutely necessary and there was a choice over whether to take the prescribed medicine orally, by simple injection, or intravenously together with a litre of isotonic fluid, the latter option was generally preferred.

It was clear that *soro* was being liberally administered outside the clinical context in a manner somewhat counter to standard biomedical practice. In some cases it was even being circulated and stored amongst villagers, a bit like a commodity. Dida had given her sister a packet which she kept stored in a drawer at home, I was told, 'just in case'. My curiosity about *soro* was reinforced during an episode when I myself became ill. In an effort to treat me, Dida offered to administer a transfusion of isotonic fluid in her front room. I declined the offer, being careful to add that I would be sure to drink plenty of fluids. But Dida would not accept this. She was concerned about my propensity for eating packets of popcorn whenever I stayed in town. No wonder I was ill, she chastised; popcorn 'does not make blood' (*não faz sangue*). Moreover, she argued, simply drinking lots of water would not help the situation. Only *soro* applied 'directly in the blood' (*direto no sangue*) would really help. Back and forth we discussed the matter until finally, in order to escape the situation, I decided to make a trip into town, with a view to visiting the doctor if need be. Dida accepted this, but only once I had promised to take a litre of *soro* with me in case I should need it at the other end. I got into my car, and just as I was about to drive away, 'forgetting' the *soro*, a bag of isotonic fluid together with a packet of tubes and needles was slung through the open window and landed on the passenger seat beside me.

As was the case in this episode, it was not all that clear whether *soro* was being prescribed by Dr Renato, by Rita the nurse, by Dida, or by patients themselves. Dida and Rita shared access to the health post cupboard where the packets of liquid were stored, and on occasion I had noted one or two other women borrow the keys in order to fetch medical supplies and distribute them to people in need. At that time (in 2002), two women in the village were trained to administer injections and insert catheters, and they shared this work according to which of them lived nearer to the patient. Dida was not able to insert a catheter, but knew how to remove one, and was often called upon for help when *soro* had been administered.

When I returned to the field some seven years later, considerable changes had occurred at the health post. Two new rooms had been added to the rectangular building, and the inside had been redecorated and refurnished with new tables, examining couches, curtains, and chairs. Eye-catching government health awareness posters jostled for attention on the waiting room walls, and the pharmaceutical cupboard appeared to be well stocked with drugs. When I asked about whether *soro* was still administered to people at home, Lourdinha, the current health post auxiliary, responded that, no, *soro* was only ever administered intravenously in the hospital or during the village clinic, and then only if it was a serious case of diarrhoea. When I asked why, in the past, *soro* had been commonly administered in people's own homes, Lourdinha brushed me off with an embarrassed laugh. Such a practice was 'wrong', she answered, and she claimed not to remember it happening. 'To have *soro* intravenously one needs a prescription from a doctor', she continued, 'and one needs to come here to the clinic. How could the doctor attend that person if anything went wrong?' Speaking to the clinic nurse yielded much the same information. Unless it is a very serious case of dehydration, she affirmed, current guidelines stipulated that *soro* should first be taken orally, and only taken intravenously in a clinical context. It appeared that in the intervening years access to state-funded pharmaceuticals had become more centralized and health practice in the clinic more regulated. The current doctor would bring a supply of isotonic bags with him on each visit to the health post every fifteen days, and whatever had not been used by the end of his shift would be taken back to the hospital in town.

Nurse Rita had since married and left the village, but I tracked her down in the town where she lived and spoke to her about these changes. Had the local health department decided to crack down on the use of *soro* in people's houses? I asked. Rita could not tell me, but she did agree that taking *soro* at home had, over the years, become 'less allowed' (*menos permitido*). After a thoughtful pause she continued: 'But I think there is also less need for *soro* than there was before'. With the new local political administration, she said, a substantial investment in health care had occurred. Pharmaceuticals were becoming more readily available, and special transportation for patients from rural areas had been implemented allowing access to the medical care on offer in the state capital, Recife. As a result, people in rural areas had become less dependent on small village clinics and ambulatory health programmes.[3]

Not everyone I spoke to viewed the changes in the health service as a wholesale improvement. Dida, for example, spoke at length about how she missed the days of Dr Renato. Dr Renato, she claimed, was the sort of doctor who had placed a high level of trust in the other health post staff, and this, she asserted, had been a good thing as it had allowed her and Rita to attend more directly to the sick of the community in his absence. Edileusa also spoke nostalgically about the days of Dr Renato, who had been 'an excellent doctor' (*um médico excelente*), prescribing *soro* as and when the people needed it. She said to me: 'The only doctor I ever liked was Dr Renato. See Maya, these days it is harder to get *soro*. Back in the days of Dr Renato it was whenever a person needed it. Back then I took so much *soro*, Virgin Maria!' I asked Edileusa if taking lots of *soro* was necessarily a good thing, and she responded that it was, because when a person becomes ill their blood 'loses strength' (*não tem a mesma força*) and the body becomes 'soft' (*mole*). 'Only *soro* gives a person back their strength', she said.

Water of life

Ruminating over a *bricolage* of Indo-European and Semitic stories about the evil eye, the folklorist Alan Dundes asks the question: what theoretical underlying principles, if any, can explain the whole range of phenomena believed to be caused by the evil eye, from the withering of fruit trees, to the loss of milk from cows, to impotence among males? The link, he suggests, is liquid, and the notion that life depends upon liquid. 'From the concept of the "water of life" to semen, milk, blood, bile, saliva, and the like, the consistent principle is that liquid means life while loss of liquid means death' (Dundes 1981: 258). Dundes illustrates this point by travelling elliptically from the Greek conception of life as the gradual diminution of liquid inside a man, the presumed thirst of the dead in ancient Egyptian funerary ritual, and from historical instances of humoral pathology in European medicine, to the metaphorical and symbolic quests for the 'water of life' in Indo-European fairy tales. His intention in doing so is to draw attention to a widespread wet-dry opposition, and to suggest that it is at least as important as the more famous hot-cold distinction with respect to folk theories of disease and well-being. Although the patchwork approach Dundes takes in this essay does not allow for a more contextualized understanding of the examples provided, his overall point is of interest. For in Santa Lucia, liquid does indeed equal life, just as dryness signals death. Although this opposition is such a truism as to hardly merit further attention, at the same time it taps into a particular historical and socio-climatic context in which the lifeblood of persons, of plants, of animals, and of the very earth itself is of exceptional concern. The specific resonance that blood has in this context comes from the fact that it is a liquid substance which, like water, has special life-giving properties which makes it precious. Moreover, in a region historically afflicted by drought, blood, like water, is conceptualized as a finite substance, often scarce, and in danger of being lost. As I hope to show in what follows, blood is central to a fluid economy particular to this region: one that links God with persons, persons with the land, persons with one another, and the land with God.

Blood, sweat, broth, and Catholicism

If cultural ideas about the body are always in flux, Santa Lucian ideas about blood are certainly no exception. Santa Lucians, like most modern Northeast Brazilians, worry increasingly about 'cholesterol' and 'blood pressure' and subscribe to biomedical understandings about the role of blood in the human body. This is particularly true among younger generations, and older people who have undergone specialized training to work in biomedical contexts. Biomedical understandings of blood, however, coexist with alternative conceptions of blood as an object of scarcity, and as a substance that carries with it the potential for spiritual redemption, love, and self-sacrifice. Most people subscribed to the idea that human blood, in the very first instance, is a gift from God. Such a gift starts out in the form of the blood-encased foetus nestling in the womb. A mother's blood is held to nourish the blood of the child she carries, causing it to grow. However, this process, it is often stressed, is both dependent upon and coterminous with another liquid gift: rain – that which comes from the heavens to become the lifeblood of the crop. The gift of rain combined with the labour and actions of people makes the soil produce food, which in turn converts into blood.

It is perhaps unsurprising that eating is said to have a direct bearing not simply on the fat content of a person, but on the volume of his or her blood. In Santa Lucia, the quantity and amount of food that a working person eats is an ongoing topic of comment and interest. Healthy men with large appetites are frequently praised as hard workers (*trabalhadores*) – their calorie requirements taken to be indexical of calories lost through work. In fact, anxieties about obesity, so prevalent in Europe and America, are largely absent among Santa Lucians, for most villagers simply refuse to believe it is impossible to eat 'too much' – particularly of the foods that make blood. Old and young are actively encouraged to pile their plates high with beans, rice, and manioc flour. These staples, together with a meat dish accompaniment, convert into the 'blood' necessary for further work – whether it be in the fields, at home, or in town. Beans are most essential to this fluid economy. 'If I don't eat beans, I start to feel weak' is a phrase I often heard. The weakness is attributable to a diminution of blood, for it is beans, above all other foods, that make blood. Such is the importance of beans in the diet that they are the first food to be ladled onto the plate. Babies, the sick, and the very elderly who may not be able to eat beans as normal will likely be offered bean broth (*sopa de feijão*) – a red-brown broth that the beans are cooked in – to fortify them.

In folk discourse, the volume of blood that a person has varies naturally over the life-course. Children have less blood than adults, for the obvious reason that they are smaller, but their blood volume will increase steadily if they are fed properly. As people age, their blood volume naturally becomes less (*menor*) and weaker (*mais fraco*).[4] The diminishing of blood with age is held to account for the loss of weight, the general slowing down, and the wrinkling of flesh in older people. Similar ideas regarding blood pertain to the sick, who, regardless of their particular illness, are often said to suffer from 'weakness' owing to 'lack of blood' (*falta de sangue*). Accordingly, those I questioned about blood donation responded that – while fine in theory – blood should only be donated by healthy, working, adults, and even then should be avoided by menstruating women. Categories of people held to be unsuitable for blood donation were the elderly, children, anyone with a medical condition, anyone with a history of evil-eye affliction, and all pregnant or lactating women. Curiously, while almost everyone I spoke to about blood donation applauded the action in principle, they tended to speculate that they, themselves, were unsuitable to donate. Reasons for this were vague, yet centred upon the notion that one's own blood was always, in some undefined sense, an endangered resource. As one woman said to me: 'I think that if you took half a litre out of me, I would fall over'.

Blood is also often spoken about as though it possessed its own cyclical seasons. Accordingly, there are certain times of year which are considered better for blood-letting than others. A bad time of year to donate blood, for example, would be shortly before the rainy season, when work in the fields is at its height, the sun is at its hottest, and when blood (in the form of sweat) flows out of the body in greatest quantities. The body of the field worker at this time of year is, in a sense, already involved in a process of liquid donation. Here I use the word 'donation' in a non-biomedical sense to denote the movement of bodily liquids out of some people and indirectly into others. In practice such flows are neither neat nor coherent. They occur through a mixture of accident and conscious struggle (*luta*), via the physical and emotional hardships of wresting a living from the baked soil. The drama of work at this particular time of year is widely conceptualized as a form of sacrifice, a veritable spillage of bodily liquids in service to others (Mayblin 2010). The excretion of sweat, the welling of tears, the seeping of wounds, the bleeding of blisters: all these bodily processes are considered part and parcel of work for the average Northeastern peasant. However, such processes clearly reach their height around the months of April and May, when the soil cries out for the rains to start, when beans are sowed, and when expectation and anxiety about the quality of rain, and the harvest to come, are at their greatest. The equation is quite simple: good rain, coupled with the sacrifice of bodily fluids at this time of year, leads directly to the production of foods such as manioc (*manioca*) and beans (*feijão*) that in turn produce the lifeblood of persons.

The flow of sacrifice in this picture is not totally unilateral. Despite the fact that it tends to be spoken about in such terms, in practice it is implicitly acknowledged that weary workers return home at the end of each day to be fed. The fluid economy is thus, in reality, like any capitalistic economy: circular, and with a constant eye on return, and on growth through circulation. Blood flows back into those who expend it via substances that enter the mouth: food and water. Men feed women and women feed men. Parents feed children and, later on, children feed elderly parents. Thus in actuality, and as any Santa Lucian will admit, labour in the fields cannot ever truly equal the scale of unreciprocated sacrifice made by Jesus on the Cross. Ordinary people must accept certain inevitable limits; nevertheless, the ideal of total Christian sacrifice is there to inspire as well as to be aspired to.

The role of blood in the spiritual and redemptive work of Santa Lucian Catholics is perhaps unsurprising given that Christ's blood as both object and symbol has long been a central focus in Christian – particularly Roman Catholic – forms of art, literature, pious practice, and theology. The sense that we are our blood, and that blood is life, recurs in debate and sermons throughout the fifteenth century, and can be derived from hundreds of devotional paintings, poems, and prayers dedicated to Christ's wounds, scourging, and crucifixion (see Bildhauer 2009; Bynum 2007). The history of Catholicism is unambiguously bloody: from the ugly violence of early crusades and missionary encounters to the beautifully rendered bleeding statues that adorn Catholic shrines and churches. Indeed, and as Bynum reveals, the blood cults and flagellants of the late medieval period elevated the soteriological qualities of blood to such a degree that blood shed posed a direct challenge to the practice of the sacraments. For example, for the crypto flagellants of Thuringia, 'one drop of blood [*una gutta sanguinis*] shed with the flail is worth more to God than rivers of the water of baptism ... or pounds of the oil of extreme unction' (Bynum 2007: 35). During the Reformation, debates intensified around the meaning and symbolism of Eucharistic liturgy, and in particular around the concept of transubstantiation, which, following the Council of Trent and the Catechism of the Catholic Church, indicate a change in the substance of bread and wine at the moment of consecration into the substance of the body and blood of Christ.

For Santa Lucian Catholics, whose houses are often adorned with images and statues of the bleeding, crucified Jesus, the bleeding sacred heart, and bloodied saints, the doctrine of transubstantiation – traditionally a 'difficult' teaching – presents no difficulty at all. Indeed I was often struck by the willingness of my friends to attest to the literal truth of this doctrine, even whilst criticizing their Protestant evangelical neighbours for pursuing excessively literal interpretations of the Bible. For them, the ritual of the Catholic Mass can only be properly described in material and aesthetic terms as beautiful (*bonita*). A 'beautiful' Mass is one in which words as well as actions have weight: that is, every part of the liturgy is clearly performed and enunciated. It is 'beautiful' for the simple reason that it is 'truth' (*a verdade*) made material. Significantly, the most 'beautiful' and 'truest' part of the Mass is cited by everyone to be the moment of the Eucharist, when the priest holds up the chalice for consecration, which thereafter contains the actual blood of Jesus.

In her historical work on blood, Bynum is careful to point out that blood was always as much about taboo as about revelation. Even within Christian art and scripture, blood is everything from dying and violation to source, birth, and origin. 'The shedding of *cruor* [external blood]', she writes, 'could be heroic, health-bringing, criminal, or polluting; *sanguis* [internal blood] could be congested and unhealthy, or the very stuff of life itself' (2007: 187). In the Brazilian context, the multiple and sometimes ambiguous meanings of blood are evident both in the ethnography presented here and in the work of Sanabria (2009). Sanabria's work on blood was undertaken in Bahia, where '*sangue* does not obey the same rules as the capillary blood described by Western anatomy. Instead it circulates in various states (thick/thin, pure/impure, hot/cold) and is the support on which a range of influences imprint themselves in bodies' (2009: 132). A notable difference between Santa Lucian notions of blood and those evinced by Sanabria's informants concerns the positive associations of blood-letting among the latter. In Bahia, strongly humoral ideas about the dangers of blood accumulation and the alleviative properties of blood-letting lead to a desire to remove blood through either menstruation or blood donation. In Santa Lucia, by contrast, blood loss is not consciously desired, nor is it deemed to have any particular health properties. Rather, it is supposed that it will naturally be lost and diminished, one way or another, and the sacrificial manner in which this happens may confer spiritual benefits. Bahian ideas about blood are likely influenced by Afro-Brazilian concepts of 'life force' (*axé*), which circulates through material substances such as blood and can be absorbed, accumulated, wasted, or cleansed in the sense of the Brazilian-Portuguese word *limpeza* (cleanliness), which connotes moral and spiritual purification (Sanabria 2009). A climatic difference can here be traced in the way Bahian ideas about cleansing seem to refer to the humidity of the tropical littoral, where, unlike the drier interior, liquids stagnate and materials age more rapidly because of the high level of moisture in the air (Sanabria 2009: 135).

Droughts and dryness, rain and tears

Unlike coastal Bahia, Santa Lucia is located in a region that is anything but humid. Climatically and geographically it is characteristic of other parts of the Northeastern interior – an area of the country described by one writer as 'a dustbowl that never ends' (Arons 2004: 25). In this area historically afflicted by drought, water is a substance that has long been in short supply. Jesuit archives record droughts in Northeast Brazil going back as far as 1559. Throughout the centuries, frequent periodic droughts in the Northeast have had calamitous effects, intensifying political conflicts, entrenching social inequalities, and decimating local populations through disease and hunger (Arons 2004; Hall 1981; Kenny 2002). The last recorded drought lasted from 1997 to 1999, and left large tracts of the surrounding land that were normally full of corn, manioc, and beans overrun by a cactus plant called *palma*. Santa Lucians recall how even in the less affected region of the *agreste*,[5] women carried tin cylinders of water on their heads for miles, and people pushing wheelbarrows lined up at wells in the centres of small towns in search of the precious resource. It is reported that even during the comparatively 'mild' drought of the late 1990s, infant mortality rates jumped by 10 per cent and there was a dramatic decline in school attendance across the region. School houses were shut down as children started being hired to collect water, 60 kilometres away. Young girls turned to prostitution as drought-stricken families resorted to desperate measures, and out of 1,552 municipalities in the drought polygon, 758 suffered 'serious problems', 336 were declared to be in 'official states of emergency', and 442 were labelled in 'critical condition' (Arons 2004).

A large corpus of popular art, music, and literature representing the drama of drought in the Northeast is today widely recognized, and examples of it can be purchased in galleries and tourist shops across the country.[6] As a consequence, the Northeast has come to be celebrated in the Brazilian imagination for its suffering, drought-ridden aesthetic. Taken collectively, notes Arons, 'the literature of drought seems like the result of a group of good Brazilian writers getting together and deciding to write the most depressing stories they can imagine' (2004: 26). For Levine, meanwhile, the Northeast's religious art 'was always the bloodiest, portraying the suffering of Christ in stark detail, celebrating, as it were, saintly pain and humiliation' (1992: 217). Drought in Northeast Brazil is simply formidable. There is little other way one can describe it, or the industry and culture that shapes its re-telling. The cultural story of drought within the Northeast is notably grafted onto the story of the Christian Passion – the heat of the interior being equivalent to that of Gethsemane, the parched suffering of drought victims equivalent to the parched suffering of Christ carrying his Cross (cf. Campos 2008).

Words such as 'inaccessible', 'cracked', 'parched', and 'austere' are often used to describe the semi-arid landscape of the interior – a landscape that for vast tracts appears thorny grey and abandoned, broken up only with occasional mud and wattle houses and fields of spiny cacti. To the eye, the village of Santa Lucia is not quite as extreme as this, but even there, anxiety about water is all-pervasive, and constitutes the ordinary backdrop to everyday existence. As in other parts of the region, 'thirst' (*sede*) carries with it a complex set of associations: of horrors past, of shame and humiliation, but also of spiritual quest and redemption. When I conversed with Father Jorge, the parish priest in 2010, he described the people of the Northeast to me as the possessors of 'great thirst' (*uma sede grande*). This exceptional thirst, he emphasized, was both physical and spiritual: Northeasterners thirsted for water, but more than that they thirsted for God. He followed this assertion with a reference to the Water of Life discourse in the Gospel of John, where Jesus meets the Samaritan woman at the well and discloses his ability to give her the 'living water' that quenches one's spiritual thirst for eternal life (John 4:14).

In fact water is a widely recognized and important symbol in the Fourth Gospel, one which theologian Larry Jones argues is ultimately symbolic of Jesus himself: '[H]e is the one who can end all thirst. He is the one who is poured out for the world. Jesus himself is the primary symbol in the Fourth Gospel, and water is a frequently recurring and constantly expanding symbol that points to him and renders him present' (1997: 230). The importance of water as a symbol of the Spirit is also evident in the way Santa Lucians make reference to John (19:34) during Easter Service readings and on *via sacra* processions, wherein blood *and water* gushes out of Jesus' pierced side. In these passages, ritually read out, the water is said to symbolize the Spirit, and the blood Jesus' Life-giving death. According to theologian John Paul Heil, the water that gushes out of Jesus is as central to the overall sacrificial narrative as the blood:

> [T]he water lends to the blood its natural cleansing and quenching qualities. That blood and water together come out of the Jesus lifted up and exalted in crucifixion brings to a climax all of the narrative's previous indications of both the salvific cleansing and quenching effects of the death of Jesus (1995: 106).

The notion that water is both life and Life Eternal resonates with a tendency for villagers to speak disconsolately about thirst as the supreme killer – particularly of infants. Dona Rosa, a woman in her seventies, once told me: 'It was with thirst that I killed my first five children'. The way she phrased it was somewhat startling, as though her infants' thirst had been all her own fault. I attempted to challenge Dona Rosa on this, but she interjected with her own explanation:

> I do not really understand such things, but back in those days we did not know that babies needed water – we thought all they needed was milk and *papa* [paste made from water and manioc flour]. See, we shoved the *papa* down them thinking they were ill from lack of solids. We never stopped to think the creatures might be thirsty. It is because of this that I say I killed my first five children – I killed them with thirst.

Dona Rosa was one of a number of women who blamed high rates of infant death in the past on thirst. An adjunctive sense of guilt often accompanied such recollections, particularly in relation to those 'thirsty infants' who had died without having felt even the cool waters of the baptismal font on their faces. The sense of perplexity and guilt among older people in relation to past thirst and infant mortality rates was one of the most discomfiting legacies of drought that I encountered during fieldwork. Particularly striking was the fact that the *quality* of the drinking-water that older generations had given to babies was never blamed for deaths. The killer was water's absence. Condensed within such painful narratives about the past, I suggest, is a peculiar layering of long-accumulated associations about drought equalling suffering, suffering equalling thirst, and more recent health campaign messages about drinking-water – or rather the microbes within it – leading to sickness and death in babies.

If there is a strong awareness that death leads from dryness, a unique mixture of associations also surrounds the advent of the rains in Santa Lucia. For just as scriptural references to storms that 'lift up the waves of the sea' (Psalm 107:25) suggest, too much wetness in the form of heavy rains and floods is also death-dealing. Curiously, many Santa Lucians swore that in the past, more babies died during the first deluges of rain in the month of May than at any other time of year. Puzzled, I asked Dida about this, and she confirmed it, enforcing her point with the words: 'My father was the village coffin maker, but the month he really dreaded was May; he would face that month with a heavy heart in anticipation of all those little coffins he would have to make'. No one

I spoke to could proffer any explanation for this reported seasonal variation in infant mortality rates, although May is clearly a significant month even to the present day, at least in terms of crop planting and anticipation of rain. As such, when the first drops are felt, people call out to one another 'Oh, good rain!' (*eita chuva boa!*), and 'Thanks be to God!' (*graças a Deus!*). Buckets of different sizes are laid out in yards at the back of houses, and basins are placed under drainpipes to collect and store rain, so not a drop is lost. The first rains are the sign that beans can be planted, for it is beans, above any other food, that must be on the table every day in order to 'make blood' (*fazer sangue*). However, bean growers will also worry that too much rain will wash away the top soil and kill off the bean crop entirely, leaving them financially impoverished, as well as bloodless and weak.

Soro vs broth: vein vs mouth

There is a certain irony in the fact that while water for crop irrigation was (and even continues to be) scarce and unreliable in the Northeast, packets of isotonic fluid were, at this time, in abundance, being so cheap to supply. It is hardly surprising that people sought to avail themselves of this liquid substance that resembled both water and blood, and that promised replenishment at such little cost. It is possible that a latent longing among the population of Northeast Brazil to join the elite of their nation, to leave poverty and underdevelopment behind, and to enjoy equal access to biomedical technology contributed to this intravenal fetishization. I mean this as much from the perspective of the doctors as from that of the patients. However, it seems to me there is more to it than this. The clue is to be found in the pervasive notion that, when administered orally, medicines and isotonic fluids count as food whereas administered intravenously they do not. The replenishment of lifeblood intravenously circumvents, to some extent, the reciprocity embedded in eating bean broth and in being fed. Why should this matter? Here, the strong theological emphasis on sacrifice and the local imperative to emulate Christ plays a central role. The technology of the drip negates any notion of being fed. It actively avoids reciprocity, avoids return, lending the emulative sacrifice of ordinary people a particular force.

Like rain that falls from the sky, isotonic fluid, too, falls down from above. It must be hooked up in order to allow it to drip, like rain, into the bloodstream. By entering the person intravenously, the bag of *soro* represents a different set of relationships and meanings. Yes, it may partake in modern biomedical idioms of illness and treatment, making 'modern subjects' of administrators and recipients, but it also steps outside of the immediate kinship relations that centre upon food. Where kin can only replenish lost blood via offerings of food that will be converted into blood, *soro* is a type of blood in itself. Its entry into the bloodstream must be facilitated by a nurse or doctor, but the substance itself is provided by the state, and comes from outside the kinship-based subsistence economy – from a diffusely anonymous source. The process of replenishment undergone is not experienced in the same way as replenishment administered orally in the form of sweet drinks and bean broths by attendant carers and relatives. Rather than returning fluid to the body that was spilt in the course of labour using the products of labour itself, isotonic fluid restores fluid lost during the production of food without undoing the sacrifice originally involved in its production. The flow, as it were, continues always in one direction. Rain and *soro* come down, blood and sweat flow out, and the food produced gives life to others.

Blood substitutes and substitutional forms of sacrifice

What is notable about blood in this particular context is that it is simply one in a sequence of liquids, including *soro*, sweat, tears, and broth, that carries symbolic weight. As one cycle blends into another – the life-course with the agricultural seasons, and the productivity of the land with longer-term climactic phases – liquids act as substitutes for the ultimate sacrifice in the ongoing sacrifice of ordinary self-giving (cf. Mayblin forthcoming). Anthropologists writing about sacrifice have identified substitution as a key feature of sacrificial rituals in different cultures (Evans-Pritchard 1956; Hubert & Mauss 1964 [1898]). As Willerslev has recently noted in relation to the topic of sacrifice among the Chukchi of northeastern Siberia: 'Sacrifice is essentially a game of displacement and replacement in that sacrifice of a thing is a surrogate act for the ultimate paradigm underlying all sacrifices, the sacrifice of oneself' (2009: 700). According to Willerslev, Chukchi reindeer herders must sacrifice themselves to their deceased, although it is not normally a human who is killed (except in certain cases of suicide) but a reindeer. However, there exists a hierarchy of acceptable substitutes, moving from the most complex and highly esteemed to the simpler and less valued. Thus a reindeer doe is more valuable than a reindeer bull, which, in turn, is more valuable than a sausage, a fish, or, in the most minimal cases, a small wooden image of the sausage or a stone. Willerslev notes that hierarchical distinctions are never lost in the process of sacrificial surrogations. Sacrificial substitution is 'guided, and indeed made possible, by symbolic resemblance, but the difference between the original and its surrogate counterparts is never forgotten by the deceased' (2009: 700).

In the Catholic context sacrifice is underscored by a different set of semiotic markers and debates, but a similar process of substitution can be said to be at work in the Santa Lucian case. Although tears and sweat are held to be bodily liquids that both derive from blood and may stand in for blood in the fluid economy of gift, flow, and sacrifice, they are not identical to blood. A hierarchical distinction is thus implicit with Christ's spilled blood as the most valued sacrificial substance, followed by the spilled blood of men and women in battle, childbirth, and/or other forms of hard physical labour, followed by tears and sweat spilled in the course of caring for one's kin. Like medieval blood obsession, which, according to Bynum, drew on a plethora of themes and images – 'washing, hiding, birthing, ransoming, suffering, punishing, living, dying' (2007: 13), amongst others – bodily fluids in the Santa Lucian context do not only stand for the individuals they derive from, but also evoke a plethora of ordinary everyday acts which are in some sense spiritualized by virtue of having forced various secretions from intact bodies. Ultimately, then, whether one loses liquid by crying for a loved one, by accidentally tearing one's skin on a sharp agricultural implement, or by sweating through labour in the fields, the net effect is the same: liquid (life force) has been lost from the body, and must be either considered a true sacrifice, or somehow replenished.

According to Willerslev, Chukchi reindeer sacrifice (and its substitutive forms) is a 'calculated action, a technology of time manipulation, so to speak, in that the delay or time lag generated through the killing of substitutes is what allows human life to continue' (2009: 699). I argue that the 'time lag' logic of substitutional sacrifice is also present in the Santa Lucian case, but for different complex reasons. In the first instance, the sacrifice that Catholic Santa Lucians allude to is merely an emulation of the most fundamental and complete sacrifice, which was Christ's crucifixion. The death of

Christ, in this view, ontologically changes the world, rendering all subsequent sacrifices by humans unnecessary and obsolete. In theory, there is no temporal urgency for Christians to self-sacrifice as Christ's self-sacrifice on their behalf is eternal.[7] The Santa Lucian notion of self-sacrifice is, perhaps in contrast to Chukchi or Nuer sacrifice, less temporally and materially instrumental, but it is so precisely because it *has* to be. As Evens (2008) theorizes, in the Abrahamic traditions, the story of Isaac and Abraham constitutes an important template for conceptualizing subsequent actions as sacrifice. The story has been widely interpreted by theologians as a lesson in the virtues of blind faith, but it may also be interpreted as an original warrant for substitution when sacrificing. As Evens puts it:

> The sort of gift Abraham set out to give is simply not for humankind to offer. The gift of death, as is the theme of Golgogotha, is God's prerogative, not man's. Hence, at the end of this story, God has to step in to make things right [i.e. by substituting the life of a lamb for the life of Isaac] (2008: 54).

In Santa Lucia, the need to self-sacrifice is hence circumscribed by a pervasive ethic of humility. The shedding of tears and sweat is not life-threatening, as in the shedding of Christ's blood, but as a (Christian) human form of sacrifice it is appropriately imperfect. That is, via the work of substitution, it remains sustainable. How does *soro* play into this substitutional logic? *Soro* increases the value of substitutional substances (like sweat, water, tears) lost in service to others in two main ways: firstly, it side-steps the reciprocity – the gesture of 'thanks' – embodied in the care given to sick kin; secondly, by working to restore the sacrificially expended body, it negates (or delays) the demand for more drastic – theologically 'perfect' and hence unsustainable – forms of self-sacrifice.

In his work on blood donation in India, Copeman (2009) has demonstrated how giving blood allows non-violent Hindu devotees to play an intimate role in the nation's military affairs via the distanciating function of the act. At play is a complex logic of 'mixing at one remove' – a 'corporeal system of concurrent intimacy and distance' in which the donor can be both present and absent (2009: 169). Copeman's ethnography elegantly demonstrates how sacrificial substitution (a measure of one's blood in place of one's life in battle) enables complex accommodations between different aims and imperatives. A similar spirit of compromise seems to exist for ordinary Catholic agri-culturalists: Jesus' act of total self-giving is the highest template for physical dehydra-tion in service to others and must, via the injunction of *imitatio Christi*, be emulated or aspired to, yet to dehydrate to the point that one's capacity for work disappears altogether is to negate God's Life-giving purpose. Taking *soro* is, then, an act of distanciation from the highest sacrificial ideal, for it is as much about claiming some-thing back as it is about giving something up. Taking *soro* in one's living-room without a biomedically diagnosed case of dehydration signifies impatience, a refusal to wait any longer for rain, for proper irrigation to arrive, for equal access to clean drinking-water and modern health-enhancing technologies. It is as if to say: 'Come, here is a liquid one does not have to wait for – let us avail ourselves of it!'

Conclusion

In Northeast Brazil, as in other parts of the world, the meaning of blood is multi-faceted, often unstable, and contextually differentiated. Carsten (2004) and Cannell (this book) are right to point out that we cannot assume that the meaning of blood is always in 'one register'. The material presented here lends a very literal slant to this observation, for if it is not always clear that the meaning of blood is always in 'one register', neither can we always assume that blood is clearly distinct from other liquid substances. In the ethnography presented, both the metaphorical and the literal capacities of blood are dependent upon the capacity of liquids in general, which are given inherently to movement, or which seem to travel outwards by their own volition, unless actively contained. Possibly there is something to be said about the molecular structure of liquid – perhaps of fluid forms in general – and their tendencies to travel. Rain, sweat, blood, tears, and broth are all substances that travel and, as with water in the Gospel of John, can expand both literally and figuratively.

To conclude, I return to the question of the isotonic drip, and its widespread popularity among Santa Lucians during my first period of fieldwork. The fact that isotonic fluid was administered intravenously so frequently is clearly a complex issue, generated not simply by the ready availability of this form of treatment and the absence of others, but by a confluence of factors: political, economic, and geographic, as well as religious and symbolic. Certainly there were some idiosyncratic elements in play: the particular personality of Dr Renato being one of these, and the micro-politics between him, the health post staff, and the clinic patients being another. One could dwell on these elements by way of explanation; one could also dwell on socio-economic factors relating to the implementation of specific healthcare strategies across Brazil, or on the politics of public health expenditure within the local admin-istration at that particular moment in time. But such a picture would surely be incomplete without also taking into account the climatic and socio-religious elements I have described. If we seek a deeper understanding of the widespread use of *soro* in the Santa Lucian context, we need to understand the place of blood in an entire sequence of liquids and flows: from the heavens, into the womb, out of the soil, into the mouth, through the body, and on.

NOTES

I am grateful to everyone in 'Santa Lucia' who made this fieldwork possible, and to all the participants of the 'Blood Will Out Workshop' held in Edinburgh (Spring 2010), for helpful comments on this chapter. Special thanks are due to Jacob Copeman, Janet Carsten, and Magnus Course for their generous intellectual contributions. Research and writing was made possible by two grants: an ESRC Ph.D. Scholarship and a British Academy Postdoctoral Fellowship.

[1] Pseudonyms have been used to preserve anonymity.

[2] Tapioca is a brilliant white pancake made from the starch of the manioc potato.

[3] For more detail on legislative changes and developments in primary healthcare in Brazil, see Cordeiro (1996) and Rosa & Labate (2005).

[4] For similar understandings of blood within the body, see Cátedra (1992) and Fairhead, Leach & Small (2006). For an overview of anthropological approaches to substances more generally, see Carsten (2004).

[5] The *agreste* is a narrow zone that cuts across several Northeastern Brazilian states, positioned between the tropical littoral and the arid interior.

[6] See Albuquerque (1999) and Arons (2004) for further detail on iconic works of literature and art concerning drought in the Brazilian Northeast.

[7] For elaboration on temporal features of Christian thought, see Engelke (2009).

REFERENCES

Albuquerque, D.M. 1999. *A invenção do Nordeste e outras artes.* Recife: Cortez Editora.

Arons, N.G. 2004. *Waiting for rain: the politics and poetry of drought in Northeast Brazil.* Tuscon: University of Arizona Press.

Bildhauer, B. 2009. *Medieval blood.* Cardiff: University of Wales Press.

Bynum, C.W. 2007. *Wonderful blood: theology and practice in late medieval northern Germany and beyond.* Philadelphia: University of Pennsylvania Press.

Campos, R.B.C. 2008. Como Juazeiro do Norte se tornou a terra da Mãe de Deus: penitência, *ethos* de misericórdia e identidade do lugar. *Religião & Sociedade* **28**, 146-75.

Carsten, J. 2004. *After kinship.* Cambridge: University Press.

Cátedra, M. 1992. *This world, other world: sickness, suicide, death and the afterlife among the vaqueiros de Alzada of Spain* (trans. W.A. Christian, Jr). Chicago: University Press.

Copeman, J. 2009. *Veins of devotion: blood donation and religious experience in North India.* New Brunswick, N.J.: Rutgers University Press.

Cordeiro, H. 1996. O PSF como estratégia de mudança do modelo assistencial do SUS. Cad. *Saúde Família* **1**, 10-25.

Dundes, A. 1981. Wet and dry, the evil eye: an essay in Indo-European and Semitic worldview. In *Evil eye: a case book* (ed.) A. Dundes, 257-312. Madison: University of Wisconsin Press.

Engelke, M. 2009. Reading and time: two approaches to the materiality of scripture. *Ethnos* **74**, 151-74.

Evans-Pritchard, E.E. 1956. *Nuer religion.* Oxford: University Press.

Evens, T.M.S. 2008. *Anthropology as ethics: nondualism and the conduct of sacrifice.* Oxford: Berghahn.

Fairhead, J., M. Leach & M. Small 2006. Where techno-science meets poverty: medical research and the economy of blood in the Gambia, West Africa. *Social Science and Medicine* **63**, 1109-20.

Hall, A. 1981. Irrigation in the Brazilian Northeast: anti-drought or anti-peasant? In *The logic of poverty: the case of the Brazilian Northeast* (ed.) S. Mitchell, 157-69. London: Routledge.

Heil, J.P. 1995. *Blood and water: the death and resurrection of Jesus in John 18-21.* Washington, D.C.: Catholic Biblical Association of America.

Hubert, H. & M. Mauss 1964 [1898]. *Sacrifice: its nature and function* (trans. W.D. Halls). Chicago: University Press.

Jones, L.P. 1997. *The symbol of water in the Gospel of John.* Sheffield: Academic Press.

Kenny, M.L. 2002. Drought, clientelism, fatalism and fear in Northeast Brazil. *Ethics, Place & Environment* **5**, 123-34.

Levine, R.M. 1992. *Vale of tears: revisiting the Canudos massacre in Northeastern Brazil, 1893-1897.* Berkeley: University of California Press.

Mayblin, M. 2010. *Gender, Catholicism and morality in Brazil: virtuous husbands, powerful wives.* New York: Palgrave Macmillan.

——— forthcoming. The untold sacrifice: the monotony and incompleteness of self-sacrifice in Northeast Brazil. Manuscript submitted for publication.

Rosa, W. de Almeida Godinha & R. Curi Labate 2005. Programa saúde da família: a construção de um novo modelo de assistência. *Revista Latino-Americana de Enfermagem* **13: 6**, 12-21.

Sanabria, E. 2009. Alleviative bleeding: bloodletting, menstruation and the politics of ignorance in a Brazilian blood donation centre. *Body & Society* **15**, 123-44.

Willerslev, R. 2009. The optimal sacrifice: a study of voluntary death among the Siberian Chukchi. *American Ethnologist* **36**, 693-704.

3

Medieval European conceptions of blood: truth and human integrity

BETTINA BILDHAUER *University of St Andrews*

Anthropologists have pioneered the academic study of blood. The founders of the discipline were not afraid to tackle the stuff of everyday life, and interested in kinship, rituals, sacrifice, violence, bodies, and pollution; all contexts in which blood had a high symbolic and practical value in many societies. Medievalists only began to follow this anthropological lead in a sustained manner around the turn of the twenty-first century (on the basis of groundbreaking work on the Eucharist, medicine, martyrdom, and bodily devotion).[1] Since then, it has become evident that blood played an extraordinarily important role in medieval Europe. The ancient civilizations on which medieval European culture was based – whether Roman, Greek, Germanic, or Hebrew – already accorded blood great significance, in blood sacrifices, heroic bloodshed, exchange of blood, and blood-centred physiology. The Middle Ages (i.e. the millennium roughly between 500 and 1500 CE) inherited this valuation of blood, and every major institution and discourse (Church, monasteries, courts, and cities; medicine, law, and the arts) stamped its own meaning on blood. In the following, I give a brief overview of the significance of blood in religion, law, courts, fiction, and especially medicine, before highlighting five characteristics of blood that are consistent across these discourses: blood as authenticity effect; blood as part of a body-soul unit; blood as defining the outlines of the person; Christ's blood as exceptional; and blood as inferior. I shall show that blood was believed to grant access to the truth as well as to hold body and soul together, separate from the external world, but always precariously so.

Ancient and medical medicine is often labelled 'humoral medicine' because it most basically understands the body as a container of four bodily fluids called humours: red blood, which was hot and moist; white phlegm, which was cold and moist; black bile, which was cold and dry; and yellow bile, which was hot and dry. Depending on the dominant humour, every human being belonged to one of four main character types or temperaments, whose names are still widely known: sanguine (with a predominance of blood), phlegmatic (dominated by phlegm), choleric (dominated by yellow bile), and melancholic (dominated by black bile). All four humours were made from food at various stages of digestion; and they were all transported through the body in blood.

Blood: Will Out: Essays on Liquid Transfers and Flows, First Edition. Edited by Janet Carsten. © 2013
Royal Anthropological Institute of Great Britain & Ireland. Published 2013 by John Wiley & Sons Ltd.

This means that there was also a second, wider definition of blood as a carrier and mixture of the four humours. Other bodily fluids, specifically breast milk, menstrual blood, and semen, were also thought to be blood at more advanced stages of digestion.

To be ill was to have an imbalance of humours, usually with one of the four dominating to an extent that was no longer merely due to the temperament with which one was born. Measures to restore balance often regulated food intake by prohibiting foods that would produce the excessive humour, and encouraged those foods as well as activities that would stimulate the production of the other three. Therapists also removed the excessive humour through blood-letting using sophisticated techniques to ensure that it was mostly the superfluous humour rather than the other three that was drawn out.

The extent to which such medical ideas were known to the wider public in the Middle Ages is uncertain, but they were familiar to the literate elite. In classical antiquity, the system of the humours had been important far beyond medicine, as the humours' qualities of hot or cold and moist or dry corresponded to those of the four elements of which the cosmos was composed: fire, earth, water, and air. They are shown as layers (with the earth as mountains), for example, in a fifteenth-century manuscript of Konrad of Megenberg's encyclopaedic *Book of Nature*, together with personifications of the planets (Fig. 3.1). This

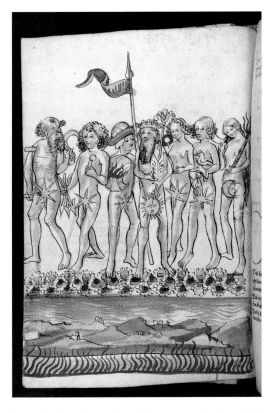

Figure 3.1. The four elements (fire, earth, water, air) and personifications of the seven planets. Konrad von Megenberg, *Buch der Natur*, Hagenau, Workshop Diebold Lauber, c.1442-8, Universitätsbibliothek Heidelberg Cod. Pal. Germ. 300, fol. 36v. (Reproduced with permission of the Universitätsbibliothek Heidelberg.)

Figure 3.2. Alexander the Great explores the bottom of the sea, knowing that the sea abhors blood and will spit him back out when he cuts himself. *La Vraie Hystoire du Bon Roy Alixandre*, France, after 1333. (© British Library Board, British Library Royal 19 D. I, fol. 37v. Reproduced with permission.)

humoral thinking continued among the medieval elites who learned to read and write (which meant reading Latin classical authors), not just among those who studied medicine specifically. Even early recipe collections in the vernacular, like the thirteenth-century German *Bartholomäus*, show an awareness of the basics of humoral theory.

The two institutions that most influenced medieval mentalities and attitudes to blood in Europe were the Church and the courts of the nobility. Christian devotion was focused increasingly on the blood of Christ and that of the saints and martyrs. In the late Middle Ages – that is, the thirteenth to fifteenth centuries – Christ's bleeding body on the cross was depicted in explicit images and texts that encouraged empathizing with his sacrifice. The Eucharist, the transformation of bread and wine into the body and blood of Christ shared between believers, also became an increasingly established part of Christian life. The Church, the community of all Christians, was often also conceptualized as Christ's body, held together by his blood.

For the medieval aristocracy, though they were obviously also Christian, spilling blood was a major way of gaining power and proving one's worth as a warrior or knight. The literature of the courts, which aimed to celebrate and shape noble culture, is preoccupied with bloody fights that prove the heroes' masculinity, but ascribes excessive blood-spilling or even blood-drinking to monsters. It also tells many stories about the special powers of blood: for example, that the explorer Alexander the Great relied on the idea that the sea abhors blood when he let himself be lowered to the bottom of the ocean in a glass container, safe in the knowledge that he would be spat out by the sea if he cut himself (Fig. 3.2).

Both the Church and lay courts passed laws, which included rules circumscribing the spilling and touching of blood. Medieval legal codes often automatically treated bleeding wounds as more serious injuries than non-bleeding ones; and various taboos regulated contact with blood and with those who touch blood, such as executioners or surgeons.

In the following, I hope to provide an overview of the main characteristics ascribed to blood that unite medical, religious, legal, and courtly discourses. It is often claimed that there is an excess of meaning in blood, that it can signify death and life, sin and salvation, sickness and health, severing and creating ties between people, kinship and violence, nobility and baseness. Some of these stark contrasts become less pronounced, however, when we see them as resulting from the importance given to blood as basically granting access to the truth and as binding body and soul to each other while separating them from the external world. For example, it should not be surprising that blood 'means' both health and sickness: if good blood is crucial for health, it is only logical that too much or too little of it will then 'mean' sickness. Because blood is believed to hold body and soul together, it is often blood contained inside the body that is valued positively, while it is a sign of danger if blood has escaped. Examples will be discussed below.

Most of my findings are true for medieval Europe and beyond: humoral medicine dominated Europe and the Arab world from antiquity and spread from there; the Church provided a pan-European umbrella of beliefs; and the culture and art of the nobility were shared across Europe and further afield. While my 2006 book *Medieval blood* concentrated on thirteenth-century German texts, I shall here predominantly deal with fourteenth- and fifteenth-century German spiritual material as most advances in research into medieval blood have since been made in this area. But I shall also contextualize this with scientific material as well as with texts and images from other areas and medieval periods.

Blood reveals the truth

'Blood is thicker than water', 'it's in my blood', and the Malaysian blood tests and Indian blood paintings discussed by Carsten and Copeman, respectively, in this volume – countless contemporary assumptions and practices still summon blood as the locus of inalienable authenticity (Bildhauer 2006: 16-50). The body and, in particular, blood are invoked as tokens of an unmediated reality imagined to exist underneath a constructed language or culture. Such representations of blood as uncovering the truth are already evident in medieval theology, science, and culture. Blood is often depicted as hidden inside the body. If it becomes visible, it is perceived as a sign which, correctly interpreted, will reveal the undeniable truth about a given issue. The Gospel of St John (19:34), for example, reports that when Christ was crucified, 'one of the soldiers with a spear opened his side, and immediately there came out blood and water'. In medieval exegesis, this gospel verse was taken to confirm that Christ had truly assumed a human body. Although John's claim that blood flowed does not prove that God was incarnated any more than any other biblical statement to that effect, the effusion of blood described in this passage was believed to demonstrate beyond doubt that Christ did not assume merely the appearance of the human body. The idea that Christ's blood revealed the truth is made literal in medieval legends reporting that the biblical soldier, often known as Longinus, was blind, but that Christ's blood made him see and realize who Christ actually was. One version of the Passion, the anonymous *Christi Leiden* (*c*.1350-60), describes this scene as follows: 'Thus, he accidentally rubbed his eyes with his hands stained with the blood; and the eyes opened and he began to see. Then he looked up and saw Christ hanging above him; and then his inner eyes were opened'.[2] Blood here reveals to Longinus, physically and spiritually, that Christ is really the incarnated son of God. Blood is shown to be something that gives immediate access to the truth, that cannot be faked, and that, as pure matter, is beyond discourse and symbolism.

Like the exegetes, most medieval people had to work harder than Longinus to decipher the truth revealed in blood. The annalist of the West Frankish monastery of St Bertin reports for the year 839 that the English king Aethelwulf of Wessex shared a terrifying bloody prophecy with the emperor Louis the Pious. An English priest predicted that pagans would soon bring devastation to the country unless the Christians repented and atoned for their shocking sins. This sinfulness is disclosed to the priest in a vision when a guide takes him to a church in a strange country to see some boys reading bloody letters:

> When he got so close to them that he could see what they were reading, he saw that their books were written not only in black letters but also in letters of blood; it had been done so that one line was written out in black letters, the next in bloody ones. He asked why the books were written out like that with lines of blood and his guide answered: 'The lines of blood you can see in those books are all the various sins of Christian people, because they are so utterly unwilling to obey the orders and fulfil the precepts in those divine books. These boys now, moving about here and looking as if they are reading, are the souls of the saints who grieve every day over the sins and crimes of Christians and intercede for them so that they may finally be turned to repentance some day' (The annals 1991: 93).[3]

The guide then adds his warning that unless the sinners repent, the pagans will attack.

A high truth value is ascribed to blood here. The vision of the bloody lines reveals that Christendom is sinful, as unequivocally explained by the guide and accepted by the priest as well as by the English king, the emperor, and the annalist to whom the vision is reported. It is specifically this bloody writing (rather than the church, the boys, or the books) that carries the central message of the vision: the sinful state of Christendom. Blood makes clear that all is not well not through the words written in it, but through its very materiality: it does not describe sins, it metonymically embodies sin. The meaning revealed by blood, however, depends on a careful process of reading and communication between the inquisitive priest, the reading boys, the interpreting guide, and later the authorities to whom the vision is reported.

A still famous example of the complicated way in which blood is meant to reveal the truth in medieval culture is the grail story, in which the knight Perceval has to ask a question about blood that would redeem the sick grail king, but fails to do so. In the seminal version, the grail romance Conte du graal by Chrétien de Troyes (c.1182), blood sometimes reveals the truth unproblematically. For instance, Anguingueron recognizes his lord Clamadeu as he approaches Arthur's court:

> He saw his lord all covered in crimson blood but did not fail to recognise him, saying at once: 'My lords, my lords, here's an amazing sight! The youth in red armour, believe me, is sending here that knight you can see. He's defeated him: I'm quite sure of that because he's covered in blood. I can pick out the blood from here and him too as being my lord, whose vassal I am. His name is Clamadeu of the Isles' (Chrétien de Troyes 1987: 411).[4]

Blood is here clearly set up as a visual sign to be read: Anguingueron asks the courtier to look at a marvel; he deduces from the fact that Clamadeu is covered in blood that he has been defeated, and he claims to recognize both the blood and the king. Blood is a trace, and with the correct prior knowledge, Anguingueron draws the right conclusions here.

But it is more difficult to decipher correctly the truth hidden in the blood at the centre of the grail mystery. Perceval is presented with the grail and a mysterious bleeding lance, but does not ask about their significance. When he first sees the drop of blood issuing from the white lance in the *Conte du graal*, the narrator makes clear that bleeding is again a spectacle, a visual sign waiting to be read:

> And everyone present could see the white lance with its shining head; and from the tip of the lance-head oozed a drop of blood, a crimson drop that ran down right to the lad's hand. The young man who had arrived there that night saw this marvel, but refrained from asking how this thing happened (Chrétien de Troyes 1987: 416).[5]

Blood is introduced into this scene as perceived by the characters: Perceval, like everyone, sees this blood drop coming out, but he fails to investigate further. He is meant to ask about 'le lance qui saignee' as well as who is served by the grail (with only the former mentioned in all eight passages referring to this event). He later finds out the answer to the first question – that the grail king is served by the grail – but never why the lance-head constantly bleeds. Blood here remains a secret, even to the recipient, pointing to the gap between the indisputable truth resident in the blood, and the impossibility of translating it into words. Later versions of the grail story link these two discourses in which blood reveals a crucial truth: that of Christ's bleeding on the cross and that of the bleeding lance. The grail here becomes a dish in which Joseph of Arimathea allegedly collected Christ's blood at the crucifixion.

In some cases, blood itself seems to be given the capacity to know something. It is a witness to the truth, irrespective of whether this is noticed by a human observer or not. This is most obviously the case in the notorious belief that blood begins to flow from a corpse if the killer is nearby. This belief was queried in most medieval texts that mention it, but became accepted as an objective test of guilt in early modern (sixteenth-century) legal codes. The theologian, philosopher, and scientist Albert the Great in 1258 provides an early example of granting some credibility to this superstition in his commentary on Aristotle's *On Animals*. But he insists on providing a logical (religious or scientific) explanation that argues against any sentience of the blood itself: it is either God who is moving the blood, or a chain starting with the killer's conscience moving his spiritual organs, which then move the air, carrying warm breath to the body that makes the blood flow again (Albert 2008: 179; Albertus 1955: book IV, question 12). Nevertheless, blood here is seen to act independently of any conscious human interaction.

Blood fuses the body-soul unit

The differentiation between material body, on the one hand, and immaterial soul, spirit, or mind, on the other, is ubiquitous in contemporary Western culture. But contrary to common belief, and unlike the invocation of blood as unmediated reality, this distinction was not of major importance in the Middle Ages. Although categories such as mind, soul, spirit, reason, senses, body, and flesh were increasingly employed in vernacular medical, religious, and literary writing in the late Middle Ages, they were nevertheless seen as belonging together. Human beings were thought of as both embodied and animated. Caroline Walker Bynum has influentially argued in *The resurrection of the body* (1995) that in the late Middle Ages the body was believed to be so essential to personal identity that it was thought to be resurrected with the soul. Just one example of how blood, soul, and body were understood as a single unit in vernacular devotional writing is a sermon by Konrad of Esslingen, transmitted in Anna of Munzingen's 1318 'sister book' (or collective spiritual autobiography) of the Dominican convent at Adelhausen in the Black Forest. Konrad describes five physical and spiritual things received through 'Our Lord's body' ('vnseres Herren lichamen') in the Eucharist: his body and incarnated holiness, his blood, his vital spirit ('leblicher geiste'), his soul, and his divinity (Anna 1880: 189). He then tells the story from Ezekiel 37 of how Ezekiel's preaching made the Israelites' scattered bones regroup, grow flesh, and come back to life (Anna 1880: 190). He interprets this story as an allegory: as the Israelites' bodies re-form and grow veins, flesh, and skin through Ezekiel's preaching, the soul's virtues are reunited and grow veins, flesh, and blood through repentance; as the Israelites' bodies are revived through the four winds, the soul is revived through God's body, blood, soul, and divinity. Thus, in this sermon, God's Eucharistic body contains his soul; the Israelites' body parts are reassembled into a living whole even after death; the human soul has veins, flesh, and blood; and the soul is revived through God's body and soul. Despite the various distinctions between body, soul, divinity, veins, flesh, skin, holiness, vital spirit, and blood, the strongest impression is one of psychosomatic unity, where all these elements combine into one, without special concern for a division of matter and non-matter.

Individual Christians were also understood to be body-soul continua held together, at least in part, by blood. In the sister book of the Dominican convent at Töss in Switzerland, first collated by Elsbeth Stagel around 1340, the nun Mechthild of Stans, for example, is given by divine grace a wound in her heart from which blood and water flow so that she can suffer with Christ on the cross. Mechthild asks God for the wound to heal over externally so that she can keep it hidden (conceiving of blood again as a secret truth that cannot be communicated in language). She remains ill with what is now only an internal wound, but one which is diagnosed as a spiritual ailment:

> And around this time a wise physician came. He was told of her condition, and when he had taken her pulse, he said that she did not have an illness, but a great yearning for an ineffable thing, and all her nature had stretched so strongly towards it that through this all her blood had flown to the heart so that it could support the heart. And he said: 'It is as impossible for her to grasp what she yearns for as it is impossible for me to grasp that the grass is green.' And she herself confirmed that this was the case.[6]

If we attempt to separate the physical from the transcendental here, Mechthild's wound now appears to be not so much biological – the physician's diagnosis is that she is not ill – but spiritual. Nonetheless, biological blood, detectable to the physician, flows in order to help her heart deal with this spiritual strain. So biological blood serves a spiritual need, or, more precisely, physical and spiritual dimensions are simply conflated. Blood flowing inside Mechthild shows her to be a psychosomatic whole, a seamless conglomerate of what we might today divide into body and soul.

In physiological thinking, blood, in particular, also connected all the material and immaterial components of the human being. Konrad of Megenberg's encyclopaedic *Book of Nature* (1348-50, from which we have already seen an image) provides a representative compendium of the biological knowledge (about humans, stars, animals, plants, stones, and wonders) that was available to non-experts in late medieval Germany. Konrad, who like so many science writers was also a cleric, clearly describes the soul and the spirit as part of human physiology. Like his sources (chiefly Thomas of

Cantimpré's *Liber de natura rerum* from the first half of the thirteenth century), he tries to combine the conflicting ideas of blood, spirit, and soul presented by Aristotle and Galen. He understands 'spirit' to be a material substance made from purified blood and transported through the arteries, but also a kind of vapour that gives biological life (Konrad 2003: 55-61; book I, chaps 39-44). Konrad further distinguishes between a natural spirit, associated with the heart, and a vital spirit, associated with the liver, with both being made from blood. There is also a third, animal spirit, associated with the brain, whose source he does not mention (originally, this name comes from the Greek *anima* for soul, but Konrad understands it to refer to animals). At least partly made from blood, spirit joins body and soul, matter and the transcendental: 'The spirit is a bond with which body and soul are tied together'.[7] That blood is a means of dealing with psychosomatic strain, as in Mechthild's case, is also in accordance with Konrad's medical knowledge. He writes of blood flowing to the heart to protect it from fear: 'If the human is afraid, the blood runs to the heart to its rescue'.[8]

Though this is still not well researched, medieval scientific and religious texts generally considered emotions to be inseparable from the body and in particular from blood in this way. In medieval physiological theory, many emotions are understood to be carried rather than signified or symbolized by blood. The theory of the four temperaments – choleric, melancholic, sanguine, and phlegmatic – suggests that the emotions and moods of anger, sadness, optimism, and laziness were fully physical and determined by blood. For example, Konrad claims that a comet forecasts bloodshed, and then explains this through its effect on the humours:

> Now you may ask why this star signifies strife and bloodshed. This is because during this time, the stars' powers draw the vital spirit out of the human being and make the spiritual blood evaporate from the human being. If the human is thus dry and hot, he is angry and fights a lot, as we see in hot people.[9]

The cosmic imbalance draws out a human being's moisture and coldness, and this makes the human hot and dry and therefore angry. The carrier of heat and dryness is traditionally defined as yellow bile in humoral medicine, but for Konrad it is part of the vital spirit (made from purified blood, as we have seen above) and of what he calls spiritual blood. No clear line can be drawn here between psychology and physiology: emotions are as much in the blood as in the spirit and the soul.

Blood defines the outlines of a person

Whether it flows to the heart or dries up under cosmic influence, blood can act independently of the will or intention of the person, or even of the rest of the body. For a mystic such as Mechthild of Stans, who was keen to surrender her will to God anyway, the fact that blood acts inside her body of its own accord to support her heart might be considered as a positive step on the mystical way. However, in Konrad's case of the comet, the agency of blood has less positive consequences: it leads to bloodshed, which of course endangers the fighters. Whether this was valued positively or negatively, the body could easily disintegrate into its parts, either when they become independent from the person or if the body comes under external attack (Bildhauer 2006: 51-83). While the distinctions between matter and spirit, body and mind, caused little debate and concern, the differentiation between the psychosomatic unit and its outside, and among its various physical parts, preoccupied many medieval texts and images. The emphasis on the continuity of body and soul did not mean that a person was perceived to be a pre-Cartesian holistic unit. The embodied human was anything but whole in its contours and its parts.

This is highlighted by Caroline Walker Bynum in her brilliant *Wonderful blood* (2007), the most significant study of blood (specifically of the devotion to Christ's blood) in late medieval Northern European spirituality, and again from a different angle in her *Christian materiality* (2011). Bynum's main point is that Christ's blood was considered to be alive, freshly flowing from the corpse, without need of the body. While Christ's body made the transition from life to death, his blood remained the same. This was taken to symbolize another instance of permanence amidst change: that Christ remained divine and eternal in his transformation to mortal humanity. Christ's immutability and his victory over death thereby became manifest in his blood. Moreover, his blood relics provided access to Christ on earth. Bynum argues that it is important that blood in most depictions is 'living blood poured out' and 'separated and shed', as her 2007 chapter headings have it, rather than still part of his body.

There was, however, also considerable anxiety about what a substance with so much independent agency could do to the body to which it belonged. If blood, so often perceived as the innermost essence of a person, can survive independently of the body, does that mean that the self disintegrates? Concerns with personal identity are often assumed to have developed only in the early modern period (e.g. Keller 2007a; 2007b). But even in the Middle Ages, each bleeding, whether it posed a danger to health or not, was perceived to be a crisis of the body conceptualized as confined within the skin. That which was suffused with blood was the person, and visible bleeding therefore meant that the external form of the person had been breached. Nevertheless, this was often interpreted as ultimately securing the body, as long as it remained limited to a brief moment of crisis. Throughout the spiritual biography of Sister Adelheit Geishörnlin in the Adelhausen sister book, for example, matter and spirit easily converge, but Adelheit's relationship to the outside of her body is more fragile in terms of excretions and food as well as blood. When souls in the shape of little people in white clothes help her to go to the latrine because she cannot stand on her own, and when God intervenes before she can frivolously devour a fried pear, the transcendental realm seamlessly meets the physical. However, taking substances like blood into, and emitting them from, the body is a more fraught process. Standing in front of the altar one day, Adelheit is granted her wish to undergo what the disciples experienced when the Holy Spirit entered them at Pentecost: a ray falls upon her, and from the great sweetness and wonder she jumps up and spins around the altar, 'vnd schoß ir das bluot ze munde vnd zuo nasen vs' ('and blood spurted from her mouth and nose', Anna 1880: 166). This is in the first instance a breach of her body, and therefore a crisis. However, because the moment was so brief, it confirms her body. A sister who witnessed the event asks Adelheit what happened, and Adelheit eventually agrees to tell her if she keeps it secret (again invoking blood as a hidden, incommunicable truth). Adelheit says:

> 'If the blood had not spurted from me, so that I had not experienced release from my body, I would have died in that moment, for nature was too weak to withstand the excessive joy and the sweetness that was in me'. She was also assured of eternal life long before her death.[10]

Adelheit claims to have been in mortal danger through her overwhelming experience (which can once more be categorized neither as spiritual nor as bodily). Blood, to some extent again acting independently of the person, leaves the body; and it is its ability to do so that protects Adelheit. Because it is limited to a moment of crisis, the blood loss here secures her body and life, and perhaps, if the following sentence suggests a causal link, even her eternal life. Bleeding here ultimately works to safeguard the body and with it the person, but only precariously so.

When it comes to lay people, blood's capacity for dissolution was more clearly perceived as a threat. The coherence both of blood and of the person which it held together was only guaranteed if blood remained inside the person, or if any appearance of blood was circumscribed as a moment of crisis. Medieval laws and taboos against bloodshed, bleeding, and contact with blood far exceed what might be practically useful for pacification, health, or hygiene. In medicine, bleeding was also disproportionately feared. Obviously, the copious bleeding of wounds was seen then, as now, as a medical problem that required treatment, but even bleeding that was considered harmless or indeed beneficial, such as menstruation and blood-letting, was viewed with suspicion and circumspection. Phlebotomy, though the most common therapeutic measure, was rigorously regulated. Late medieval pocket calendars and diagrams recommended where and when to draw blood in order to remove more or less of one of the essential humours and restore health by bringing these back into balance. Konrad's *Book of Nature*, for example, in a fifteenth-century illustrated version, opens with an image of the so-called 'blood-letting man', perhaps the most widespread medical diagram indicating the appropriate points at which to let blood in order to cure particular diseases (Fig. 3.3). The lack of detail indicates that this particular diagram was included to signal learnedness rather than to act as an actual guide. This man is unperturbed by the fine bloodlines emanating from sixteen wounds on his body; his serene face and heavily drawn outline retain his integrity.

A more practice-orientated example is the blood-letting and recipe book of Asang from 1516-19, which details standard rules for blood-letting (*Das Asanger Aderlaß- und Rezeptbüchlein* 1967: 27-35). It prescribes from which side of the body to let blood, according to the seasons, the affliction, and its duration. It advises not to let blood when the weather is too hot or cold, if the urine is red or the veins too large; to consider whether the person is used to blood-letting, and in what phase and sign of the zodiac the moon lies; not to let much blood when the patient is old or ill; to let generously when the blood is black and thick; if possible, not to let blood on the fifth, tenth, fifteenth, twentieth, and the last five days of each month; under no circumstances to let on 1 August, 31 December, and 18 April, but to do so on 17 March and 11 April; to let blood from certain veins after eating and urinating and some before; to choose the veins from which to let according to the disease to be treated; and to take special precautions for five days after blood-letting.

Exchanging blood only rarely created bonds – as it could between Christ and Christians – and it was therefore normally feared rather than encouraged. In the *Book of Nature*, it is not mystics who long for blood, but monsters: the mermaid Scylla who 'desires human blood'; the cave-dwelling Cyclopses who 'eat blood'; and the Comani people who 'drink horses' blood'.[11] Taking in blood is also depicted as decidedly negative in the case of the leech that sucks so much blood that it bursts, which is compared to the way in which greed kills the human soul (Konrad 2003: 336; book III.F, chap. 21).

The special status of Christ's and pious Christians' blood
When outside the body, blood is usually represented as a diffuse liquid without clear limits, and is known for its power to destroy both the body to which it belongs and

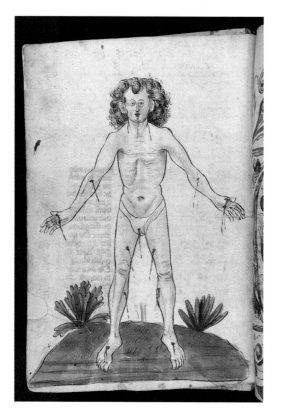

Figure 3.3. Blood-letting man. Konrad von Megenberg, *Buch der Natur*, Hagenau, Workshop Diebold Lauber, *c*.1442-8, Universitätsbibliothek Heidelberg Cod. Pal. Germ. 300, fol. 3v (title page). (Reproduced with permission of the Universitätsbibliothek Heidelberg.)

other bodies. Blood can only in exceptional cases remain coherent, and make bodies coherent: when bleeding is limited and marked as a crisis, as in Adelheit's case, or when it is affirmed and brought to a higher level, like Christ's blood. Christ embraces the bleeding that would normally dissolve his body, and opens up to become the collective body of Christendom. For example, the *Book of Nature* characterizes Christ's blood as corrosive. It compares the blood to a worm which can break stone and hard glass:

> Thamur or samier means Salomon's worm. It says in the book called *Scholastic History* that Salomon divided and broke the temple stone with it and that an ostrich broke a hard glass with it, so that it could take out its young chick. The worm can signify our Lord Jesus Christ, for our Lord's blood, which he shed on the holy cross, has such great power that it softens the stony hearts to suffer with Christ in the Passion.[12]

Christ's blood is described here as dissolving and softening even stony hearts. Konrad also mentions the well-known belief that a he-goat's blood can break an otherwise indestructible diamond (in other texts this is likened to the power that Christ's blood has over hardened human hearts: Konrad 2003: 468; book VI, chap. 3). Though this rupturing is entirely positive, neither the blood nor the hearts can be said to show any unity here. Blood is not self-contained but enters and softens believers' hearts.

Christians' blood is not always coherent either. According to the *Book of Nature*, the white snail, for example, is born from putrid grass and can change completely into blood, a capacity which is compared to the behaviour of pious Christians:

> It is born from putrid grass with excess moisture and heat. The worm-like creature is grey, lethargic, and fat and has much blood of its kind. If one sprinkles salt on it, the worm flows apart almost completely and entirely, so that almost nothing of it remains, and it becomes mere blood of its kind. This is good as medication. Consider this to signify the people who have tried the salt of wisdom, who flow apart in meditation and regard themselves as nothing in the world. I mean divine wisdom, but human knowledge makes the impudent masters conceited and inflated. In this regard Paul says 'scientia inflat', which means 'science inflates', and he means it in the sense that I said.[13]

This snail can dissolve into blood, becoming 'almost nothing', and the same happens when people devote themselves to divine wisdom. The dissolution of the body in God's wisdom is here again depicted as something positive, especially in contrast to the inflated ego of those devoted to worldly matters. However, it is also clear that mystical becoming nothing means death for the snail, and in any case the comparison to a snail's blood drags spiritual dissolution down from its lofty heights.

This passage makes clear not only that blood is as often dissolved as it is coherent, but also the exceptional nature of the devotional model of embracing bodily dissolution. Mystics ingeniously appropriate Christ's manner of welcoming blood and the disbanding of the body, often much more so than Adelheit in the blood-spilling episode. Much of the devotion to Christ's blood aims at becoming one with Christ. Margarethe Ebner, a Dominican nun at Maria Medingen, for example, experiences the satisfaction of becoming one with God's blood not only by pressing a large crucifix onto her heart (again, interior and exterior, body and soul, are not distinguished), but also through the Eucharist:

> During the day, when I receive our lord, God's true presence is given to me internally with such a strong Christian love, which I have received nakedly and without mediation in my soul from the love that pressured my soul, and I know that I have in me the living power of God, his holy blood and flesh.[14]

Christ's Eucharistic blood enters Margarethe's body and soul here, and this causes not concern, as in most secular contexts, but bliss. Konrad of Esslingen also advocates unity with Christ's blood as an ideal for the nuns. He describes Christ's Eucharistic blood as hot, liquid, and red – the chief characteristics of blood as a humour, as mentioned above: 'Das ander stucke, dz man enpfahet, das ist sin heiliges bluot; an dem sint die 3 stuck: es ist heis, es ist flussig, es ist rot' ('the other part one receives is his holy blood, which has three qualities: it is hot, it is liquid, it is red', Anna 1880: 190). Konrad then interprets each of the three qualities received with Christ's blood as a spiritual effect on the believer: like fire, heat purifies, while moisture cleanses and redness imprints God's image into the soul:

> From these three qualities the human profits in the following ways: from the heat, the rust is burned from the soul. ... Secondly, it is liquid, for that which is liquid cleanses. ... Thirdly, the redness, for the colour of the blood rejoins and renews the divine image imprinted into our souls.[15]

This suggests that Christ's blood here enters the soul (as part of a unified psychosomatic person). Again it is exceptional that the taking of someone else's blood by the devout Christian is blissful rather than threatening. Blood enters the body through the mouth and then works on the transcendental soul through burning, cleansing, and imprinting it. These are all highly positive, rather than painful or dangerous, effects of Christ's blood within the believer.

Increasingly, ordinary believers attempted to emulate the nuns' and mystics' fervour in their devotional practices, and commissioned or bought manuscripts and images that actively encouraged devotion to Christ's blood. A psalter produced around 1480-90, perhaps for a woman in Kent, for instance, opens with eleven pages completely painted bright red or black with a regular pattern of blood drops. Onto three of these pages, woodcuts of the Passion are pasted. In the one shown in Figure 3.4, Christ's suffering body is reduced to his five wounds that stream with red blood. The vividly coloured image creates a visual invitation to submerge oneself in the bloody suffering of Christ, and experience it with him as immediately as possible.

The incoherent blood and bodies of women and Jews

Some people could never hope to achieve a coherent body which neither emitted nor took in blood on a regular basis. Women were not able to contain their blood, medically speaking, because of their insufficient warmth; and therefore they could not have a coherent body. Their blood flowed out, according to medical views, because they had to emit superfluities from food that they could not burn off like men. Only men could

Figure 3.4. Christ's five wounds. Psalter, c.1480-90. (© British Library Board, British Library, Egerton 1821, fol. 9r. Reproduced with permission.)

achieve coherent fluids: it was a well-known sign of a male foetus, cited also by Konrad, that under its greater heat 'a woman's milk is so thick and viscous that if it is sprinkled on a glass, the drops stand like egg-white and won't flow, but if the woman is carrying a girl, her milk is thin and watery and its drops flow apart'.[16]

For the men on whom this blood encroached, it was often polluting. While a neutral or nuanced view of menstrual blood is evident in practical medical guides (Green 2005), the vernacular German texts, less designed for pragmatic advice than for the collection of knowledge, clearly distinguish between men's and women's blood and frequently refer to menstrual pollution. Konrad of Megenberg, for example, in his short chapter on the eyes, finds it necessary to mention the well-known belief that menstruating women cloud new mirrors, infect eyes, and can throw a camel into a ditch with their poisonous gaze (2003: 33; book 1, chap. 5). When female mystics embraced their own uncontrollable bleeding, mingled Christ's blood with theirs, desired and drank it, they to some extent only enacted what was medically and socially open to them. In so doing, they both re-valued bleeding as a spiritual activity allowing access to God, and perpetuated the belief that women were never self-contained.

Women's lack of self-containment also informed the belief that they needed men's blood (preferably in the purified form of semen) to warm them. Semen was the most refined form of blood, whitened through several stages of purification. Many popular texts warned men against sexual intercourse, which would allow women, driven by their impure menstrual blood, to draw the precious fluids out of them. On occasion, this is described as 'sucking' (see Bildhauer 2002). Mystics again re-valued as well as perpetuated this stereotype by sucking and drinking blood out of Christ's wounds. Together with ideas of the evil eye caused by menstrual pollution, this idea of blood-sucking women contributed to later conceptions of women as vampires and witches.

While women were believed to bleed incontinently and to want men's refined blood, virgins were partially exempted from this in some texts. They were perceived not to have bled yet (as the first blood of defloration was often conflated with first menstrual bleeding; Bildhauer 2006: 103-25). Menopausal women did not regain the same status, as their blood-retention was regarded as fraught with dangers to themselves and others. A return to the non-bleeding, coherent body of a virgin was thus as difficult as it was desirable: consider, for example, what happened in the case of Adelheit of Brisach of the Adelhausen convent:

> This same sister, Adelheit, was very worried about her virginity, because she was a widow, and she cried day and night for her virginity. When she had done so for many years, an angel came and said to her: 'Very well, God wants to grant you your wish, as much as is possible.' And he led her into the air; and there were other angels, too, who had a wine press, and they laid her into it and pressed her so hard that she thought that not a drop of blood remained in her body. And they said to her: 'We have pressed out of you all the blood that has sinned in you, and we shall pour virgins' blood into you, and you shall become as much like a virgin as you possibly can, but you cannot become a virgin.' And when she came to, she lay soaked in blood.[17]

It is striking that the bleeding, the pressing out of corrupt blood, is dwelt upon here, but not the insertion of virginal blood. As a deflowered woman, Adelheit bleeds and cries copiously and incessantly; as a virgin, she does not bleed or cry any longer. The blood of real virgins should presumably remain entirely in their bodies, which can only be approximated in this case through the reinsertion of blood that then remains in the body. Deflowered women's blood is here shown to flow excessively and dissolve, whereas virgins' blood might retain some of the integrity ascribed by medical theory to men's blood.

Similarly excluded from the possibility of having a coherent body that did not bleed uncontrollably were Jewish people. Like women, Jewish men were believed to menstruate and to need Christian men's blood. Again, this is a surprisingly frequent accusation in the later medieval and early modern period (Bildhauer 2006: 94-6). Even the *Book of Nature* manages to establish a tenuous link between Jews and a snake that draws men's blood:

> Several Latin books have a chapter about that which shall be described now, and this chapter tells of a snake called emorois, that is, in German *emoroi* or strength-sucker, for as Isidore says, a person who is bitten by this snake sweats out his own blood until all his veins pour out, and whatever life is in him flows out with the blood, for the Greek word *emach* means blood, from whence the name *emorois* comes and also the word haemorrhoids, which are the veins ending at the human's anus; and from those veins in Jews flows the red flux and also in several Christians, according to the changes of the moon.[18]

Konrad claims that Jews bleed unintentionally and uncontrollably, having incoherent bodies. Moreover, Jews are here associated with a blood-sucking snake that also effectively takes blood and thereby life, another common accusation against Jews, women, and various vampiric monsters (Bildhauer 2006: 119-25). While women could at least theoretically gain cohesion on a higher level by becoming one with Christ's body, this was not open to Jewish people. Rather, they were only believed to enable the greater coherence of Christ's body by temporarily making it bleed in host miracles (which often occurred at the outer periphery of the Corpus Christi of the Church), as they were thought to have done to Jesus in the Passion.

Conclusions

Blood was credited with remarkable power in late medieval German science and religion, and beyond. While in medical and secular thought bleeding (however minor) was predominantly viewed with suspicion as a threat to the person, such crisis moments were also valued as chances for healing and heroism. Christianity went furthest in embracing bleeding and the dissolution of the person it entailed, as a chance for opening up to, and becoming one with, Christ and with a community of believers. Although blood was in this respect part of the whole person rather than just of the body, a slightly different school of thought relies on blood being purely physical matter, outside discourse and culture, so that it is able to reveal the innermost essence and truth about a variety of issues without having to be mediated through language (at least in theory). Contradictory beliefs about blood were held simultaneously, but blood was rarely viewed as insignificant.

Such medieval ideas about blood are remarkably close to the contemporary conceptions of blood explored elsewhere in this volume. Maya Mayblin, for instance, observes similar anxieties of how best to let blood, and investment in its health-giving and sacrificial powers in Northeast Brazil. This overlap can be explained in three ways. In part, it is certainly due to the persistence and spread of European and Middle Eastern science and religion shaped in premodernity, including ideas about blood based on ancient Greek humoral medicine as well as Christian, Muslim, and Jewish views about blood sacrifice, martyrdom, and shared blood.

Some of the similarilies, however, may also result from the shared tools of anthropologists and historians for understanding blood. Studies of medieval cultural history have always been strongly influenced by anthropological work such as that of Claude Lévi-Strauss, Victor Turner, and especially Mary Douglas; and now both disciplines have embraced anti-essentialist theories of the body. This gives both medievalists and anthropologists a heightened sensitivity to the limits of the body, to blood prohibitions, to ritual and symbolic uses of blood, to blood exchanges and kinship bonds. This focused attention may mean that, despite our best intentions, we overlook other attitudes to blood that would differentiate the cultures we study more strongly from one another.

There is, however, one crucial difference between medieval and contemporary attitudes to blood. Anthropologists may be surprised by what is not there in the Middle Ages: a preoccupation with blood to define hereditary bonds of race or nobility. 'Blood relatives' is a term used in both Latin and some vernaculars in the Middle Ages, and the idea that kinship groups shared a common blood was known and confirmed through the dominant theories of conception. But it was much less frequently invoked than, say, the association of blood with sacrifice or violence. The medieval idea that some blood is better than that of others (male blood better than female, Christian better than Jewish) is only later worked into the notion that a special kind of blood constitutes race or nobility, as in 'blue blood' (see de Miramon 2009; Nirenberg 2009). Similarly, the distinction of human from animal blood that bothered early modern scientists (Schaffer 1998) is not a prominent issue in medieval culture. Instead, various animals' blood could stand unproblematically for Christ's and Christians' blood and its powers. I have already mentioned several examples of this above; another is the widespread belief that pelicans feed their young with their own blood, which is often compared to Christ's self-sacrifice for Christendom (Fig. 3.5).

Finally, some of the continued popularity of seeing oneself as a container of blood, pierced at one's peril, surely stems from the usefulness of this model of identity both for medieval people and for modern ones. The human being as an autonomous, cohesive, embodied entity ending at the skin (thought of as an ideally impermeable barrier, whose breaching is highly circumscribed) is the basis of medieval and modern notions of what

Figure 3.5. Pelicans feeding their young with their own blood. Bestiary, England, 1230-40. (© British Library Board, British Library Harley 4751, fol. 46. Reproduced with permission.)

a person is. This only becomes problematic on an extremely detailed level (Which atom exactly still belongs to my skin and which to the surrounding air or dust? Are the bacteria in my intestines part of me or not?) and on an extremely broad one (Can the self exist without the body after death? Is it ever fully independent from God's providence?). The idea of the self as a blood-infused entity, whose breaching is so obviously dangerous, guards against fears of the self and the outside merging. In the Middle Ages, these fears might have taken the form of worries about sharing one's bodily space with demons and food, of losing part of oneself through shedding fluids and solids, and of all knowledge coming from God. Today, they might centre on sharing one's bodily space with germs, pollutants from the environment, donor organs or implants; or on losing control of oneself through food intake and emission, or through being manipulated in a virtual reality run by machines and conspirators; and certain individuals may still faint at the sight of blood outside the body. Demarcating oneself off clearly from the outside through guarding against blood flow still helps to uphold a sense of self.

NOTES

This chapter is a substantially rewritten, updated, and expanded version of Bildhauer (2012). I thank the Leverhulme Trust for the award of the Leverhulme Prize, which allowed me to take research leave during which I reworked this chapter.

[1] On medieval blood, see, for example, Bildhauer (2006); Bradburne (2001); Bynum (2007); Cohen (2004); Faure (1999); Frantzen (2004); McClive & Pellegrin (2010); McCracken (2003); Miller (2010); Salisbury (2004); Vincent (2001).

[2] 'Also streich he die hende von ungeschiete mit deme blude ubir die augen unde die augen gingen yme uf unde wart sehende. Da sach her ubir sich unde sach Xristum ober yme hangen, unde da wurden yem die ynnern augen uf gedan' (Christi Leiden 1936: 46). All translations from medieval German are mine.

[3] 'Et cum ad illos adpropinquaret ut uideret quod legerent, perspexit libros eorum non solum nigris litteris uerum etiam sanguineis esse descriptos, ita uidelicet ut una linea nigris esset litteris descripta et altera sanguineis. Cumque interrogaret cur libri illi sanguineis lineis descripti essent, respondit ductor eius: "Lineae sanguineae, quas in istis libris conspicis, diuersa hominum christianorum peccata sunt, quia ea quae in libris diuinis illis precepta et iussa sunt minime facere et adimplere uolunt. Pueri uero isti qui hic quasi legendo discurrunt animae sunt sanctorum quae cotidie pro christianorum peccatis et facinoribus deplorant et pro illis intercedunt, ut tandem aliquando ad poenitentiam conuertantur; et nisi iste animae sanctorum tam incessanter cum fletu ad Deum clamarent, iam aliquatenus finis tantorum malorum in christiano populo esset" ' (Annales 1964: 29).

[4]   'Son seignor tot de sanc vermeil
         vit covert, nel mesconnut pas,
         ainçois dist tot isnellepas:
         "Seignor, seignor, veez merveilles.
         Li vallés as armes vermeilles
         envoie cha, si m'en creez,
         cel chevalier que vos veez.
         Il l'a conquis, j'en sui tot cers,
         Por che qu'il est de sanc covers.
         Je connois bien le sanc de chi,
         et lui meïsmes autresi,
         qu'il est me sire et je ses hom.
         Clamadeus des Illes a non" ' (Chrétien de Troyes 1993: 2764-76).

[5]   'Et tot cil de laiens veoient
         le lance blanche et le fer blanc,
         s'issoit une goute de sanc
         del fer de la lance en somet,
         et jusqu'a la main au vallet
         coloit cele goute vermeille.
         Li vallés voit cele merveille

qui laiens ert la nuit venus,

si s'est de demander tenus

coment ceste chose avenoit' (Chrétien de Troyes 1993: 3196-205).

[6] 'Und under disen zitten do kam ain wiser artzet her: dem ward ir wandel gesait, und do er ir audren gegraif, do sprach er sy het en kainen siechtagen: sy het ain grosse sennung nach ainem ubergriffenlichen ding, und were alle ir natur als fast dar uff gedennet das da von alles ir bluot zuo dem hertzen was gesigen, das es dem hertzen ze hilf kem, und sprach: "Es ist als unmuglich das sy das begriffen mug darnach sy sennet, als unmuglich mir ist das ich begriffen mug das das gras gruen ist." Und des verjach sy selb das es also wer' (Stagel 1906: 66).

[7] 'Der gaist ist ain pand, da mit leib vnd sel ze samen sint gepunden' (Konrad 2003: 56; book I, chap. 39). On Konrad's Christian interpretations of natural phenomena, see Nischik (1986: 266-94).

[8] 'Wenn der mensch sich fuerht, so lauft daz pluot tzuo dem hertzen sam zuo seinr enthaltung' (Konrad 2003: 59; book I, chap. 43).

[9] 'Nv maht du fragen, warvmb der stern streit bedaeut vnd pluot vergiessen. Daz ist darvmb, daz ze den zeiten der stern chreft die lebleichen gaist auz dem menschen ziehent vnd machent daz behend pluot ausduenstend auz dem menschen. So nu der mensch truchen ist vnd hitzig, so ist er zornig vnd vicht gern, als wir sehen an haizen lauten' (Konrad 2003: 104; book II, chap. 11).

[10] 'Were das bluot nut von mir geschossen, daz mir nút entlibung were worden, ich wer in der selben stund tod, wann die nature wz ze kranke gegen der vbrigen froyde, vnd gegen der süssigkeit, die in mir was. Si wart ouch gesichert lange vor irme tode des ewigen lebennes' (Anna 1880: 167).

[11] 'ist den scheflaeuten vnd allen menschen veint vnd ist lustig vnd girig dez menschen pluotes vnd seins flaisches' (Konrad 2003: 267; book III.C, chap. 18), 'di ezzent pluot' (Konrad 2003: 527; book VIII, chap. 3); 'trinkent pfaerds pluot' (Konrad 2003: 527; book VIII, chap. 3).

[12] 'Thamur oder samier, der haizt Salomons wurm. Da von sagt man in der geschrift, die scolastica hystoria haizt, daz Salomon dez tempels stain da mit tailt vnd zeprach vnd daz ein strauzz ein hertes glas da mit zerprach dar vmb, daz er sein iunges straeuzzel her auz naem. Der wurm mag vnsern herren Ihesum Cristum bedaeuten, wan vnsers herren pluot, daz er vergozz an dem heiligen chraeutz, hat so grozz chraft, daz ez die staineinn hertzen erwaicht zuo dem mitleiden vnsers herren marter' (Konrad 2003: 337; book III.F, chap. 23). In the *Historia scholastica* by Petrus Comestor (d. *c.*1178), it is actually the worm's blood that splits the stone and the glass.

[13] 'Der chumt von faulem gras mit vebermazz der faeuhten vnd der hitz. Der wurm ist gar traeg vnd vaizt vnd hat vil pluots nach seinr art. Wenn man saltz auf in sprengt, so zerflevzt er vil nahen aller gantz vnd gar, also daz sein nahent nihtz mer beleibt, vnd wirt eytel pluot aus im in seiner art. Daz ist guot zuo mangerlay ertzney. Da pey verste die laeut, di versuocht habent daz saltz der weizhait, die zevliezzend ze mal in andaht vnd achtend sich selber nihtz in der werlt. Ich main die goetleichen weizhait, aber die menschleich chunst macht die veppigen maister hochvertig vnd zerplaet. Da von spricht sanctus Paulus: Scientia inflat, daz spricht: Die chunst ze plaet vnd maint ez in dem sinn, vnd ich gesprochen han' (Konrad 2003: 338; book III.F, chap. 25).

[14] 'des tagez so ich unsern herren enphahe, so wirt mir inwendik geben mit ainer as starken christenlicher minne diu war gegenwertket gocz, die ich da blozzklichen in min sel enphangen han an mitel und von der minne, diu min sel gezwungen hat, und ich waiz, daz ich die lebenden craft gocz in mir han, sin hailigez bluot und flesche' (Margarethe & Heinrich 1882: 89).

[15] 'Von den drien stucken enpfahet der mensche dise nutze: von der hitze veget er den roste abe der sele ... Das ander: es ist flussig, wann wz flussig ist, dz weschet ... Das dritte die röte: wan die farwe sines bluotes wider verwetet vnd wider nuweret das götlich bilde, das in die sele getruckt ist' (Anna 1880: 190).

[16] 'der frawen milch dick ist vnd zaeh, also der sie sprengt auf ein glas, so stend die tropfen als dic arwaizz vnd vliezzend niht. Aber so die frawe mit eim dirnlein get, so ist ir milch duenn vnd waezzerig vnd zervliezzend ir tropfen' (Konrad 2003: 64; book I, chap. 47).

[17] 'Die selbe swester Adelheit hatte groß leid vmb den magtuom, wan si wz ein wittwe vnd weinde tag vnd nacht vmb den magtuom. Do si dis vil jar getreib, do kam ein engel vnd sprach zuo ir: "Wolluff, Gott wil dich erhören, also vere es muglich ist." Und fuerte si in den lufft, da warent ouch ander engel, die hatten ein trotten vnd leiten si darin vnd trotteten si also sere, das si duochte, das in irme libe niena troppff bluotes blibe. Vnd sprachen do zuo ir: "Alles das bluot das in dir gesundet hatt, dz hand wir vss dir getrottet vnd sollen dir megde bluot ingiessen vnd solt megden also glich werden als du iemer macht, aber du enmacht nut maget werden." Vnd do si wider kam zuo ir selben, do lag si in bluot besöppfet' (Anna 1880: 155).

[18] 'Etleich puoch ze latein hat ein capitel vor dem, daz nun geschriben ist, vnd daz selb capitel sagt von einr slangen, dev haizt emoroys, daz ist ein emoroy oder ein chraftsaugerinn ze daeutsch, wan, sam Ysidorus spricht, welher mensch von der slangen gepizzen wird, der switzet sein aigen pluot auz im selber also lang, daz sich all sein adern entsliezzent, vnd waz lebens in im ist, daz get auz im mit dem pluot, wan emach in chriechischer sprach

haizt pluot, dann chuemt der nam emoroys, vnd da von chuemt auch daz wort emoroydes: daz sint die adern, die sich zuo dem aftern aendent an dem menschen, vnd auz den selben adern flevzt den iuden der rot fluzz vnd auch etleichen christen nach dez monn aendrung' (Konrad 2003: 299-300; book III.E, chap. 13).

REFERENCES

ALBERT THE GREAT 2008. *Questions concerning Aristotle's On animals* (trans. I.M. Resnick & K.F. Kitchell). Washington, D.C.: Catholic University of America Press.

ALBERTUS MAGNUS 1955. *Quaestiones super De Animalibus* (ed. E. Filthaut) (Alberti Magni Opera Omnia **12**). Münster: Aschendorff.

ANNA VON MUNZINGEN 1880. *Die Chronik der Anna von Munzingen* (ed. J. König). Freiburger Diöcesan-Archiv **13**, 129-236.

ANNALES DE SAINT-BERTIN 1964 (eds F. Grat, J. Vielliard & S. Clémencet). Paris: Klincksieck.

THE ANNALS OF ST BERTIN 1991 (trans. J.L. Nelson) (Ninth-Century Histories **I**, Manchester Medieval Sources Series). Manchester: University Press.

DAS ASANGER ADERLAß- UND REZEPTBÜCHLEIN 1967 (eds G. Eis & W. Schmitt) (Veröffentlichungen der Internationalen Gesellschaft für Geschichte der Pharmazie (N.S.) **31**). Stuttgart: Wissenschaftliche Verlagsgesellschaft.

BILDHAUER, B. 2002. Bloodsuckers: the construction of female sexuality in medieval science and fiction. In *Consuming narratives: gender and monstrous appetites in the Middle Ages and the Renaissance* (eds) L.H. McAvoy & T. Walters, 104-15. Cardiff: University of Wales Press.

———— 2006. *Medieval blood.* Cardiff: University of Wales Press.

———— 2012. Blood, bodies, Bynum. In *Blood-symbol-liquid* (eds) C. Santing & J. Teuber, 17-36. Louvain: Peeters.

BRADBURNE, J.M. (ed.) 2001. *Blood: art, power, politics, and pathology.* Munich: Prestel.

BYNUM, C.W. 1995. *The resurrection of the body in Western Christendom, 200-1336* (Lectures on the History of Religions (N.S.) **15**). New York: Columbia University Press.

———— 2007. *Wonderful blood: theology and practice in late medieval northern Germany and beyond.* Philadelphia: University of Pennsylvania Press.

———— 2011. *Christian materiality.* New York: Zone.

CHRÉTIEN DE TROYES 1987. *Arthurian romances* (trans. D.D.R. Owen). London: Dent.

———— 1993. *Le roman de Perceval ou le conte du graal* (ed. K. Busby). Tübingen: Niemeyer.

CHRISTI LEIDEN IN EINER VISION GESCHAUT 1936 (ed. R. Priebsch) (Germanische Bibliothek Zweite Abteilung: Untersuchungen und Texte **39**). Heidelberg: Winter.

COHEN, J.J. 2004. The flow of blood in medieval Norwich. *Speculum* **79**, 26-65.

DE MIRAMON, C. 2009. Noble dogs, noble blood: the invention of the concept of race in the late Middle Ages. In *The origins of racism in the West* (eds) M. Eliav-Feldon, B. Isaac & J. Ziegler, 200-16. Cambridge: University Press.

FAURE, M. (ed.) 1999. *Le sang au Moyen Âge: Actes du quatrième colloque international de Montpellier Université Paul Valéry 27-29 novembre 1997* (Les cahiers du CRISIMA **4**). Montpellier: CRISIMA, Université Paul Valéry.

FRANTZEN, A.J. 2004. *Bloody good: chivalry, sacrifice and the Great War.* Chicago: University Press.

GREEN, M. 2005. Flowers, poisons and men: menstruation in medieval Western Europe. In *Menstruation: a cultural history* (eds) G. Howie & A. Shail, 51-64. Basingstoke: Palgrave Macmillan.

KELLER, E. 2007a. *Generating bodies and gendered selves: the rhetoric of reproduction in early modern England.* Seattle: University of Washington Press.

———— 2007b. 'That sublimest juyce in our body': bloodletting and ideas of the individual in early modern England. *Philological Quarterly* **86**, 97-122.

KONRAD VON MEGENBERG 2003. *Das Buch der Natur*, vol. II: Kritischer Text nach den Handschriften (eds R. Luff & G. Steer). Tübingen: Niemeyer.

McCLIVE, C. & N. PELLEGRIN (eds) 2010. *Femmes en fleurs, femmes en corps: sang, santé, sexualités, du Moyen Âge aux Lumières* (L'école du genre: nouvelles recherches **4**). Saint-Etienne: Publications de l'Université de Saint-Etienne.

McCRACKEN, P. 2003. *The curse of Eve, the wound of the hero: blood, gender, medieval literature.* Philadelphia: University of Philadelphia Press.

MARGARETHE EBNER & HEINRICH VON NÖRDLINGEN 1882. *Ein Beitrag zur Geschichte der deutschen Mystik* (ed. P. Strauch). Freiburg: Mohr.

MILLER, S.A. 2010. *Medieval monstrosity and the female body.* New York: Routledge.

NIRENBERG, D. 2009. Was there race before modernity? The example of 'Jewish' blood in late medieval Spain. In *The origins of racism in the West* (eds) M. Eliav-Feldon, B. Isaac & J. Ziegler, 232-64. Cambridge: University Press.

NISCHIK, T.-M. 1986. *Das volkssprachliche Naturbuch im späten Mittelalter: Sachkunde und Dinginterpretation bei Jacob von Maerlant und Konrad von Megenberg.* Tübingen: Niemeyer.

SALISBURY, J.E. 2004. *The blood of martyrs: the unintended consequences of ancient violence.* New York: Routledge.

SCHAFFER, S. 1998. Regeneration: the body of natural philosophers in Restoration England. In *Science incarnate: historical embodiments of natural knowledge* (eds) C. Lawrence & S. Shapin, 83-120. Chicago: University Press.

STAGEL, E. 1906. *Das Leben der Schwestern von Töss* (ed. F. Vetter) (Deutsche Texte des Mittelalters **VI**). Berlin: Königlich Preußische Akademie der Wissenschaften.

VINCENT, N. 2001. *Holy blood: King Henry III and the Westminster blood relic.* Cambridge: University Press.

4

The blood of Abraham: Mormon redemptive physicality and American idioms of kinship

FENELLA CANNELL *London School of Economics and Political Science*

> One could, after all, easily imagine a whole book on American notions of blood.
>
> Carsten 2001: 31

This chapter is concerned with idioms of blood as they occur in the daily life and religious thinking of American Latter-day Saints.[1] The contexts in which blood comes to mind for LDS people are various, and not all directly connected to each other. Sharing in wider American and Christian culture, Mormon conceptions often look familiar from one angle, but have a distinctive logic, which I shall try to unfold.

The material presented here may be read as one gloss on a suggestion made by Janet Carsten in relation to Schneider (1968), that it is not clear that 'blood' in American kinship actually constitutes a single register, or that 'biogenetic substance' is not itself a metaphor for something else (Carsten 2001: 31). I have argued elsewhere (Cannell 2013) that both 'blood' and the 'law' are themselves historically constituted and in part religiously derived categories in the United States, and that the meaning of 'blood' cannot be divorced from its historical context. In this chapter, I hope in part to show that 'blood' is not a single register even within American Mormonism, but both reflects a series of partly mutually contradictory historical positions and constitutes repeated versions of the articulation of a mystery central to Mormon religious experience.

A bloodless Communion?

I am sitting with friends and acquaintances in the pleasant ward chapel in a small town in upstate New York on any Sunday morning of my fieldwork. Out of the three hours that we will all spend in church each Sunday, one hour (the first, while I was there) is given over to the Sacrament Service, which is how Latter-day Saints ('Mormons') refer to their Eucharist.

The ward chapel in which we are sitting is a well-built, inconspicuous low-level building, surrounded by grass and an adjoining parking lot, in a quiet, residential area slightly outside the centre of town. It is built not for architectural drama, inside or

Blood: Will Out: Essays on Liquid Transfers and Flows, First Edition. Edited by Janet Carsten. © 2013 Royal Anthropological Institute of Great Britain & Ireland. Published 2013 by John Wiley & Sons Ltd.

outside, but for practicality and a certain feeling of faultlessly maintained, plain but prosperous comfort, which Latter-day Saints seem to value. There is a wide, spotlessly carpeted entrance lobby with chairs and side tables furnished with some church magazines. There are passages with plenty of hanging space for storing heavy outdoor coats and boots during the deep snow months of winter. There are a number of meeting rooms for the various Sunday School classes and other functions, and a large hall where receptions are sometimes held after weddings. But the most imposing room is the part of the building which corresponds to most Christians' idea of a church. Here there are blue carpets and blue upholstery on the long seats arranged as pews on either side of a central aisle. There is softly filtered light coming in from side windows, but no stained glass, and no distracting views in or out. At the front of the church, where the altar would be in most Christian places of worship, there is instead a raised platform, with a centrally placed lectern equipped with an adjustable microphone, and behind that some few rows of raised seats that look back towards the main congregation. There is a small organ, a piano, and a high screen to one side of the platform, with a table in front of it covered in a white cloth. The wall behind the platform is decorated with high, polished wooden panels of a rich mid-tone, and the platform and all the benches are also made of solid wood. There are no statues, no religious pictures except those used to decorate the little printed orders of service which the ushers give out as you enter, and no crosses anywhere in the room. The effect, therefore, is in some ways more like a school hall than a church, to those who are used to other Christian traditions. The overall feel of the building is slightly corporate, and LDS chapels are mostly variations on this theme, but it also includes subtle local touches – I know that this meeting house was actually one of the last ones to be built by the local ward members themselves in the late 1970s, and that the beautiful timber used in its furnishings and decoration, for example, was sourced from the surrounding New York forests.

Latter-day Saints have church authorities, but they do not have a division between laity and clergy in the sense that Catholics or most Protestants have one: that is, they do not have a professional priest or minister who conducts the liturgy or mediates between the ordinary congregant and the divine. Each ward (the LDS equivalent of a parish) has a 'bishop' who is the local ward leader, but this is a non-professional office which a man holds in addition to his normal day job, and each individual generally only serves as bishop for a few years at a time before the office passes to someone else. The bishop is assisted by two male counsellors, and by a number of other men and women serving in the ward on the same voluntary basis, including the organists and Sunday School teachers. In addition to those with these specific ward 'callings', every man, woman, and child over the age of 6 can expect to be asked from time to time to contribute to the Sacrament Service, by giving a short prepared talk, saying a prayer, singing, or bearing testimony of their faith; all these contributions are made from the central lectern at the front of the chapel, where the importance of the adjustable microphone quickly becomes clear, given the varied heights and ages of the congregation.

Despite these organizational differences, the Sacrament Service is in many ways familiar to anyone who has attended 'low-church' Protestant services in England or elsewhere. LDS congregations always sing hymns, and while some of these were written since the foundation of the LDS Church and address distinctive doctrinal and church-history issues, there are also a good number which are shared with the English and American Methodist and other Protestant repertoires from which, historically, the LDS Church developed and from where it recruited many of its founding members, including its first Prophet, Joseph Smith Jr. Mormons (like some Methodists and Baptists) are strict avoiders of alcohol, and do not use Communion wine. They also do not use Communion wafers. Instead, during the administration of the Sacrament, little plastic trays holding a number of miniature individual paper cups of water and small pieces of ordinary bread are brought to the end of each pew by teenage boys (serving as 'deacons') and then passed from hand to hand down to the end of the pew. Everyone, including children and non-members, may take the Sacrament, unless for some reason they feel that they should not do so on a given day.

It is also the job of one of the 'deacons' (who are at a stage of progression within the LDS Church known as the Aaronic Priesthood) to say the dedicatory prayer each week as the Sacrament is prepared on the cloth-covered side table. This prayer (usually uttered in a respectful but slightly sing-song voice by the teenage boy concerned) runs as follows (italicized words are those on which the pattern of emphasis is often placed):

> O *God*, the Eternal *Father*, we ask thee in the name of thy Son, Jesus Christ, to *bless* and *sanctify* this bread to the souls of all those who partake of it, that they may eat in remembrance of the body of thy Son, and *witness unto thee, O God*, the Eternal Father, that they are willing to take upon them the name of thy Son, and *always remember him* and keep his commandments which he has given them; that they may always have his *Spirit* to be with them. Amen (Doctrine and Covenants 20: 77 and Moroni 4).

The prayer on the water follows:

> O *God*, the Eternal *Father*, we ask thee in the name of thy Son, Jesus Christ, to *bless* and *sanctify* this [water] to the souls of all those who drink of it, that they may do it in remembrance of the blood of thy Son, which was shed for them; that they may *witness unto thee, O God, the Eternal Father*, that they do always *remember* him, that they may have his *Spirit* to be with them. Amen (Doctrine and Covenants 20: 79 and Moroni 5).[2]

For anyone who has attended a Roman Catholic, Episcopalian, or Church of England Mass or Eucharist, the differences in this LDS approach to the Sacrament will be striking. In an Anglican service, of course, the priest will invite the congregation to approach the altar after taking the Sacrament himself, and will then administer both wafer and wine. Although the means of offering the Sacrament vary slightly in different styles of Anglican liturgy, the identification of the Communion wine with the blood of Christ is always made very clear; generally, the priest will say to each communicant as the wafer and then the cup are offered, 'The body of Christ; the blood of Christ'. In High Anglican services, the treatment of the Sacrament prior to the administration of Communion approaches that of Roman Catholicism, in which the wafer and wine are understood miraculously to become the body and blood of Christ, and not just to represent them. In either Anglican or Catholic services, and also in some low-Church Protestant traditions, there is almost certain to be some iconography which represents the sacrifice of Christ and/or the saints for the redemption of mankind, and most usually there will be a crucifix of some kind, or at the minimum a plain cross. In all these Communion liturgies, the Last Supper is recalled before the Communion, and Christ's words equating the bread and wine with his sacrifice, are quoted. The idea of the identification between the blood of Christ shed to save the world, and the Communion as a recapitulation of that sacrifice, is therefore clear both visually, in the words of the liturgy and in the sensory equation between blood and wine.

The Mormon Sacrament Service looks at first glance as if it could be understood simply as an extremely austere extension of nineteenth-century low-Church Protestant traditions, including teetotalism, a distaste for iconography, a deliberate distancing from any suggestion of Catholic readings of the Mass as transubstantiation, and so on. The blood of Christ, which receives multi-sensory emphasis in other forms of Christian Communion, figures only briefly in the dedicatory prayer for Latter-day Saints (and in some of the hymns where these overlap with the wider Protestant canon), and the water which the congregation drinks does not recall blood in the way that wine does. Certainly, as I have already mentioned, these traditions do play into the formation of Mormon church aesthetics in important ways. It is also perfectly clear that there is no complete disjuncture between Mormon and other Protestant Christian readings of the Atonement of Christ; although Latter-day Saints are sometimes described pejoratively by others as being 'not really Christians', they are in fact extremely Christocentric, and the Atonement is a vitally important teaching for them. While different readings of the relationship between human responsibility and Christ's redemptive grace have been one of the key issues of division between the various Protestant, Orthodox, and Catholic traditions in Christianity, the Mormon reading of the Atonement is, however, even more distinctive and is contextualized in a way which is probably unique. For Mormons, Christ's death on the Cross was a voluntary ransom which could only have been made by the Son of God, and which freed all humans from the sin of Adam, and brought about the gift of physical resurrection for all human beings. However, Mormon teaching is that each individual is still responsible for the consequences of his or her own sins, and needs to live in obedience to God in order to attain the highest level of post-mortal life, the Celestial Kingdom, in which man can fulfil his destiny of becoming of the same kind as God (although never equalling God in the degree of his progression). In addition, LDS understanding posits not only a life after death, but also a life before this mortal life (the 'premortal' existence); at this time, all humans agreed to play a part in the development of human agency according to God's plan. In this plan, both the Fall of Adam and Eve and the redemptive death of Christ were agreed and foreordained, and all humans accepted the task of furthering God's plan by exercising obedience in their own mortal lifetime, although they would forget their premortal existence at birth.

In addition, Latter-day Saints believe that Joseph Smith restored to them certain aspects of the divine truth, which had been lost since the time of Christ's disciples, and which for them are recorded in those books of the Mormon Scriptures which are additions to the normal Christian Old and New Testaments. Worthy adult LDS men become inheritors of the Melchisedeck Priesthood, which in theory means that they may access powers of healing and other saving blessings which had been lost for many centuries. It is because of this universal male priesthood that Latter-day Saints do not need a professional clergy to administer the Sacrament; instead, young men distribute it under the auspices of the adult bishop who presides over the Sacrament Service. If a deacon stumbles in pronouncing the dedicatory prayer, the bishop will stop him and, if necessary, repeat the prayer correctly himself. Thus the Sacrament service is conducted, in other words, by the restored Mormon priesthood at its junior and senior levels.

The appearance of Protestant anti-ritualism in a Mormon Sacrament Service is therefore partially misleading, since there is a discreet but powerful and distinctive logic of ritual efficacy by which the service is actually organized. Similarly, the fact that the symbolism of blood is, relatively speaking, downplayed in the Sacrament Service is not solely accounted for by the affinities between Mormon and low-Church Protestant liturgical tastes. Rather, Mormon worship does not choose to dwell always on the blood of Christ because, as other authors have also noted (cf. Davies 2000: 52, 95) and as LDS acquaintances sometimes pointed out to me themselves in commenting on their services, they are focused instead on the resurrected body of Christ, not his broken and suffering body on the Cross. By extension, the services also focus on the hope of progression towards the resurrection of the perfected body for all believers, and the continuity of the resurrected body and indeed of kinship, marriage, and the birth of children in the highest levels of salvation which is central to all Latter-day Saints (see, e.g., Cannell 2005).

This usually muted focus on the sensory and emotional centrality of Christ's blood and suffering is connected to an often-cited aspect of Mormon teaching, that both God and Christ have glorified bodies of 'flesh and bones'.[3] This teaching, along with the assertion that God the Father and God the Son are two distinct personages (rather than being aspects of the Trinity), formed part of the First Vision of Joseph Smith (Doctrine and Covenants 130: 22), and is central to the LDS Restoration Gospel – the idea that the visions of Joseph Smith restore and complete Christianity, which had been languishing in partial error for many centuries. Pictures of the First Vision, which show the adolescent Joseph encountering God and Christ in the grove of woods near his home in Palmyra, generally emphasize the power of the revelation of this divine physicality by portraying the bodies of God and Jesus in a blaze of light. Such portrayals, although they are not used to decorate chapels, are in fact very popular among Latter-day Saints, and are used both in official Church venues such as Church museums and galleries and as much-loved home decorations. The Church bookstore, Deseret Book, sells many reproductions, prints, and small-scale statues of figures of Christ, God the Father, and Joseph Smith which people display in cabinets in their living-rooms and elsewhere. The originals of these decorations are not all created by LDS artists – many Protestant artists are also very popular, although Catholic images are not[4] – but the market is defined by an LDS taste. Thus perhaps the best-loved statue of all, often on the Church's official website (www.lds.org) and elsewhere, is the Christus, the statue of Christ which is the central feature of the North Visitors' Center in Salt Lake City, a replica of an original by the Danish Romantic period sculptor Bertel Thorvaldsen.[5] The LDS Christus is much visited by Church members and non-members alike. The statue shows a more than human-sized (3.4 m tall) figure of Christ, conventionally portrayed with a flowing beard and gentle expression, and with his arms half-outstretched in what seems to be a gesture of welcome. On closer inspection, one can see the wound in Christ's side, and it becomes obvious therefore that this is a depiction of Christ resurrected, as he showed himself to his disciples in bodily form after the crucifixion. However, the wound is hard to see, and the marks of the crucifixion are not the elements to which one's attention is first directed (in contrast to many Catholic traditions of statuary). The LDS Christus is carved from intensely white marble; since I have never been to Copenhagen, I cannot say for certain whether the stone is actually whiter than that used in the original, but the setting certainly makes it seems so. It is positioned against a blue and violet spiral mural depicting the Mormon cosmos, and is lit by a large window, so that it literally glows with a pure light (Fig. 4.1).

This statue is deeply loved by most Latter-day Saints I know, who experience it as resonant with meaning and affect. It is clear that the portrayal of Christ in vividly physical but resurrected form is deeply moving in part because it permits an imaginative identification with the First Vision experience of Joseph Smith, and in part because

Figure 4.1. Mormon *Christus* statue in the North Visitors' Center in Temple Square, Salt Lake City. (Photo by the author.)

it brings to mind the promise and hope of physical resurrection in glorified bodies for all the Saints, in the life to come. At the same time, it must summon up associations with the physical miracles possible for the Restored Priesthood,[6] which themselves both witness the living presence of the divine and of present-day revelation, and also pre-figure the idea of the resurrected body, 'glorified' and redeemed from suffering and death.

It also seems to me clear that there is a powerful association of ideas between the *Christus* and the First Vision description of a Christ and God 'of flesh and bones' – and not 'flesh and blood', as in the more common phrase. When I commented on this to LDS acquaintances, the response would usually be of the type 'ah yes!' – that is, a confirmation, combined with some hesitation about taking the matter further in explicit discussion. Much of Mormon conversation circles around such hesitations (especially conversation with non-members like myself) because Latter-day Saints are highly aware of the injunction of their Church to draw a distinction between state-ments which are Scriptural and/or authorized by the Church hierarchy, on the one hand, and statements which are 'speculation', on the other. 'Speculation' covers a vast range of topics of intense interest to LDS members, and by no means illegitimate to discuss, but the answers to which cannot be certainly known. Thus the 'ah yes!' of my friends clearly communicated to me something which they did not spell out: that Joseph may have glimpsed something about the mysterious nature of the divine and glorified body itself. That something, I would say, is evoked by the statue of the *Christus*, whose wound is not a source of human pain, but a witness to others of redemption achieved. The wound does not bleed. One might imagine that in the veins of the Divine Persons flowed not blood, but pure white light or liquid – one imagines this, but one does not know for sure; it is a mystery the understanding of which is for the future.

In this context, one can see the LDS Sacrament as having a different construal of the Communion in Christ than is constitutive of Catholic and Protestant sensibilities.

Mormons do remember and evoke the Atonement, and Christ's suffering, but their thoughts, perhaps more than those of other Christians, are focused ahead on the resurrected body of Christ, rather than his suffering and bleeding humanity. One could say that the 'white' symbolism of Mormon Sacrament has an affective 'rightness' in this framing because in one sense the Latter-day Saint Communion with Christ is envisaged as a sharing in his resurrected and glorified physicality in the life to come, and not or not only in his blood. Thus the Sacramental water looks both ways – it is the symbol of the blood of Christ, but who knows of what nature the blood of Christ may be?

The blood of Abraham

If the 'blood of Christ' has unexpected forms and resonances for Mormon Christians, then so too does the blood of Abraham and of the Tribes of Israel, which plays a central if sometimes perplexing part in Latter-day Saint life and thought.

All Latter-day Saints have a religious duty to compile their genealogy (on both Mother's and Father's sides) to the level of great-grandparents, and further if possible. The purpose of so doing is to take the names of these ancestors to the Mormon Temple (not to be confused with the ordinary ward chapels described above), where salvation and blessings can be offered to them through ritual means (see Cannell 2005). In this way, Latter-day Saints strive to open the Celestial Kingdom to those who did not have the opportunity to join the Church in their lifetimes, or who were born before Joseph Smith restored the priesthood. For most converts to the Church, this work has to be started from scratch, but long-standing LDS families have often completed their own genealogies over several centuries, so as well as updating them, they work on genealogies and blessings for unrelated persons whose names are 'extracted' from historical (e.g. parish) records. Genealogy is thus also an aspect of the Church's wide-ranging missionary aspirations (Cannell 2005).

For this reason, Latter-day Saints are usually highly aware of their own family histories, and often consider themselves in relation to what they might have inherited from their ancestors. Utah Mormons may trace their membership in the Church right back to its foundation, and most people recognize groups of families descended from the founding leaders of the Church (including Joseph Smith himself) as forming part of a religious-social elite. For these people, the Mormon version of the pioneer story, in which the persecuted Church fled westwards over several decades before its members finally settled in Utah, is a key reference point. Many family histories use the phrase 'born of goodly stock' to characterize the initial convert to the Church in their past, but also stress the element of personal choice, persistence, and sacrifice often demanded of those who became Latter-day Saints in the nineteenth century. The phrase 'of goodly stock' implies that the family was of a religious and spiritual strain that prepared them to hear the truth of the Mormon message, and that the Church was their destiny (of which more below). However, Mormonism places intense emphasis on individual agency, and on the idea that personal dedication is needed to take up the opportunities that may be offered. Thus the effects of being of 'goodly stock' are never automatic, but require a person to, in a favourite LDS phrase, 'choose the right'. For recent converts, the meaning of family history is obviously different, but is equally of interest, as they reflect on how it was that the message of the Mormon Gospel was something that spoke to them, and consider (variously with respect, regret, or in a vein of repudiation) the different practices or traditions of the families in which they were brought up.[7]

In addition to the attention paid to one's own personal ancestry and its relation to the Church, there is another register in which Latter-day Saints are given a way to think about their identity in an idiom of descent, and this is through the attribution of membership to one of the Tribes of Israel. This attribution does not derive from your family history, but is given through a separate mechanism, the Patriarchal Blessing which every Mormon boy and girl receives, usually as a teenager, when their bishop considers them to be spiritually ready and to have a good foundation in the Gospel.[8] Those going for a blessing should also feel ready and eager to receive it themselves, although parents often may urge teenagers to get their blessing if they feel it would be helpful to them, perhaps during a difficult phase of adolescence.

Patriarchal Blessings are very personal documents, and, as Douglas Davies notes (2000: 150, 197), are not available to be researched in any routine fashion, or through statistical analysis of an archive. People only share the contents of their blessings with others when they wish to do so and feel it's appropriate. The blessing is revelation, and is understood to be of the Holy Spirit, channelled through the patriarch, but each blessing is designed for the enlightenment and inspiration of the particular unique individual to whom it is given. Latter-day Saints sometimes talk about their Patriarchal Blessings as a 'road-map for life', although it would be wrong to understand it as laying out unequivocal instructions. People will often read and re-read their blessings at times of difficulty, and may return to them at different times in their lives and see different meanings or possibilities in what is written. The blessing therefore requires the active participation of the person receiving it, in prayer and interpretation. It also requires that the recipient does his or her part to allow the blessing to be fulfilled, again placing emphasis on the role of individual agency in Mormonism. Typical examples, often found in blessings, would be promises that a girl would become a mother in Israel (marry a faithful Saint and have children within the Church), or that a boy would become a leader or judge in Israel (hold office within the Church). These two promises refer to the major aspirations of most young men and women within the Church, each of which is understood as the fulfilment of a spiritual role, so it is not surprising that they occur often. However, it would be possible for an individual to neglect their opportunities and so prevent the blessing from being fulfilled.

It is more usual for blessings to make general statements (you will become a mother) than to make specific ones (you will have six children), but specific prophecies of this kind are found. Where Latter-day Saints who strive to live faithfully find that these predicted blessings have not unfolded in their lives, they do think about what this means; often, people may feel a sense of hope that even if they are denied marriage or parenthood in this mortal life, the blessing means that they will certainly be given that opportunity in the life to come. If a woman is told she will have six children, but medical or financial reasons mean that she has a smaller family, she might anticipate the possibility that her 'other' children might be those she will raise in heaven. Several people also have mentioned using their Patriarchal Blessings as a source of inspiration and courage, one resource which they may draw upon. For example, one person persists in looking for a partner despite romantic disappointment, another keeps striving for a university education despite wrestling with dyslexia and lack of money – and both these people ultimately succeeded. In these cases, people are obviously working against the odds to help make the blessings come true.[9]

The attribution of lineage in Israel is another aspect of these revealed truths given to a specific individual. A person is told that the Holy Spirit has revealed that they are 'of

Ephraim' or 'of Manasseh', for example. Everyone has a general idea of what this means, but the level of knowledge varies considerably from person to person, and in addition the official and doctrinal explanations do not capture all the aspects of how people think with these ascriptions in practice, or how understandings have changed historically in the Church. I will try to account for both the 'official' and the 'lived' meanings in the rest of this section.

These lineage ascriptions refer to the claim made in Mormon Scripture that the inhabitants of America are in fact descended from the Lost Tribes of Israel.[10] The LDS prophet Lehi is said to have travelled to the New World, and to be descended from Ephraim, son of biblical Joseph, and related by marriage to descendants of Joseph's other son, Manasseh. As Jan Shipps (1987, 2000) and others have noted, this claim is important because it both situates Mormonism as an indigenous American religion and combines this with the claim, also made by many other groups at the time, including Calvinists (Cooper 1990), to be inheritors of the 'covenantal' promises made by God to Abraham and his seed. American Latter-day Saints expect most of their number to be descendants of Ephraim and Manasseh, but believe that diaspora and migration caused descendants of the other tribes to be scattered among the 'Gentile' nations of the Old World, whence they might join the LDS Church as converts.

Insofar as LDS lineage ascriptions are known at all to commentators outside the Church, they have tended to be associated with claims that Latter-day Saints have a particularly racist history. There have indeed been racist episodes in the Church: most notoriously, perhaps, the refusal until 1978 to admit Black Church members to full male adult ritual status ('priesthood'), but also including attitudes to and actions towards Native American people, now widely viewed as wrong.[11] The relatively low number of Black American Mormons is a lasting legacy of these earlier prejudices.[12]

As the LDS historical sociologist Armand Mauss (2003) has pointed out in an important history of lineage ascription, it is less clear that these painful events were indicative of any greater propensity to racism among Latter-day Saints than among other groups of contemporary Americans. Mauss's argument, which probably finds broad LDS support, is that racist views were a deplorable historical episode, and a distortion of the central tenets of Latter-day Saint teaching, which aimed to make the restored Gospel available to the whole world. For Mauss, racist thinking about lineage was influenced by general nineteenth-century and early twentieth-century thinking in Europe and the United States, including 'Anglo-Saxon triumphalism', but was also hardened by the persecution of Mormons themselves by the American mainstream. Assertions of an identity as a superior 'chosen people' were a form of compensation. A key period, for Mauss, was just after the establishment of the Saints in Utah, when 'pulpit literature' began to elaborate a certain version of ideas about the premortal life, 'as a phase in divine history during which God had assigned his spirit children to the more favored lineages, the less favored or the disfavored ("cursed"), depending on their merits during premortal life' (2003: 269). Mid-nineteenth-century Utah Mormons came to think of Black Americans as the descendants of Cain (the 'cursed'), of Native Americans as descendants of Manasseh, possible key actors in the Second Coming of Christ but also associated with apostasy in Mormon Scriptures, and of white Mormons as predominantly the descendants of Ephraim, the tribe to whom a special leadership role had been given. Further, they thought that these racialized lineages reflected premortal merit or demerit. Fortunately, argues Mauss, Mormon engagement with worldwide mission and LDS encounters with people from many lands eager to embrace the Gospel eventually rendered these racialized conceptions void for most Latter-day Saints. 'The purging of the preoccupation with lineage has been the gift of the world's peoples to Mormonism' (Mauss 2003: 268). He notes with gratitude that recent Church authorities and patriarchs have returned to 'Christian universalism', often giving a more inclusive reading in which tribal ascription has nothing to do with literal ancestry (Mauss 2003: 34-5).

As Mauss rightly states, the ways in which early Mormon writers deployed the language of 'blood' were themselves often ambiguous. Sometimes, blood was thought of in a physical register, while at others people would speak of inherited traits as ' "in the blood" ... even traits of a spiritual kind' (Mauss 2003: 23).

A physical idiom of blood could in fact be bent towards either inclusion or racialized exclusion, because Mormons believe that physical bodies can be powerfully ritually changed. Both Joseph Smith and Brigham Young had argued from the inception of the religion that converts did not always have to be literally descended of the 'blood of Israel'. Most converts would be of the 'blood of Abraham' by physical descent, but there might also be righteous gentiles. Gentile converts, however, would experience their blood being physically changed by the Sacrament of Mormon baptism, so that after the ritual, the blood of Abraham would indeed flow in their veins (Shute, Nyman & Bott, 1999: 63). Conversely, the association of Blacks with the 'curse' of Cain led to a notion that their physical blood was somehow spiritually tainted. Susan Lederer has noted that LDS hospitals were the second in the country to recognize the importance of blood banks, but that from 1943 to 1978 separate 'black' and 'white' blood stores were kept, because of the fear among white Mormons that even one drop of 'black blood' might render one ineligible for the priesthood. Reportedly, some Mormons continued to request and receive 'white' blood even after the admission of Blacks to the priesthood (Lederer 2008: 197), presumably because popular understandings lagged behind the change of doctrine for some Utah Mormons.

It is not surprising that this history leaves traces in the ways that contemporary Mormons understand lineage ascriptions. I did not hear racist views from people I met on my fieldwork, and I think such views are now uncommon among Latter-day Saints, although middle-aged people recalled witnessing racist attitudes in past decades, and noted that conservative rural Utah took time to adjust. A less racialized version of implied lineage 'ranking', however, still remains, if only in the way that people mention it to dismiss it: that is, people generally know that Ephraim is the lineage of Mormon leadership, although they may construe that knowledge in various ways. Joseph Smith himself was 'of Ephraim' and declared to be a direct descendent of the biblical Joseph, as well as having descent from Judah by another line, thus uniting the New World and the Old World Israel in his person (Shute *et al.* 1999: 65). The numerous descendants of Joseph Smith, Brigham Young, and the other early leaders of the Church,[13] sometimes referred to with varying degrees of irony as the 'Mormon aristocracy', would therefore be expected to be 'of Ephraim' also. Although levels of theoretical knowledge about lineage vary widely, many people would recognize the expectation, derived from early Mormon thinking about the 'gathering of Israel' before the Second Coming, that the descendants of Ephraim and Manasseh will be identified first, then those of Judah (sometimes associated with converts from Judaism), then the other Tribes, then the Gentiles. The feeling that many 'of Ephraim' or 'of Manasseh' are taking a lead in the unfolding of Scriptural time is therefore still present for people, although without any necessary racial denigration of other identities. A patriarch in California gave this example:

Almost every tribe has been recorded in Patriarchal Blessings, but mine are mostly Ephraim and Manasseh. They're mostly Ephraim; there are ten Ephraims to one Manasseh. I worried [about this] sometimes ... and I spoke to a General Authority [of the Church] and he said, 'You ought to be very, very careful ... [because] the other tribes aren't really accepting now in mass, but they will. Eventually'.[14]

This same patriarch also had a somewhat unusual lineage attribution, that of 'Joseph. They didn't tell me Ephraim or Manasseh, but I didn't care. I could receive another patriarchal blessing to find out if I'm Ephraim or Manasseh. But I know that I could have Manasseh because I have Cherokee blood in me, and they're probably Manasseh.'

The social identity of this patriarch is 'White', but his comment suggests the possibility that he received his own blessing from someone who themselves was aware of his rumoured 'Cherokee blood', and for whom 'Joseph' represented a compromise between 'Ephraim' (the expected 'White' attribution) and 'Manasseh' (the expected 'Indian' attribution). Also interesting is the patriarch's distancing of himself from the need to identify as definitely Ephraim: 'It's nice to know that you've inherited the challenge to give temple sealing blessings' (the special role of Ephraim), he says, 'but Israel is the Lord's chosen. Ephraim received the birthright, but Israel is the one who'll be the blessing for all the world, ... and that includes all twelve tribes'.

Friends in New York told me of another patriarch who had been asked to give a blessing to a convert identified as 'White', but felt an inexplicable desire to defer doing so. When he eventually gave the blessing, the patriarch was inspired to give the highly unusual attribution 'of Abraham'. This implied that, although coming within the covenant, the recipient's line of inheritance could not be identified, and imaginably might not be of the line of Jacob/Israel. It later emerged that the recipient had a number of African-American ancestors of whom he only became aware for the first time when doing his family history. In this story, therefore, even more strongly than in the preceding one, it is understood that patriarchs may 'see' hidden elements of the history of 'race' by means of prophetic inspiration.[15] This observation, however, was not in itself racist. Indeed, several people took the moral of this story to be that very many Americans, perhaps especially anyone with a history in the American South, probably had mixed heritage if they looked into their pasts. Thus 'whiteness' was recognized as a social construct, not an essentialized quality. There are also instances where the discovery of hidden complexity in apparent race works the other way around: a Church member identified as Native American was discovered through her blessing not to be 'of Manasseh' as expected, but instead 'of Ephraim'. The patriarch, the recipient, and the recipients' family were all recorded as being startled by this, but they all accepted it as true. 'How could it not be Manasseh if she's an Indian? But it was Ephraim'.

The sense that lineage ascriptions might reveal invisible, complex aspects of inheritance emerged also in relation to differences in lineage between members of the same family. For the California patriarch,

Well, I gave a blessing to four children in a family. The first three were Ephraim, and a lot of times you have this impression and you say, 'No, it can't be that, because all the Youngs are Ephraim', but I had the impression that he was Manasseh, so: Trust in the Lord.

Many people to whom I talked, and especially newer converts, were somewhat troubled when I asked them to explain what the link might be between tribal identity and family history; several answered hesitatingly to the effect that these were separate kinds of identification. Certainly, for many Church purposes, the two issues are treated separately; perhaps as well these answers reflected the recent trend towards claims by Church authorities that ascription simply identifies the 'channel' through which a Church member's blessings flow, and has nothing to do with literal lineage or descent (Faust 2005; Mauss 2003: 32). Nevertheless, in other contexts it was clear to me that people found the disjuncture between 'lineage' and 'family history' potentially jarring; several people referred to the idea of the physical 'gathering of Israel' at the end of time, in which the righteous are supposed to be called together in one place under their tribal affiliations. People were puzzled and a little worried by being asked to consider whether they would be together with their own immediate families within their 'tribe', or not – a question to which most people didn't feel they had an answer.

Like red hair or brown eyes, lineage mostly runs in families, and mostly confirms your social expectations; the exceptions, however, are exceptionally important, suggesting as they do that there is a complex interplay between individual identity and descent identity, and that transmission of any quality is neither automatic nor predictable. For me, therefore, the importance of lineage ascription is not exhausted by the debate about race and Mormonism, but speaks to an even wider set of issues about inheritable characteristics.

In some measure, perhaps, these issues are influenced by changes in popular understandings of scientific views of heritability. Many Mormons are well educated; they know that contemporary genetics does not propose a one-to-one correspondence between 'genotype' and 'phenotype'.[16] What is perhaps more intriguing is that the idea of 'surprise' lineage is not only a modern one. In 1855, Brigham Young could invoke the idea of the 'scattering' of the tribes of Israel among the Gentiles to explain why the Church would sometimes attract one member of a family as a convert, but not other members of the same family.

> Take a family of ten children ... and you may find nine of them purely of the Gentile stock, and one son or daughter in that family who is purely of the Blood of Ephraim. It was in the veins of the father or mother and was reproduced in the son or daughter, while all the rest of the family are Gentiles. You may think it is singular, but it is true (Brigham Young, *Journal of Discourses*, vol. 2: 268-9, 8 April 1855, quoted in Shute *et al.* 1999: 83).

Here, Brigham Young speaks as if informed by some primitive version of Mendelian theories of inter-breeding, as if 'the blood of Israel' were a recessive gene in the parents, which might combine and emerge in some offspring, and yet be absent in others. I do not know with what theories of plant or animal breeding Brigham Young was conversant. Presumably, however, some forms of thinking about both were current among the Utah Mormons of this period, whose most urgent task it was under Brigham Young's direction to coax the desert to produce enough crops, fruit, and animals to feed the growing population.

The crucial difference between Brigham Young's analogy and those used by my acquaintances is perhaps that Brigham Young does not here think about the parents of the convert as individuals of 'mixed' identity; it is as if their Gentile blood occluded the blood of Israel until it combined to make one individual with the pure blood of Abraham. For the contemporary Latter-day Saints I know, however, the idea of an individual being composed of mixed heritage – both in terms of ethnicity and national derivation, on the one hand, and in terms of mixed lineage, on the other – is clearly to the fore. As the California patriarch put it:

> If I find out some day that I missed [the correct lineage attribution in a blessing], I think the Lord will be lenient on me. But if I said, that … someone was from Manasseh, but he really had more Ephraim in him … they, they're all mixed. If you're from Ephraim you probably have a lot of Manasseh in you too.

Perhaps, therefore, it is not so much that popular understandings have changed because of scientific advances, but that the social capacity to tolerate the idea that 'blood' (or genetics) might not give an unequivocal answer to the identity of an individual has increased between 1855 and today.

Exclusivist versions of lineage thinking in any case always had to contend not only, as Mauss suggests, with the Mormon strain of 'Christian universalism' and the powerful missionary impulse to bring the message to all, but also with the logic of cognatic kinship, which, always present, became increasingly formalized with the growing emphasis on religious genealogy since the 1880s.[17] One logical development of Mormon thinking on kinship is the recognition that the universe of kin of any individual is potentially infinite. Although this thought may be effectively ignored or repressed in many Western cognatic contexts (e.g. Edwards & Strathern 2000: 157), Mormon thinking about heaven and the ritual work which is done for the related dead frequently confronts Latter-day Saints with the tenuousness of any principles of 'family' selection (surname basis, etc.) which they may, temporarily, adopt for their genealogical research.

In addition, the LDS sense of appropriate lineage ascription does, at least for some people, also reflect other registers of closeness in kinship. One friend in upstate New York feelingly told me that she and her daughter, to whom she is very close, have the same lineage, Manasseh. It interested me that she emphasized this, since her daughter both is adopted, and considers herself of Latin American background, while the mother is socially 'White'. Latter-day Saints sometimes think of kin, including adopted kin, as having 'chosen' each other in the premortal existence (Cannell 2013), a notion which limits the idea that kinship is simply physically determined, or that adoption is 'less' than biological kinship. In this relationship between adoptive mother and daughter, lineage seems to underline that sense of a 'meant' connection which exceeds, rather than underwrites, racialized or biologized classifications. Mother and daughter share a form of physical connection through the lineage of Manasseh, which is made visible to them through the power of revelation.

Thus in my view, Mormon lineage has not lost its salience with the fading of closed conceptions of race since Black members were finally admitted to the priesthood in 1978. Associations of tribes with ethnicity seem presently to suggest deep historical processes and profoundly 'American' connections, rather than to reinscribe crudely bounded racial categories.[18]

Perhaps one central element of what Latter-day Saints acquire as they think about lineage is instead a sense of heredity as itself a mystery, despite (or even because of) its seeming contradictions; a truth requiring illumination through revelation. In this sense, lineage thinking reinforces the experience of kinship as sacred, which is also pursued through genealogical work and many other aspects of LDS practice.

It may be evident from the foregoing that Mormon notions of transmission are governed by a characteristic form of reduplicative logic, or redundancy. Joseph Smith himself, for instance, asserted his right to be recognized as Prophet of the Restored

Church by means of: (1) the receipt of direct divine revelations allowing him to utter present-day prophecy; (2) the angelic gift of lost Scriptures written in an unknown language; (3) the inspired translation of those Scriptures by means of divine revelation (Scriptural authority plus direct revelation); (4) the claim to be the recipient of a spiritual office of the priesthood by transmission of birthright going back to Abraham; and (5) physical blood descent from Abraham, via both Jacob and Judah. As well as all these claims, Joseph Smith is understood to have been one of the 'noble and great' intelligences of the premortal existence, who, like Christ himself, agreed to carry out the work of God in the mortal world at a given time and place.

I have sometimes asked Latter-day Saints whether it is possible to transmit goodness in a family line; people usually pause, then answer that it is not. People with a distinguished family history in the Church have sometimes added that they feel, rather, an intense burden of responsibility not to let their ancestors and wider family down. The Mormon emphasis on the centrality of individual agency, on the responsibility for 'choosing the right', makes ideas of pure ancestral determination impossible. At the same time, the pause before the answer acknowledges the idea of elite lines, of chosen lineages, and of noble intelligences whose destiny was fixed before the moral world began, and also of social elites whose wish has been to embody and exemplify these qualities within the leadership of the Church. If one is 'of Ephraim', does this mean that one's ancestors were 'of Ephraim'? Or some of them? If so, which? Such questions surely fall into the LDS category of 'speculation', and as such, I would argue, they epitomize the sense in which Mormon thinking about transmission, which appears to be so dedicated to the projection of religious answers, actually serves in the end to hold open kinship as an arena of mystery, in which agency, relatedness, creation, and destiny endlessly collide.

Conclusion: resurrected and unborn

As Janet Carsten has suggested in the introduction to this volume, blood as a symbol seems particularly suited to, and capable of, carrying the transformation of meaning. But, as she also points out, it may be an error to think that there is any single register of blood in a given context. The symbolism of blood is historically constituted in any given place and time, and successive historical constructions may overlap, sometimes jaggedly.

In the Mormon example, we see both these propositions illustrated. There is a 'flow' of meanings of Mormon blood, which after all partakes of the wider Christian understanding that the shedding of Christ's blood fulfils and transcends the promises made to the blood of Abraham. But Mormonism makes a distinctive attempt to recuperate the 'closed' blood of Israelite lineage, while simultaneously extending the offer of Church membership through universal mission. The outcome is, firstly, the generation of episodes and instances of contradiction, particularly around the blood of nineteenth-century 'race'. More recently, Latter-day Saints have imagined a blood shared by and flowing between all, though distant, connections. Nevertheless, logical gaps remain. My perspective is that cognatic kinship, especially in Christian variants, rests on and works through a sense of the mystery of transmission.[19] Genealogical thinking, as Jeanette Edwards has rightly observed, 'is more than the reductionist or essentialist exercise that its stereotype would have us believe' (2009: 152).

Unlike most Christians, Mormons do not dwell on the contemplation of Christ's spilled blood as a sign of suffering, but focus on a resurrected Christ whose mysterious physicality exceeds 'blood' or 'biogenetic substance' completely. I would like to conclude with one further reflection which links the issue of perspectives on transmission to the centrality of the resurrected body with which I began. Harold Bloom (1993) has spoken of 'American Religion' as being characterized by a 'Gnostic' focus on the individual as being essentially coeval with and coexistent with God. Something like this indeed can be discerned in Mormonism, where, for instance, it is asserted that 'Man was also in the beginning with God. Intelligence, or the light of truth, was not created or made, neither indeed can be' (Doctrine and Covenants 93: 29). Bloom identifies the experience of an essential aloneness with God as central to the American religious, and he suggests that it may be for this reason that Americans have adopted the central image of the human foetus (portrayed as floating alone within the womb, rather than as a trope of human connection) in so many political and religious battlegrounds, most obviously in the pro-Life versus pro-Choice debates.

In several ways, Latter-day Saints have aligned themselves with socially conservative Protestants in recent years, and have sought common ground in their central valuation of 'the family'. It might therefore seem self-explanatory that official Church statements deplore abortion as the taking of human life, and countenance it only in circumstances of extreme medical adversity (risk to life from continuing pregnancy) to mother or child – and even then, not as an automatic decision. The LDS attitude to the unborn, however, is not in fact the same as the conservative Protestant position that every fertilized embryo is a human life. In fact, LDS authorities draw on various statements of their founders which assert that human life does not begin with conception, and suggest that it begins when the baby 'quickens' (i.e. is felt to move in the womb for the first time by the mother), understood as the soul entering the body. This reading would potentially be compatible with a more liberal attitude to abortion, but this is not what is happening at present. In addition, authorities usually argue that in order for the child to have accomplished the mortal stage of human progression according to God's plan, he or she must take at least one breath on earth; just one will suffice, but babies who are stillborn do not meet this criterion. Although stillborn babies are expected to be listed on family records,[20] the Church stipulates that no rituals are to be carried out for them, but deliberately leaves moot the question of whether they will be made part of their parents' eternal family. Opinion varies on what happens to the spirits of stillborn babies: some people think it possible that the spirit may return to the family in the body of the next child born by the mother. Where a baby dies after taking a breath, however, the spirit is understood to have completed its needful time on earth, however brief, and to have progressed to the next stage of existence and be waiting in the spirit world. Such spirits are often said to be especially valiant, in need of almost no mortal learning.

It is presumably this distinctively LDS reading of the embryo which has enabled a number of Mormon Senators to vote in favour of human stem cell research (Thompson 2005: 270), although the official LDS website remains carefully neutral on this question.

The above, however, is a Mormon leadership (elite male) view. Mormon women (and sometimes their husbands), in conversation and in many blogs which discuss this problem, tend to treat all 'lost' children together, whether they die shortly after birth, or are stillborn or miscarried.[21] Most women will spontaneously refer to the widely held notion that all such children are near presences in the spirit world who can still be felt by their mothers, and also that they will be returned to their parents in the resurrected existence, to be raised by them as they could not be on earth. Women are also aware of the 'official' teaching on stillbirth, but sometimes seem to bracket this out, and at other times to struggle painfully with its implications.

In this final example, therefore, we see that, even within Mormon teaching itself, the meaning of human biogenetic substance may not be stable, and may in fact be deeply inflected by gender and hierarchy. And this division is not simply reducible to differences in male and female experiences of and intuitions about early pregnancy. For Mormon women, mothering children has a profound religious as well as social significance; the Church often presents motherhood as a counterpart to the male priesthood, although many Mormon feminists and scholars have begged to differ. But the comparison is not only chauvinistic, since the act of giving birth is profoundly significant within Mormon progressionist doctrine. Here's how one (male) blog poster expressed this recently:

> Birth is simply a transition. Thus, when God organised the intelligences into their respective spheres ... that would be man's spiritual birth. When these spiritual beings gained physical bodies, baddabing [sic; i.e. 'Hey Presto!'] ... physical birth. Ultimately we will transition into eternal bodies, so is our resurrection a type of eternal birth? Finally, those who obtain celestial bodies will need to be transitioned into that phase, so maybe there is a type of Celestial Birth?[22]

When Mormon women refuse to think of stillborn babies as any less their children, they may be reflecting wider American Christian social values, but they are also expressing a sense of a distinctively female contribution to creation, where the sense of the body as resurrected, rather than as abjected, is always present in the most intimate experiences of mortal physicality, casting a luminous shadow of itself to come.

NOTES

The research on which this chapter is based was funded by an Economic and Social Research Council grant (Competition Award R000239016) and by a London School of Economics Staff Research Fund Seed Money Grant, both gratefully acknowledged. Particular thanks are due to John Dulin for research assistance, and to Janet Carsten for editorial guidance.

[1] Members of the Church of Jesus Christ of Latter-day Saints are popularly called 'Mormons' but usually refer to themselves as 'LDS'.

[2] LDS.org Family Guidebook, 'Priesthood ordinances and blessings' (available on-line: *http://www.lds.org/manual/family-guidebook/priesthood-ordinances-and-blessings?lang=eng*, accessed 15 January 2013). See also Green (2009) for an interesting LDS discussion.

[3] Only the Holy Ghost is considered 'a person of Spirit' in Mormon teaching.

[4] Occasionally LDS artists do display and sell statues of Mary as mother of Jesus which recall Catholic iconography (see Lloyd 2011), but I have never seen one in a Mormon home.

[5] The original statue and statues of Christ's twelve disciples stand in the Copenhagen 'cathedral', the (Lutheran, once Catholic) Church of Our Lady.

[6] The LDS Church considers itself as the holder of truths and powers from the time of Christ, lost for millennia under historical Roman Catholicism (viewed as a period of apostasy), but now restored; these include the various powers of its universal male priesthood.

[7] Fuller discussion of conversion stories will be given in future work (Cannell n.d.).

[8] I have heard of blessings given to children as young as 11, but it is usual to receive them at ages 15-19. The bishop signs a 'recommend' before the person may go to the patriarch.

[9] Patriarchal Blessings do also sometimes mention less generic matters, and may refer to particular concerns in the person's life which are not publicly known. Everyone concerned (patriarch, recipient, and the young person's parents) will understand this as being the work of the Spirit. However, the Spirit is not thought of as being lacking when the blessing concerns general aspirations, as the form of words used is always slightly different from one text to another, and people find much meaning in these particularities.

[10] After the conquest of Israel by the Assyrians in 732BC, many of the original twelve Tribes of Israel, named after the twelve sons of Abraham, seem to vanish from the biblical record, and only Judah (incorporating Simeon), Benjamin, and the non-territorial priestly Levites continue to be mentioned. (Note that numerical anomalies are the result of the splittings and combinations of tribes, which cannot be detailed here.)

[11] For example, the programme of the mid-twentieth century by which 'Indian' children were sponsored in education at the price of being separated from their own families and sent to live with white Mormons.

[12] On the experiences and testimonies of Black Mormons, see, for instance, Embry (1994).

[13] Numerous partly because polygamy was practised by both Joseph Smith and Brigham Young, although then banned by the Church in 1890.

[14] My acquaintances agree that small numbers of attributions to all the tribes are found in the present time, but I have personally only heard of Rueben, Levi, and Judah.

[15] Cf. Palmié (2007),who argues that contemporary attempts to 'decide' racial identity through genetic testing are identical in their logic to divination.

[16] Although both Nash (2002) and Palmié (2007) argue that misconstrual of genetic evidence along the lines of social preconception is very widespread, including by those using 'DNA research' to trace family history.

[17] For a fuller explanation of this statement, see Cannell (2013).

[18] One could imagine lineage without race in Mormon logic, since the uncommon tribal ascriptions (Isaachar, Asher, etc.) which are expected to emerge in the end times have never been racialized, but are to be gathered from among the Gentiles, where they are 'scattered'.

[19] My use of 'cognatic kinship' has a different theoretical focus than the 'double descent' discussed by Davies (2000: 149).

[20] Stillborn babies (labelled as such), but not miscarriages, may be entered on some Church genealogical records.

[21] See, for example, Guest Post 'Grieving for Gus' on the blog *http://www.mormonmommywars.com??p=1049* (accessed 24 January 2013).

[22] Dustin, posted 17 August 2009 under 'Intelligences and spiritual birth' at *http://www.eternalrounds* (last accessed 15 May 2010).

REFERENCES

BLOOM, H. 1993. *The American religion: the emergence of the post-Christian nation*. New York: Simon & Schuster.

CANNELL, F. 2005. The Christianity of anthropology (Malinowski Lecture, 2004), *Journal of the Royal Anthropological Institute* (N.S.) **11**, 335-56.

——— 2013. The re-enchantment of kinship. In *Vital relations: kinship and the critique of modernity* (eds) F. Cannell & S. McKinnon. Santa Fe, N.M.: School for Advanced Research Press.

——— n.d. Conversion as kinship thinking. In *The religion of kinship: Mormon genealogical thinking in secular America* (working title). Unpublished manuscript.

CARSTEN, J. 2001. Substantivism, antisubstantivism and anti-antisubstantivism. In *Relative values: reconfiguring kinship studies* (eds) S. Franklin & S. McKinnon, 29-54. Durham, N.C.: Duke University Press.

COOPER, R. 1990. *Promises made to the fathers: Mormon covenant organization*. Salt Lake City: University of Utah Press.

DAVIES, D. 2000. *The Mormon culture of salvation: force, grace and glory*. Aldershot: Ashgate.

EDWARDS, J. 2009. Skipping a generation and assisting conception. In *Kinship and beyond: the genealogical model reconsidered* (eds) S. Bamford & J. Leach, 138-59. New York: Berghahn.

——— & M. STRATHERN 2000. Including our own. In *Cultures of relatedness* (ed.) J. Carsten, 149-66. Cambridge: University Press.

EMBRY, J.L. 1994. *Black saints in a white church: contemporary African American Mormons*. Salt Lake City: Signature Books.

FAUST, J.E. 2005. Your Patriarchal Blessing. *New Era*, November (available on-line: *http://www.lds.org/new-era/2005/11/your-patriarchal-blessing?lang=eng*, accessed 24 January 2013).

GREEN, J. 2009. Mormon prayer and Mormon art. Times and Seasons, 19 August (available on-line: *http://timesandseasons.org/index.php/2009/08/mormon-prayer-and-mormon-art*, accessed 16 January 2013).

LEDERER, S. 2008. *Flesh and blood: organ transplantation and blood transfusion in twentieth-century America*. Oxford: University Press.

LLOYD, R.S. 2011. New scriptural art: 'Seek My Face' exhibit opens at Church History Museum. *Church News*, 19 March (available on-line: *http://www.ldschurchnews.com/articles/60623/New-scriptural-art-Seek-My-Face-exhibit-opens-at-Church-History-Museum.html*, accessed 24 January 2013).

MAUSS, A.L. 2003. *All Abraham's children: changing Mormon conceptions of race and lineage*. Urbana: University of Illinois Press.

NASH, C. 2002. Genealogical identities. *Environment and Planning D: Society and Space* **20**, 27-52.

PALMIÉ, S. 2007. Genomics, divination, 'racecraft'. *American Ethnologist* **34**, 203-20.

SCHNEIDER, D.M. 1968. *American kinship; a cultural account*. Englewood Cliffs, N.J.: Prentice Hall.

SHIPPS, J. 1987. *Mormonism: the story of a new religious tradition*. Urbana: University Press.

———— 2000. *Sojourner in the promised land: forty years among the Mormons*. Urbana: University Press.

SHUTE, R.W., M. NYMAN & R.L. BOTT 1999. *Ephraim: chosen of the Lord*. Salt Lake City: Millennial Press.

THOMPSON, C. 2005. *Making parents: the ontological choreography of reproductive technologies*. Cambridge, Mass.: MIT Press.

5

Who is my stranger? Origins of the gift in wartime London, 1939-45

NICHOLAS WHITFIELD *McGill University*

In the penultimate chapter of his classic study of blood transfusion, Richard Titmuss returned 'to the theme of "the gift" '. He did so within the frame of a question, 'Who is my stranger?', which titled his inquiry and captured his model of altruistic free giving, an ideal that anchored the essence of virtue to the anonymity of 'stranger relationships' (Titmuss 1997 [1970]: 276-304). In the context of modern blood transfusion systems this alignment of gift and stranger was provocative. Whilst Titmuss both admitted and embraced the impossibility of personal contact between givers and recipients, his reference to '*my* stranger', and his wish to know 'who?', implied a sense of exclusivity and intimacy, the idea that a donor, discrete and singular benefactor of a blood gift, gave to an equally discrete, equally singular beneficiary, and that each fluid gesture, after a protracted flow through an extended sequence of clinical and technical mediation, arrived unmixed in the veins of a thankful recipient.

Even in 1971, the year *The gift relationship* became available in London and New York, the passage of blood was rarely so simple (Copeman 2005: 469-70; Fontaine 2002: 418; Titmuss 1997 [1970]: 73-6). As all blood collectors, and probably most blood donors, knew, the image of singularity was for the most part an illusion. In Britain, complex systems of blood transfusion became common during the Second World War with the founding of London's Emergency Blood Transfusion Service in 1939, an organization whose practices of pooling, cold storage, and plasma production derived from innovations in America, Russia, and Spain (Coni 2007: 69-80; Elliott, Macfarlane & Vaughan 1939). Titmuss, Professor of Social Policy at the London School of Economics, was well aware of the technical particulars of blood transfusion therapies when he composed his comparative analysis. As such, he described and idealized a modernized system of blood transfusion in terms that were directly and deliberately unfaithful to its practice. Between gift and stranger was a paradox this chapter sets out to explain.

My aim is to use history to make sense of the discord between the rhetoric of the gift, which implied singularity, and the reality of blood transfusion, which denied it. The position I will defend is that the gift arose strategically, not on the pages of *The gift*

Blood: Will Out: Essays on Liquid Transfers and Flows, First Edition. Edited by Janet Carsten. © 2013 Royal Anthropological Institute of Great Britain & Ireland. Published 2013 by John Wiley & Sons Ltd.

relationship in the twilight era of the welfare state, but in London on Homefront recruitment propaganda of the 1940s, less as an attempt to capture the realities of blood transfusion than as a motivational device for a disparate panel of volunteers irrevocably split from the human consequences of their generosity (Lederer 2008: 55-62). The gift appeared in the consciousness of anonymity, and with the belief that if obscurity was an unassailable feature of blood donation, plurality was not. It also arrived bound to representations of singular recipient figures, figures comparable to what Georg Simmel defined as the strangers of modern societies, transient wanderers who embody a 'union of closeness and remoteness ... strangeness indicates that one who is remote is near ... with the stranger one has only certain *more general* qualities in common' (1950 [1908]: 185-6, original emphases). Here I argue there could be no gift without the stranger, without the abstract figures evocative of missing kin – child, husband, sweetheart, brother – whose images multiplied in the representational settings of wartime Britain.

Focusing on the situation in London, the argument begins from the historical recognition that gifting, with its fetish for one-to-one connectedness, was not always a self-evident or appropriate way to characterize an act of bodily donation. In the 1930s, calls for volunteers were limited to selective public lectures and intermittent radio broadcasts, and presented blood-giving as a humanitarian enterprise above and beyond the cause or gratification of individuals. Consistent with the ethical precepts of a domineering voluntary sector, humanity was the target of altruism, and organizers of the London Red Cross Blood Transfusion Service limited donors' contact with recipients and prohibited remuneration (Collini 1979: 49; Harris 1992: 134-5; Lewis 1999: 14-16). During the Second World War, blood transfusion publicists spread an alternative view, which differed in its reliance on images of fictive recipients. By the early 1940s, the figures of the solider and the child civilian, replete with written and visual biographies, occupied the imaginary end-points of a donor's 'gift of life'. Transfusion propagandists pressed volunteers to enlist these figures when making the decision to donate, and when configuring their identities as donors. The central observation of this chapter is that the gesture towards an image of one-to-one transfusion in wartime publicity occurred at precisely the moment when the large-scale reorganization of the blood supply began rendering the reality of a fixed, singular recipient untenable. As well as describing this parallel transition (first and second sections), I will argue for its significance in interpreting the historical relations of anonymity and altruism, rationality and 'the gift of life' (third and fourth sections). Here I confront the present-day tendency to oppose modern blood supplies with romantic connotations of a 'gift relationship', to label the gift anachronistic and claim of its proponents false divisions of economy and virtue, with a story of historical coincidence and mutual complicity (Healy 2006: 126-30; Schwartz 1999; Waldby & Mitchell 2006: 182-4). Similar to Jonathan Parry, who, interpreting Mauss, contended that an 'elaborated ideology of the "pure" gift' was a contingent invention, 'most likely to develop in state societies with an advanced division of labour and a significant commercial sector' (Parry 1986: 467), this chapter relates the rise of a particular version of free giving to the advent of a modern medical technology. From 1939, industrial processes began first to demarcate, then to consolidate, a new domain of the gift. The fates of anonymity and altruism were fused.

The blood bank and *The gift*

Between 1921 and 1939, the Red Cross Blood Transfusion Service (RCBTS) was London's premier organization for supplying volunteer blood donors to surgeons and recipients at city hospitals.[1] In the first five years of its (unofficial) operation, its panel of donors grew from a handful of volunteers to 450 registered members in 1926, by which time 68 hospitals subscribed to the Service, making an annual 737 calls for the treatment of numerous conditions – duodenal ulcers, stomach carcinomas, septicaemia, and the various forms of anaemia most common among them. Expansion continued throughout the interwar period. By 1938, the last year of the Service's full operation before its succession by London's emergency medical arrangements, a panel of 2,698 volunteers answered 6,628 calls from 200 hospitals in and around the city, exclusive of private houses and nursing homes. These figures upheld the RCBTS's claim to be among the world's largest and most successful voluntary donor organizations, indispensable to the London surgeon, exemplary for provincial imitators, and recognized internationally.[2] Under the direction and moral perspective of its founder and honorary secretary, Percy Lane Oliver (1878-1944), out of whose rented house in Camberwell the Service operated, the RCBTS began to define and propagate a discrete category of blood donor, an ethical vision that functioned variously to regulate hospital practices, justify the expansion of the Red Cross Service to provincial districts, and promote an ideal of citizenship generally.

At the time of its dissemination into London medicine from 1918, blood transfusion was a relatively unconventional surgical procedure viewed with suspicion by those unaccustomed to its therapeutic applications (Pelis 2007). Its techniques fell between two categories, the so-called direct and indirect methods (Keynes 1922: 107-12). The first involved the surgical transfer of unmodified blood from donor to recipient by vessel anastomosis – that is, by attaching an artery to a vein with a three-point suture or with a small silver cannula – and required the unobstructed contact of live tissues (Crile 1907; Lewisohn 1924: 733; Starr 1998: 31-6). Indirect methods, which began surpassing direct techniques from around 1911, involved drawing blood into graduated metal or glass containers with a cannula syringe (Maluf 1954: 94-101). In 1915, Richard Lewisohn, a surgeon at the Mount Sinaii Hospital in New York, proposed mixing withdrawn blood with a diluted sodium citrate solution to prevent clotting, an innovation that simplified the technique of blood transfer and allowed surgeons to preserve blood outside the body, clot free, for longer periods (Lewisohn 1915; Wain 1984).[3] In all cases, transfusion involved the issuing of blood from one individual to another at the time of an operation, usually in close, if not immediate, proximity.[4]

To ensure the reliability of volunteers, Oliver devised elaborate selection and enrolment methods, resisting large-scale 'stunt appeals' on the wireless or through the national press in favour of giving low-key lectures in which '[n]o appeals for donors are made ... Listeners are asked to consider in all its bearings the project of enrolment, and no encouragement is given to joining in the enthusiasm of the moment', lest enthusiasm engender false self-expectations (Oliver 1933: 699). During enrolment, donors agreed to comply with various conditions of membership, including, importantly, the requirement not to pursue contact with recipients of their blood. Despite the one-to-one connection, Oliver insisted that blood-giving was above all a service to humanity generally, not a private relation between individuals, and by limiting recipient-donor contact he sought to restrict and regulate, though not eliminate entirely, the one-to-one dimension of blood transfusion.[5] According to Oliver, blood-giving was less about the singularity of personal gratification than about a duty to a community (1933: 699). In the pages of the RCBTS quarterly newsletter, distributed freely from 1933 to all volunteers, he reminded readers that 'every donor should realise that he or she is a unit of an organisation created and functioning for the benefit of humanity generally, at the direction of surgeons, and not at the behest of a single individual'.[6] Strategic anonymity was at the heart of interwar altruism.

From April 1939, planners of London's Emergency Blood Transfusion Service (EBTS) began to assemble an alternative scheme, in which blood would not be given on a one-to-one basis but taken from multiple volunteers and preserved in giant refrigeration units at four newly established 'blood depots', located in satellite towns on the city's periphery. It would be extracted as it would be administered: not by a surgeon but by emergency nursing staff with simplified and standardized apparatus. It would be procured, finally, from a panel of over 100,000 volunteers selected on the sole basis of their physical suitability. The business of donor organization was no longer the exclusive preserve of the Red Cross, whose interwar service continued to function on a much-reduced scale throughout the war, but was now under the centralized jurisdiction of the Medical Research Council (MRC) and the financial control of the Ministry of Health (Gunson & Dodsworth 1996: 12-16). The structure of this scheme arose above all from the expected nature and effects of air raids on London:

> The disorganization of means of communication caused by aerial bombardment makes it impossible to call upon donors at those times when blood is most needed. Medical and surgical personnel will be required to attend to patients during severe air raids or at periods of active fighting. They must administer blood and not spend time withdrawing blood. Donors obviously cannot be sent up to the front-line dressing stations. It will be absolutely essential, therefore, to have adequate supplies of stored blood (Vaughan 1939: 933).

Each depot would tend both to civilian emergencies and to disasters incurred through direct enemy action. Recruitment of an estimated 100,000 volunteers began on a national scale on 3 July, with announcements in all major national newspapers and a radio broadcast on the British Broadcasting Corporation (BBC) Home Service.[7] On 29 July, notices in the medical press detailed 'the Transfusion Scheme to date', and reported the testing of 50-60,000 volunteers across the city at eighty designated 'testing stations'.[8] On 12 August, *The Times* announced the registering of the first 100,000 blood donors, an achievement that owed largely to a consistent emphasis on the practical accessibility of blood donation, and an associated dropping of morally orientated criteria for the selection of donors.

Although many London medics of the 1930s were not inclined towards wholesale systems of blood storage – 'The feeling in England is that this is carrying change too far' (Horsley Riddell 1939: 299) – almost all granted the value of stored blood for wartime emergencies. The depot directors and architects of the EBTS therefore faced little opposition to their plans, and drew on a range of international exemplars. One notable source was the 'blood bank' of the Chicago Cook County Hospital, innovated by the director of therapeutics, Dr Bernard Fantus. Fantus was not the first to use techniques of blood storage, but what distinguished his system was its moralized principle of debt and repayment. Importantly for this essay, his use of a fiscal metaphor achieved a synthesis of reciprocation and solidarity, and imposed an obligation between donors and recipients. 'Just as one cannot draw money from a bank unless one has deposited some, so the blood preservation department cannot supply blood unless as much comes in as goes out' (Fantus 1937: 128). Since blood-giving was intended as a form of deposit or reimbursement, it followed that Fantus was in favour of 'the healthy volunteer donor' as the 'main source of blood', and made no reference to remuneration. As such, his blood bank concept was not merely compatible with the theory of the gift as conceived of by Mauss – a society-building activity and method of sustaining relations between groups and individuals (Mauss 2010 [1925]; Murray 1990: 207-9) – but provided an explicit embodiment of it:

> Any one who owes his life to blood transfusion clearly owes some blood to some one else who is in great need of this restorative ... It should be the plain duty of the one who has recovered from such a disease to donate some of his blood to save the life of a fellow man in the hour of his desperate need. Surely one whose life has thus been saved owes some of his now curative blood to another victim of the same kind of infection (Fantus 1937: 129-30).

True to Mauss, the soul of the giver was preserved in the vaults of Fantus's blood bank (Mauss 2010 [1925]: 84). It travelled to the veins of recipients, wherein it stayed until a time of repayment by donation. Proof of a resilient soul was found above all in the racial segregation of 'white' and 'Negro' bloods in many American hospital blood banks, a policy that physicians at the Johns Hopkins Hospital admitted had no 'biologic or physiologic ground', but which they enforced anyway, shying away from an overt justification. As Dr Mark M. Ravitch commented: '[I]t has been deemed best to avoid the issue' (1940: 171).

There were, besides, many advantages of the blood bank, such that its proponents felt it right not to dwell too long on its failings. Admirers and imitators remarked on its self-sustaining quality and significant practical benefits: '[A] blood bank provides immediate availability of blood of various types, a safe blood from the standpoint of the transmission of syphilis, an economical blood ..., a lightening of the labors ... and an increased efficiency in collecting blood' (Barton 1941: 176). Whilst in Britain the terminology of banking was never so explicit and the racial division of donations generally frowned upon, collectors faced the same problem of how to moralize the act of blood-giving for practical ends, and themes of insurance and recompense became quickly central to the new language of gift. These themes will be reviewed in a later section. For now it suffices to reiterate the profound impact of blood conservation methods on transfusion practice, most importantly the growing distance, spatial and temporal, they imposed between recipients and volunteers. From 1940, the introduction of pooled serum and plasma products compounded and complicated this distance, substituting a one-to-many/many-to-one relation for the immediate one-to-one connections of the interwar period (Vaughan 1942: 20). In such conditions of obscurity and separation, images of recipients began populating publicity and recruitment materials, attesting a fictional bond and singularity that was newly redundant.

Knowing strangers
Representations of recovered war heroes, tales of salvaged children, voices of returned veterans crackling across the wireless or sounding from the stage; quite suddenly these once-forbidden 'others' began to dominate all mass communication formats, nationally or locally directed, coming into rapid and close association with themes of 'the gift'. Recipients appeared first in writing, in newspaper announcements and in transcripts of radio broadcasts. The wireless then gave them a spoken presence, whilst visually they appeared from the summer of 1940 on photographs and posters, displayed in town halls, taped to factory walls, hoisted to prominence on banners and pasted to the sides of derelict buildings destroyed by German bombs (Fig. 5.1). They appeared on cinema newsreels too, in national press features, and on blood donor enrolment forms

Figure 5.1. 'Will you become a blood donor?' The ambiguous image invites the role of imagination to personalize the faceless figure, donor or recipient. The same image appears in other publicity materials, and the walking stick is suggestive of a war veteran: that is, a living example of a blood beneficiary, also a blood donor who gives in the name of reciprocity. See the final section for themes of donor motivation, repayment, and insurance. (Imperial War Museum, London, © IWM. Reproduced with permission.)

(Fig. 5.2). Janet Vaughan, director of the Slough depot, remarked in a government memo that '[i]t has also proved successful to have speakers from the stage stressing the importance of the service and the need for a full response from local donors. The most successful appeals are made by returned wounded men who have themselves received transfusions'.[9] A file containing drafts of the first proposed radio broadcast in 1939 is the earliest piece of documentary evidence:

> Before a blood transfusion a patient may be unconscious, breathing heavily and irregularly, the pulse may barely be felt and the face have the peculiar muddy pallor associated with sudden blood loss. But when a transfusion takes place and the new blood passes into the vein the breathing of the patient becomes normal, the pulse is readily felt again, colour comes back to the face and the patient may open his eyes and appear to take an interest in his surroundings. Patients themselves have described a transfusion as giving them 'a sense of having life pumped into them'.[10]

What, then, accounts for the rapid rise of recipient figures, virtual beneficiaries of the anonymous gift? Primarily it is the blood bank that explains their new frequency; or, rather, the mediated system of collection, treatment, storage, and redistribution that the blood bank imposed, as well as the alleged bad effects of the obscurity it cast around the process of transfusion. Long before historians and psychologists of the later twentieth century rediscovered it, contemporaries of the Second World War understood full well the potentially devastating impact of such mediated, bureaucratic organizations

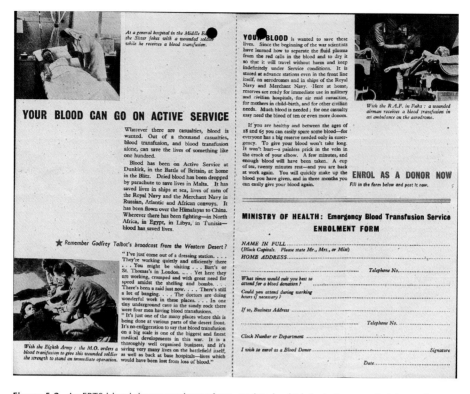

Figure 5.2. An EBTS blood donor enrolment form, undated, which includes several pictures of medics administering blood to wounded soldiers. (Wellcome Library, London.)

upon individual moral consciousness (Bauman 2000 [1989]; Ginzburg 1994: 56; Lachs 1981). Ironically it was Percy Oliver, typically opposed to conceptualizing blood-giving in terms of a single 'other', who first and finally gestured to the stultifying threat of technical mediations upon the dependability of collective goodwill. 'The wholesale use of stored blood', he warned in 1938, 'would tend to dry up the springs of altruism ... as there would be difficulty in identifying [blood's] ultimate destination and effect, an important factor to most voluntary donors'.[11] The same would be the likely effect of pooling techniques adapted from the Spanish Civil War:

> One drawback from the point of view of a voluntary service [is] whether the [transfusion] method finally adopted ... will make it impossible for a donor's blood to be identified with any particular case or patient. In Spain the blood of six separate donors is mingled in order to 'average out' minor individual incompatibilities. Many donors in this country regard the report on the utilisation of their blood as a matter of great personal interest, and if it were impossible to obtain this it might detract from their willingness to volunteer.[12]

During the planning phase of the EBTS, however, the new distance imposed by a modernizing blood supply had appeared genuinely threatening only to those familiar with an alternative scheme. With the exception of H.F. Brewer, formerly Medical Officer to the RCBTS, the depot directors had little experience organizing panels of blood donors and conceived of their problem independent of Oliver's precedent, as a new and autonomous task invigorated with the urgency of conflict. It was only in January 1940, when donors began querying the need for blood in the absence of air raids, that the directors began awakening to the problem of volunteers' motivation. Montague Maizels, director of the blood depot at Maidstone, told Dr Chalmers of the MRC about the possibility of a BBC radio broadcast, the point of which would not be recruitment, but a general explanation of the need for blood collection: 'There is a considerable amount of puzzlement amongst our volunteers as to why we are asking them to give their blood in the absence of air-raid casualties'. Insofar as puzzlement posed a threat to co-operation, 'I think we should consolidate our present panels and obtain many thousand new volunteers if the position were made clear'.[13] 'Making clear' was exactly the point, the cardinal object of an organization steeped in obscurity: making clear the research objects that necessitated blood procurement in the absence of civilian need, and, more important, making clear the figures of the recipients and the processes responsible for their invisibility.

Behind the general problem of clarifying obscurity, recipient rhetoric was bound to the concrete task of ensuring that blood donors attended bleeding sessions when called. In July 1940, in the final days of the 'bore war' and in the absence of bombs, Dr Solandt, then director of the Sutton depot, had noted with dismay the lack of reliable volunteers in a letter to the MRC: '[The] response from donors at Sutton yesterday', he wrote in a request for support, 'was 22 out of 60. This is the worst response that we have had, with the exception of one or two very bad days during the winter'.[14] The solution came just two months later with the commencement of air raids on Britain, notably on London, and proof that blood transfusion was indeed a vital therapy for the critically injured. Solandt and his colleagues could now verify their claims that the EBTS was a 'life-saving service', and therefore imposed an obligation on its members. 'The most important aspect is that when a donor enrols he should appreciate that he has joined a life-saving service and must present himself when called upon for bleeding'.[15] In its early guise, the recipient was an instrument for enforcing obligation, for encoding a duty to respond to calls to give blood.

The most effective way to demonstrate the life-saving potentials of blood-giving, and to 'make clear' the necessity of the EBTS, was photographically. At least since 1938, with the establishment of *Picture Post*, a weekly, left-of-centre, illustrated periodical, which drew heavily on interwar developments in typography, layout, and photographic documentary,[16] the project of 'making clear' had, in the evolving conventions of British media, been twinned with the related and much more widespread project of 'making real'. *Picture Post*'s first editor, Stefan Lorant, a refugee Hungarian Jew with strong anti-fascist views, had pursued photographic journalism for its promise of factuality, and believed wholeheartedly that the British public could and would respond to serious, popular news presentation. Presaged by the documentary movement of the 1930s, and indebted to its sombre associations with realism and its rejection of sensational narratives (Webster 2005: 39), *Picture Post* represented not only a break with traditional contemporary British journalism, but also a culmination of emerging journalistic strategies and news values in an age that recognized new and powerful linkages between media and democracy (Hall 1972: 71-4; J. Taylor 1991: chap. 1; P.M. Taylor 2003: 349-52). Bearing in mind the pains taken to distinguish democratic from totalitarian propaganda by a commitment to the virtue of truth (Bartlett 1941; Rogerson 1938), we can see in Lorant's use of photograph-as-mediator-of-reality a timely and strident political gesture: '[T]hrough photographic realism the great themes of freedom were constantly reified' (J. Taylor 1991: 54). In deliberate contrast to popular newspapers like the *Daily Mirror*, according to historian Michael Bromley, 'Britain's first truly tabloid newspaper', and 'the quintessential graphic newspaper of the 1930s and 1940s' (1999: 114),[17] often condemned for its bombastic sensationalism and irresponsible use of images (1999: 97), *Picture Post* strove to resist populism in favour of a purportedly neutral presentation of truth through the ideal of objective photography (Hall 1972: 77).

In the summer of 1940, as German bombers began the attack on RAF Fighter Command, it was in *Picture Post* that recipients made their public debut (Calder 1991: 33). In an August issue, on the back of widespread and prescient expectations that London would be Hitler's next target, the journal broached the issue of 'The air-raid', what it involved, the official response procedure, how best to survive. 'The thing that most distinguishes this war from all previous wars', began the editorial, 'is that to-day everyone is in it. Distance means little, boundaries and seas are no protection, for this is a battle of air-power. And to the ordinary person, air-power finds expression in air-raids'.[18] Describing blood transfusion as among 'the most remarkable, and typically inconspicuous, lines of Civil Defence',[19] the piece focused less on personalized tales of imperilment and restoration than on the necessity of blood transfusion for helping 'the severely wounded' in general: '[B]lood is stored ready for use in special refrigerators, kept at between 2 and 4 degrees centigrade. When a call for blood comes, it is sent out at a moment's notice in special refrigerator vans, together with the necessary apparatus for administration, already sterilised'.[20] Where text conveyed operational and quantitative details, two images inserted blood transfusion within the general cycle of the air raid. The first was of a blood bank refrigerator, and revealed an internal invisible stage in the process of transfusion (see the final section). Beneath it, a caption avowed the proven magnitude of blood transfusion services in war: 'Profiting by the lesson of the Spanish war, when 10 per cent of the population needed transfusion, the Blood Transfusion Service has set up Blood Banks, has stores of blood classified, refrigerated, ready for instant use'.[21] The sequence then continued to a second image, a picture of the recipient (Fig. 5.3). Not only demonstrating the life-saving potentials of blood transfusion, the arrangement of the photograph in sequence alongside the Auxiliary Fire Service, Women's Voluntary Services, and Casualty Rescue Squads placed blood transfusion within an effective structure of civilian defence, completing the marriage of individual action to collective outcome. If indeed 'distance means little', this was due not only to the military technology of the aircraft bomber but also to the mobile, reproducible photograph (Mirzoeff 1999: 71-3).

As the use of recipient images on enrolment forms suggests, the depot directors relished these emerging pictorial strategies, particularly the realism of photographs. Janet Vaughan was especially enthusiastic. Through substantial involvement with recruitment campaigns and the creation of transfusion-related publicity, Vaughan, trained as a haematologist and expert in the anaemias, had come to understand a great deal about the most effective means for sustaining an interested and reliable panel of blood donors. She stressed the relation of persistence to success – 'No donor panel will maintain itself at full strength without constant care' – and saw the need for tenacious continual emphasis, through a spectrum of media, on the relevance of blood-giving to victory. Vaughan reckoned above all on the value of depicting recipients: 'Any shots of the administration of blood appearing in news items have always pleased and interested donors'. She believed images of blood administration to be so crucial, in fact, that she criticized the central organs of national propaganda (with the obvious exception of

The A.F.S. Fight a Fire

An incendiary bomb has set fire to a house. 180,000 A.F.S. men are on duty day and night, ready to handle trouble like this, with any of their 20,000 pumps. They are trained to the minute.

The Rescue Squads Get Busy

Recruited mostly from the building trades, these husky men (there are 10,000 of them in the London area alone) are specially skilled in making wrecked buildings safe.

direct to the Chief Constable, and is at once radiated to each Divisional Police Headquarters, and all sub-stations where there are sirens—there are about fifty in a moderate-sized town. It is also transmitted at once to the Fire Brigade Super-intendent, who is in charge of both the regular brigade and of the A.F.S. Immediately, the fire services stand to. Theirs may be a colossal task.

A single heavy bomber can carry upwards of a thousand incendiary bombs—a squadron can carry nearly ten thousand—each one potentially a source of fire. It has been calculated that a bombing 'plane passing over a district and releasing its bombs in series would be able to cause perhaps as many as ten to fifteen actual fires in every 100 yards, along the track of the 'plane, which might

have a width of about 400 ft. To meet this possible situation, fire services are organised into com-paratively small areas, each containing emergency units capable of handling outbreaks until reinforce-ments arrive. These areas are determined by careful calculation, based on the actual road mileage, multiplied by a factor determined by the fire risks in each locality. Each area has its own

Doctor Gives an Emergency Blood Transfusion

Profiting by the lesson of the Spanish war, when 10 per cent. of the population needed transfusion, the Blood Transfusion Service has set up Blood Banks, has stores of blood classified, refrigerated, ready for instant use.

Troops Guard Against Looting

While householders leave home to take shelter, squads of soldiers patrol the streets, to protect property against possible looting after wreckage. Their work is co-ordinated with Police and A.R.P.

21

Figure 5.3. Blood transfusion as a critical stage in the response to air raids. *Picture Post,* 17 August 1940. (Reproduced by kind permission of the Syndics of Cambridge University Library.)

radio) for failing to include enough. Articles in the daily press, she insisted, 'unless accompanied by pictures of the blood being actually used [lack the] ... appeal of the [wireless] broadcast', which offered a more personal means of exhortation (O'Sullivan 1995). Cinema trailer films could prove equally limited for the same reason. So, wrote Vaughan, 'it is essential [at] enrolling centres to have a fine window display to attract the passer-by: experience has shown that for this purpose actual photographs of the blood being given under War conditions are greatly appreciated.[22]

The photograph was also amenable to a second format for representing the gift, also mobile, reproducible, and visual: the poster (Fig. 5.4). The striking creations of the war artist Abram Games, who produced work for several wartime propaganda campaigns and who was the acknowledged master of spelling out connections between cause and effect, are among the most memorable examples of Second World War posters. Games' designs won widespread acclaim in the early 1940s, and one historian insists that 'few would dispute that on balance it was Abram Games' war', so striking and prolific were his designs (Rickards 1971: 34). He created three blood transfusion posters between 1939 and 1945, two displaying recipient figures, the third using a clock motif, emphasizing the convenience of blood-giving and its minimal demands on volunteers' time (Fig. 5.5). As much as any other propaganda format, these posters, displayed in post office windows or taped to factory walls, and synchronized to the schedules of recruitment and blood collection campaigns, encapsulate the central dynamics of the gift: that it was intended to reveal an invisible other, a recipient rendered strange by modernization; that it depended upon narrative or illustration or both; that it was mass-produced, scrupulously timed, and locally encountered; and that it was both necessary and possible only because of the same technologically induced mediations that it confronted and was intended to reduce.

Figure 5.4. Consistent with broader propaganda themes in wartime Britain, the wounded soldier represents a singular recipient of a life-saving blood gift, the absent 'someone ... somewhere'. A version of the image also appears on the front page of the EBTS blood donor enrolment form shown in Figure 5.2. (Wellcome Library, London.)

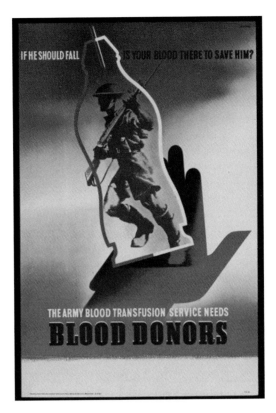

Figure 5.5. The singular soul of the gift? A poster by Abram Games for the Emergency Blood Transfusion Service, undated, depicts a soldier recipient figure within a blood bottle. (Wellcome Library, London.)

Knowing donors

The outstanding advantage of fictive recipients was that they coerced the energy of imagination in response to anonymity. Like nationalism and the idea of a nation, a singular recipient was ultimately an imagined entity, conceived of as part of 'a deep, horizontal comradeship' (Anderson 2006 [1983]: 7). Empty in the sense of being no one in particular and yet richly suggestive of kinship and blood, these abstract imagined figures claimed the same quality of simultaneous 'remoteness and nearness, indifference and involvement', that Simmel assimilated to the figure of the stranger, a modern wanderer who 'comes incidentally into contact with *every* single element but is not bound up organically, through established ties ... with any single one' (1950 [1908]: 186, original emphasis). Like the blood bank, which sought a system of reciprocity through a monetary language of obligation, the aim of the stranger was to enact the soul of the gift by personalizing the gesture of blood donation.

As such, the strangers of 1940s blood transfusion propaganda were linked, as well as to the specific problem of reliability, to a more widespread practical problem of moral motivation: what could be the appeal of a particular action which, experienced in isolation, appeared inconsequential (Bauman 2000 [1989]: 101)? The question was common to a whole range of wartime civilian issues. Why work in factories? Why 'Dig for Victory'? Why turn out the lights? Why sacrifice pots and pans and other household items? The problem, it seemed to Tom Harrisson, co-founder of the Mass Observation social research organization,[23] was the obscure relation between effort and outcome. 'There was a general atmosphere of "What is the use?" ', Harrisson had remarked after visiting a wartime munitions factory: 'What appears to be wanted is a National consciousness that each is part of the greater whole, that each has a definite stake in winning the war, and that every person, however indirectly connected with the War Effort, is part of an essential War machine' (Harrisson 1943: 124). In another study he had insisted that '[o]fficial propaganda, almost invariably, asks you to do something from which you will not benefit immediately in a concrete way, and which will often entail actual sacrifice of your own immediate interests' (Mass Observation 1941: 57). The feeling of making a contribution, where it could be enforced, was therefore a delicate and painstaking priority, as in the war factory which eventually established 'an exhibition of finished sets in the canteen, so that the machine-shop girls could come and see what it was that they were contributing to make' (Harrisson 1943: 44).

Exhibiting, showing, seeing: historians writing on a range of issues have seen the task of media to reduce distance, to act 'as the vital conduit between those fighting and those more distantly participating in – or vicariously experiencing – war': '[T]he primary role of media in wartime in the Anglo-American world has long been to maintain the ties of sentiment between the soldiers in the field and the home front' (quoted in Carruthers 2000: 5-6). In Second World War Britain, the need for such campaigns demonstrating the connectedness of remote actions sprung from the contemporary understanding of an urgent danger of moral indifference within technologically advanced societies, societies in which human action can be effective at a very great and still growing distance (Bauman 2000 [1989]: 193; Lachs 1981: 12). To grasp how widespread was this project of reconciliation – a project of making clear and making real – one need only recall the persistent efforts, through posters and other illustrated public notices, to persuade civilians that their 'idle chat' might prove fatal to soldiers fighting abroad: the 'Careless Talk Costs Lives' campaign that ran throughout the war. One of the most famous images on this theme was designed by Games, and depicts an arrow spiralling from the mouth of a background civilian to impale three soldiers in the foreground of the image: 'YOUR TALK MAY KILL YOUR COMRADES'. Just as anti-Semitic and depraved representations could distance and de-personalize the subjects of Nazi propaganda (Bauman 2000 [1989]: 216) – what Ian Kershaw describes as its ultimate and most terrible triumph (2002 [1983]: 275) – so could the emotive depiction of soldiers, children, or air-raid casualties (the cardinal victims and heroes of wartime Britain) intensify the humanity of the distant other, bringing back to the forgetful civilian the human face and aim of conflict.

Moreover, the fact that posters, narratives, cinema newsreels, and so forth, *did* represent the cardinal victims and heroes of wartime Britain sheds light on another aspect of the gift, namely its gendering,[24] the fact that it partook of all the elements of wartime propaganda contrived to coax, prompt, and motivate the domestic woman. Soldiers and children predominated the hoardings, figures which, as Lucy Noakes has shown in her study of recruitment to the Auxiliary Territorial Service, dwelt on the supposedly intrinsic nurturing and maternal qualities of women, an assumption as common to civilian wartime recruitment campaigns as to general media rhetoric of the 1940s (2006: 104). The pursuit of housewives that began in summer 1939 became a motif for recruitment for the next six years, emphasizing their suitability and playing on their (presumed) emotional tendencies. Excepting one photograph in the August 1940 issue of *Picture Post* (which depicts a middle-aged woman receiving a blood transfusion, and which was unofficial),

Figure 5.6. A publicity photograph taken at the blood depot in Slough, 1940. A woman reads a poster emphasizing the potential blood benefits for a 'husband, brother or sweetheart'. Most likely a staged encounter, it represents the ideal blood-giver, motivated by a concern for distant, singular others. (Wellcome Unit for the History of Medicine Library, Bodleian Libraries, University of Oxford. Despite the author's best efforts, the copyright holder remains unknown.)

the majority of surviving visual and written materials refer either to men at war or to young children on the Homefront – and this in spite of the fact that a strong proportion of civilian recipients of blood transfusions were women. Consider the proposals for a film of 1942, for instance, and the case of 'Little Johnnie':

> [T]he treatment of a case of shock could be indicated solely by a recipient's face and an accompanying sphygmomanometer in which the ebb and flow of life is shown by the fall and rise of the mercury column, which of course finally attains a satisfactory level. A 'flash back' to anxious relatives waiting for news in an anteroom and their relief when little Johnnie is saved, might bring the human element before the public.[25]

Note not only the implication that 'the human element' has been somehow removed from public view but that its retrieval becomes an appropriate problem for the tools of publicity and propaganda. Images alone could 'bring before' the public a 'human element', represented in figures of vulnerable children and fighting men, and otherwise lost in the cold stores of the blood bank. Figure 5.6 is demonstrative in this respect, and captures more fully the gendered quality of stranger relationships. The image of a potential blood-giver reading a poster that promotes consideration for distant soldiers encapsulates the ideal blood-giver and the ideal woman at war, and attests to a trend amongst middle-class housewives, recorded and encouraged by Mass Observation, of doing things for an imagined 'other'. In June 1940, Harrisson had commented on this phenomenon with the example of knitting, a popular pastime for many wartime women:

> [H]ere the personal element may appear again; the socks or scarves are for a man, perhaps her own husband or son, or alternatively for someone else's. An example has been given of the type of woman who devotes much of her time and energy to sewing, organising, canvassing for the local WVS [Women's Voluntary Service], and here also she is able to identify her efforts with the object – sick people in hospitals, the Sailors Home, all definite people who will make use of and appreciate her work.[26]

In her history of women factory workers, Susan Carruthers notes the consistent and ongoing efforts of propagandists to promote precisely these themes to female audiences. To take just one example, Carruthers examines the Ministry of Information film *Jane Brown changes her job*, a propaganda short that addressed a residual prejudice against factory work and aimed to entice women away from traditional areas of female employment to the war industries. The film told the story of Jane, who trades office work for aeroplane construction, then progresses quickly up the ranks. Notably at odds with the factory workers of the Mass Observation study, who were apathetic and wholly uninterested with the outcomes of their collective efforts, Jane finds deep satisfaction in her role, 'proudly carrying the card which "means she is doing work of national importance" '. The strongest appeal of the film, writes Carruthers, 'is to women's sense of patriotism, of doing things for others – hence Jane's final flush of pride as the finished aircraft is wheeled out of the factory and her satisfaction in knowing that she has helped "to put another plane in the shed for the boys" ' (1990: 240). Whether it be a plane, a scarf, or a pint of blood, it was the preoccupation with the distant object that mattered, that should matter, that was made to matter (and made visible) by the techniques of written and photographic publicity.

The curiosity both to know and to assist a distant stranger was, according to an EBTS booklet of 1944, a pervasive and normal characteristic of wartime donors. *LifeBlood*, 'the official account of the Transfusion Services', stood out among other propaganda materials for its emphasis on unity above diversity, on the ability of a shared occupation – blood donation – to transcend social divisions (Webster 2005: 24-5). In contrast with other materials, *LifeBlood* underemphasized the gendered aspect of the gift and instead told the stories of six unexceptional characters: a soldier, a workman, a railway goods guard, an elderly man with an Air Raid Precaution (ARP) badge and a limp, a plump, middle-aged woman, and a young red-haired girl – a diversity of typical situations and shared interests convoked to express the multiple appeal and widespread suitability of blood-giving to a so-called 'general public'. As for the soldier, Corporal Evans: 'He can never forget how his best friend, just before they were evacuated from Dunkirk, had the lower half of his body crushed by some falling masonry. [Corporal Evans had] watched on the beach while the medical officer dripped in a pint of blood', and was forever impressed by the way in which his friend's 'lifeless form revived as some unknown person's blood began to refill his veins'. Ever since then, 'Corporal Evans repays the debt of his friend'.[27] A comparable sense of debt motivated Jim the workman, also the friend of a blood transfusion recipient injured through falling into a 60-foot-deep tank in a munitions factory: 'his pelvis broken, the base of his skull fractured, three or four ribs crushed in, and a good many face wounds'. Moved by the severity of his workmate's injuries and the miracle of his survival, 'Jim has come to return some of that blood'.

'After all, it might have been me', he says.[28] This notion of virtual insurance was shared by Harry Robinson, the railwayman, who 'knows what happens if a man gets crushed between two trucks on shunting operations – or smashed in an air-raid'. 'For all you know', says Harry, 'they may be pumping it back into your own body one day'.[29]

As for the elderly ARP man and the two women, rather different motives compel them to give. The ARP man had been seriously wounded in the Great War. Without blood transfusion, it had taken him months to recover. Now, with three sons fighting in the army, he draws consolation from modern medical techniques (if his sons are wounded 'they need not suffer as he suffered'), and so contributes to the service that could save their lives. The middle-aged widow, Mrs Alice Edwards, mother of four and with one son in the army, gives blood for related reasons. What is more, she finds that regular 'blood-letting seemed to do her good, to overcome a feeling of heaviness'. Also for the sake of an absent other, and on his encouragement, the red-haired Mabel Adams donates to the spirit of the soldier she will one day marry, and others like him:

> Well, there they are, these six ordinary men and women, samples of the million and four hundred thousand ... who have enrolled as blood donors from one end of Britain to the other ... All over the country people like Mrs. Edwards, Corporal Evans, Mabel Adams, and Jim, with very little trouble to themselves, have given their pints of blood. In every one of the fighting forces at this moment, and in all the bombed towns and cities, there are men and women who owe their lives to these gifts.[30]

Not content with a mere display of outward normality, however, *LifeBlood* also proposed how normal folk thought or *should* be thinking: 'When, on the morning of the 6th of June, 1944, the news reached every home, office and factory in Britain that the invasion of France had begun, three questions came to our minds. How will it turn out? Will the casualties be very high? Will *he* come through all right?'[31] Such instructive imagining was not restricted to soldiers fighting overseas but applied also and equally to strangers closer to home:

> *Imagine yourself there* as they hurried the three victims from the blacked-out street into the warm casualty ward. Take a look at Bert Hiss, as he lies on the stretcher. His left foot is crushed, his left leg deeply lacerated, his left thigh and right leg badly torn. There is only one thing that can possibly save him ...[32]

As well as demonstrating the role of imagination in creating strangers, these narratives reiterate the lesson that the image of the normal donor implied preoccupation with a distant and otherwise unknown recipient: 'If Jim and Mabel and Mrs. Edwards and the A.R.P. man with the limp and Corporal Evans and Harry the railwayman could have been present when a small group of ten men and women gathered together one Tuesday morning in a hospital board room', the narrative continued, 'they would have seen the fruits of their small, personal sacrifice'. That they, like all blood donors, could not see first-hand the fruits of personal sacrifice put the onus upon the pamphlet to compensate. What miracles of rejuvenation these donors could not witness, *LifeBlood* would dutifully recount:

> [T]hose crushed wrecks that had lain on stretchers with the life draining out of them two years before are now fit, useful members of society, trained as skilled engineers and carrying on in the very factory where the explosion had taken place. It took the blood of thirty-seven donors to perform this miracle.[33]

In its display of personalities and motives, *LifeBlood* pressed on its readership an image of blood donors coextensive with a general public: individuals noted only for, and exactly because of, their ordinariness. Binding these people, what they had (or could have) in common, was the gift, and its direction to a broader war effort, the defence of sovereignty. As well as tying giver to recipient, the rhetoric of the gift bound strangers to one another, dimming individual differences through light of a common pursuit (Rose 2003: 2-7; Webster 2005: 21-5). But above all the gift was an appeal to women. Drawn, written, spoken with wives and mothers in mind, the recipient rhetoric of the gift appealed to and reinforced an idea of the wife and woman on the Homefront. Knowing the outcome of a blood transfusion in interwar London was one thing (and the outcome was often not good); but knowing the (fictive) recipient of a gift in wartime was something else altogether. This 'something else' placed a painstaking, mass-produced emphasis on a so-called 'human element', it took the idea of a one-to-one connection where none existed, it appealed to imagination for the task of realizing strangers, and it was thoroughly gendered.

Journeys of the gift

The argument so far has examined the invention of the gift alongside systems of preservation and pooling, its connection to recipient figures, and its attachment to specific practical problems of reliability and moral motivation. It was, however, to the question of the internal operation of the blood bank that the depot directors finally turned in 1943, when they first began plans for *LifeBlood*, originally titled, 'The gift in the battle line'. By this stage, the display of fictive recipients was an obligatory component of effective publicity, and through a marriage of textual and visual techniques the depot directors aimed to be explicit about the connection between donors and patients: 'We are anxious to include a ... section, built up from "human documents" from the regions and depots, giving, if possible, some indication of what part of the country each story comes from'.[34] *LifeBlood* was to provide, above all, a means to trace the multiple consequences of a singular deed through a compendium of stories, the abstract sum of which was *the* story 'From blood-giver to battlefront'.[35] The plan was to include details of 'a number of civilian air-raid casualty and armed forces blood recipients, explaining the reasons why the blood has to be transfused and describing the wounds [and] diseases from which they would probably not otherwise have recovered'. Next, it would 'describe the technique of the blood service from the time of the donation to the time of the transfusion'.[36] Hence *LifeBlood* traced the 'gift of life' from genesis to destination, from the dreary humdrum of the bare parish room with its pockmarks and patchy ceiling to the first Allied landings at Sicily on 10 June 1943:

> [V]ery soon a man here and a man there, hurrying across the beaches, dropped to the ground. Stretcher parties raced towards them and carried them to the improvised first aid post. One or two had suffered damage to arteries, or had had their legs fractured by machine-gun bullets, and within an hour of the first man coming ashore, the equipment taken from the biscuit tins was being used to drip the pale golden liquid [plasma] into the veins of these serious casualties. The result merits the description 'miraculous'. In almost every case the seemingly lifeless body began to revive. It was like putting a half-dead flower in water on a hot day.[37]

Appearing alongside the heroes in the drama of Sicily were examples from the younger generation enrolled in the domestic dramas of the Homefront. As a modern medical therapy with the potential for dramatic restorative effects, blood transfusion left ample room to exploit these younger patients to their full emotive extent:

James, aged ten, was riding his bicycle along the village street when he was knocked down by a motor bus, of which the wheels passed over both his legs. One leg was almost severed, the other was severely lacerated. There were severe bruises on various parts of his body ... On arrival at the hospital he was comatose and the blood pressure could not be measured ... and in the surgeon's own words 'he became very restless ... it appeared as if he must soon die, he became deathly pale, cold, pulseless'. Improvement began almost as soon as plasma was given ... The almost severed leg, naturally, had to be amputated, but the other injuries were dealt with successfully and the child recovered ... During the critical period he had received three-quarters-of-a-pint of blood, and five pints of plasma.[38]

Accompanying the narratives, photographs visualized the transformation of blood into blood products, and included images of procurement, cold storage, spin freezing, right through to the administration of plasma on the battlefields. Thus through written and visual means *LifeBlood* worked to dissipate the 'mental blackout' associated by one Ministry of Information official, Professor Ifor Evans, with the catastrophic effects of civilian despondency, by presenting to donors in its full functional specificity the very system of operations obscuring from them the immediate practical or moral relevance of their gift (Mackay 2002: 55). 'Neither the donors nor the recipients see the complicated processes and all the careful work that make the vital blood gift possible', began the chapter on 'The secret of plasma'. So at the centre of *LifeBlood* a sequence of six images revealed the transformation of raw blood into a series of storable, mobile products (Fig. 5.7), whilst a written account of the manufacture and distribution of plasma gave an answer to

a question blood donors very often ask. 'Why,' they say, 'can't we know the actual soldier or sailor to whom our blood gift goes?' If the donor's whole blood were used for a transfusion, it would be possible for the donor and the recipient to know one another ... But when blood transfusion takes the form of transfusing the plasma alone, this is not possible, for the plasma of many donors has to be pooled.[39]

What began in 1939 as a tentative gesture towards a humane 'other' had, by 1944, become a full-scale dramatization of donors, recipients, and their bond of the gift. *LifeBlood* was, in the most literal sense, a revelation, seeking in visual display and narrative the restoration of moral faculties feared blunted by a technological onslaught. That during the Second World War London donors began giving blood 'with fictive recipients in mind' (Healy 2006: 117) – *Who is my stranger?* – owed to the modernization of the blood supply in a double sense: first, because modernization provided the conditions of separation and strangeness that rendered this image necessary; and, second, because the dissemination of these images required multiple means of (targeted and local) mass communication.

The gift comprised various elements: it was bound to a notion of a stranger, an illusory and singular recipient; it was scheduled, reliant on a timetable and parasitic on the rhythms of the wartime factory; it was deliberately gendered, arising in a culture of recruitment that targeted women, and proclaiming their motives of sacrifice for men and children; at the same time it was avowedly universal, alleging a transcendental quality that cut across social divisions, finding unity amongst diversity, bespeaking the commonality of a shared fate and purpose; and finally it was visual and widely propagated, based around the new conventions and ambitions of an expanding media culture. Through the early 1940s, knowing the fate of one's gift became more than knowing the likely conditions for its administration. It was a matter of being responsive to the human face of blood transfusion, a matter of knowing and of wanting to know the humanity of the recipient and, by extension, of the act itself. Attached inextricably to the technological heritage of a modernized blood supply, and, by extension, a modernized emergency medical service, the gift appeared first by dissolving the visibility of the blood transfusion process and then

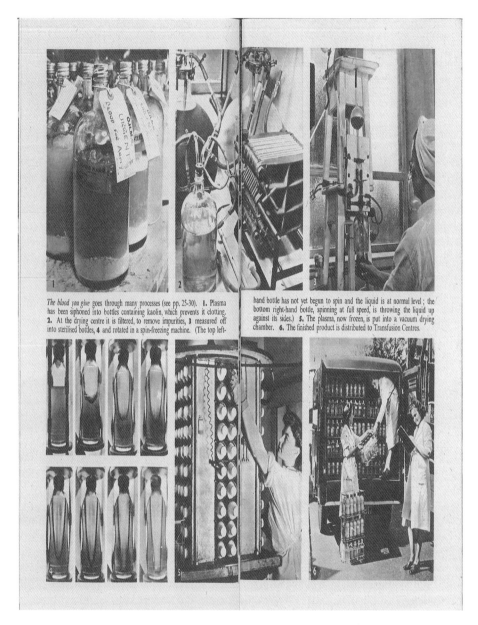

The blood you give goes through many processes (see pp. 25-30). **1.** Plasma has been siphoned into bottles containing kaolin, which prevents it clotting. **2.** At the drying centre it is filtered, to remove impurities, **3** measured off into sterilised bottles, **4** and rotated in a spin-freezing machine. (The top left-hand bottle has not yet begun to spin and the liquid is at normal level ; the bottom right-hand bottle, spinning at full speed, is throwing the liquid up against its sides.) **5.** The plasma, now frozen, is put into a vacuum drying chamber. **6.** The finished product is distributed to Transfusion Centres.

Figure 5.7. The centrefold of *LifeBlood* (1944), revealing the creation of blood plasma products and the otherwise invisible processes of siphoning, filtration, spin-freezing, and vacuum drying. (Reproduced by kind permission of the Syndics of Cambridge University Library.)

by compensating the product of that dissolution. Invisibility could not but be treated as a temporary inconvenience, an aberration tended to most effectively by the self-same technologies of which it was born. The war of visibility against obscurity was replicated by the battle of the fictive recipient against the anonymity of the blood bank – and true to Parry's conjecture of free giving and its self-interested antithesis, above all things it was the blood bank that went in parallel with the gift.

The Allied victory of 1945 brought an end to the work of the EBTS. In 1946, a National Blood Transfusion Service for Britain continued the practical innovations of its emergency predecessor. Two decades later, Richard Titmuss was composing his comparative study of voluntary and commercial systems of blood procurement, and through his research efforts in Britain and America was well aware of the fundamental disruptions wrought by the modern production and storage technologies of the early 1940s. Despite shifting ideological landscapes and political priorities, he was also aware of how those disruptions had continued into peacetime practice. At this point we may return to the paradox that opened this essay. The troublesome concept of a 'stranger relationship', which lay at the heart of Titmuss's thesis, was deliberately ambiguous, parasitic on the fiction of a singular beneficiary it knew full well to be missing. 'Who is my stranger?', the title of his penultimate chapter, was intended not as a pure or complete description, but as the question we *should* ask as we partake of an activity which, fundamentally, lacked the singular equivalent to which the term 'stranger' gave a disingenuous nod. Moreover, and more generally, it was, according to Titmuss, the question that distinguished the amorphous domain of unquantifiable altruistic behaviour from the quantifiable transactions of the economic sphere. In contrast to the claim of his most astute critic, the eminent economist Kenneth Arrow, who insisted that 'an expression of impersonal altruism is as far removed from the feeling of personal interaction as any marketplace' (1972: 360), these anonymous transactions were *not* impersonal, since with imagination donors could ascribe to the stranger – to '*my* stranger' – the lost faces of comrades, the familiar stories of separation and survival, the personal qualities of missing kin. Put simply: Titmuss's theme of the gift, like its wartime precursor, used the strangeness of the blood bank in order precisely to deny it, to overcome its blinding imposition, to defy the impersonal terms it thrust upon an activity whose safe continuation depended upon the mentality of the unrequited deed.

Recently there has been a tendency for commentators to believe the fictional singularity of the gift relationship which Titmuss's ideal playfully invoked, to take at face value a concept of giving which, to all intents and purposes, was mythical and strategic. So I have attempted to throw light on the gift's true ancestry, the fact that it emerged at a time of conflict when the simple, singular connection was already a bygone reality, a remnant of traditions of the 1930s and before. Titmuss was not the first to ask about strangers or to promote a wider curiosity about otherness. The history of that curiosity is the history of the gift itself. And the question *Who is my stranger?* makes sense only in light of another, its precursor and forebear: Why give blood to a service that lacks an immediately perceptible relevance, be it practical or humane? Because blood is a gift of life, and because its value can be gauged, if not in the immediacy of a donor's day-to-day activities, then in the images, narratives, and human stories presented by collection authorities and imagined by their volunteers. *Here* is your stranger. *He* is your stranger.

NOTES
[1] Secondary accounts used: Gunson & Dodsworth (1996); and Pelis (2007).
[2] *Blood Transfusion Quarterly Circular (QC)*, no. 22, January 1939, National Archives (NA), London, FD 1/3245. For a comparison of blood transfusion services in London, Paris, and New York in the 1920s and 1930s, see Schneider (2003: 197-207).
[3] Lewisohn was not the only surgeon to suggest citrate as an anti-coagulant, but he received greater credit in America for suggesting a volume of 0.2 per cent solution for transfusion. For a more detailed account, see Keynes (1949: 37-9).

[4] Partly for the sake of volunteers' emotional welfare, Oliver insisted that donors should not at any time come into contact with their recipient (Pelis 2007).

[5] The RCBTS required hospitals to complete one-page forms detailing the outcome of a blood transfusion; these were then forwarded to blood donors (Pelis 2007).

[6] 'Private calls', *QC*, no. 13, October 1936, Red Cross Archives (RCA), London, Acc 345.

[7] Memorandum, 'Suggested requirements for one central blood transfusion depot', Wellcome Library (WL), London, GC/186/1.

[8] *The Lancet*, 29 July, 1939: 263.

[9] Janet Vaughan, 'Publicity and propaganda', WL GC/186/2.

[10] 'Blood Transfusion' wartime emergency memo, 1939, NA FD 1/5883.

[11] 'Storage of blood', *QC*, no. 20, July 1938, RCA Acc 345.

[12] Report of the Blood Transfusion Service for the year ended 31 December 1937, NA FD 1/3246.

[13] Letter from M. Maizels to Chalmers, 17 January 1940, NA FD 1/5885.

[14] O.M. Solandt to A. Drury, 27 July 1940, NA FD 1/5885.

[15] A. Drury to D. Landsborough Thomson, 18 December 1940, NA FD 1/5885.

[16] Within six months of its first edition, *Picture Post* boasted a print run of over a million copies per week; two months later, the figure was 1,350,000 (Bromley 1999: 105; Cameron 1967: 149; Hall 1972: 73).

[17] On the *Daily Mirror*'s pioneering use of graphic devices, see Cudlipp (1953: 69-77).

[18] *Picture Post*, 17 August 1940: 10.

[19] Ibid.: 27.

[20] Ibid.

[21] Ibid.: 21.

[22] All quotations from Janet Vaughan, 'Publicity and propaganda', WL GC/186/2.

[23] Established in 1937 by Tom Harrisson, an anthropologist, and Charles Madge, a reporter for the *Daily Mirror*, Mass Observation was a British social research organization committed to the anthropology of everyday life. During the Second World War it recruited panellists to keep diaries and complete directives, and produced commentaries on various aspects of civilian life (Summerfield 1985).

[24] Fantus cited 'the antepartum clinic' as a major source for the blood bank, and one most evocative of its philosophy: 'Here the blood bank function expresses itself most simply' (1937: 129).

[25] M. Maizels to A. Drury, 15 January 1942, NA FD 1/5885.

[26] Mass Observation File Report 290, June 1940.

[27] *LifeBlood*: 6.

[28] Ibid.

[29] Ibid.: 7.

[30] Ibid.

[31] Ibid.: 3, my emphasis.

[32] Ibid.: 29-30, my emphasis.

[33] Ibid.: 30.

[34] S.F. Wilkinson to depot directors, 7 October 1943, WL GC/107/1.

[35] The title of the introductory chapter; others included 'Transfusion: a life-saving service' and 'The gift works miracles'.

[36] Synopsis of book on blood transfusion, from S.F. Wilkinson to A. Drury, 7 October 1943, WL GC/107/1.

[37] 'The gift in the battle line', draft, 1943, WL GC/107/1.

[38] Synopsis of book on blood transfusion, 7 October 1943: 4, WL GC/107/1.

[39] *LifeBlood*: 23.

REFERENCES

ANDERSON, B. 2006 [1983]. *Imagined communities: reflections on the origin and spread of nationalism* (Second edition). London: Verso.

ARROW, K. 1972. Gifts and exchanges. *Philosophy & Public Affairs* **1**, 343-62.

BARTLETT, F.C. 1941. *Political propaganda*. Cambridge: University Press.

BARTON, F.E. 1941. The management of a blood bank at the Massachusetts Memorial hospitals. *The New England Journal of Medicine* **225**: 5, 176-9.

BAUMAN, Z. 2000 [1989]. *Modernity and the Holocaust*. Cambridge: Polity.

BROMLEY, M. 1999. Was it the Mirror wot won it? The development of the tabloid press during the Second World War. In *Millions like us: British culture in the Second World War* (eds) N. Hayes & J. Hill, 93-124. Liverpool: University Press.

CALDER, A. 1991. *The myth of the Blitz*. London: Cape.

CAMERON, J. 1967. *Point of departure: an attempt at autobiography*. New York: McGraw-Hill.

CARRUTHERS, S.L. 1990. 'Manning the factories': propaganda and policy on the employment of women, 1939-1947. *History* **75**, 232-56.

————— 2000. *The media at war: communication and conflict in the twentieth century*. London: Palgrave Macmillan.

COLLINI, S. 1979. *Liberalism and sociology: L.T. Hobhouse and political argument in England, 1880-1915*. Cambridge: University Press.

CONI, N. 2007. *Medicine and warfare: Spain, 1936-1939*. London: Routledge.

COPEMAN, J. 2005. Veinglory: exploring processes of blood transfer between persons. *Journal of the Royal Anthropological Institute* (N.S.) **11**, 465-85.

CRILE, G. 1907. The technique of direct transfusion of blood. *Annals of Surgery* **46**, 329-32.

CUDLIPP, H. 1953. *Publish and be damned! The astonishing story of the Daily Mirror*. London: A. Dakers.

ELLIOTT, G.A., R.G. MACFARLANE & J. VAUGHAN 1939. The use of stored blood for transfusion. *The Lancet*, 18 February, 384-7.

FANTUS, B. 1937. The therapy of the Cook County Hospital. *Journal of the American Medical Association* **109: 2**, 128-31.

FONTAINE, P. 2002. Blood, politics and social science: Richard Titmuss and the Institute of Economic Affairs, 1957-1973. *Isis* **93**, 401-34.

GINZBURG, C. 1994. Killing a Chinese Mandarin: the moral implications of distance. *Critical Inquiry* **21: 1**, 46-60.

GUNSON, H. & H. DODSWORTH 1996. Fifty years of blood transfusion. *Transfusion Medicine* **6**, 1-88.

HALL, S. 1972. The social eye of *Picture Post*. *Working Papers in Cultural Studies* **2**, 71-120.

HARRIS, J. 1992. Political thought and the welfare state 1870-1940: an intellectual framework for British social policy. *Past and Present* **135**, 116-41.

HARRISSON, T. 1943. *War factory*. London: Victor Gollancz.

HEALY, K. 2006. *Last best gifts: altruism and the market for human blood and organs*. Chicago: University Press.

HORSLEY RIDDELL, V. 1939. *Blood transfusion*. Oxford: University Press.

KERSHAW, I. 2002 [1983]. *Popular opinion and political dissent in the Third Reich: Bavaria 1933-1945*. Oxford: Clarendon Press.

KEYNES, G. 1922. *Blood transfusion*. London: H. Frowde; Hodder & Stoughton.

————— 1949. The history of blood transfusion. In *Blood transfusion* (ed.) G. Keynes, 1-40. Bristol: John Wright & Sons.

LACHS, J. 1981. *Responsibility and the individual in modern society*. Brighton: Harvester.

LEDERER, S. 2008. *Flesh and blood: organ transplantation and blood transfusion in twentieth-century America*. Oxford: University Press.

LEWIS, J. 1999. The voluntary sector in the mixed economy of welfare. In *Before Beveridge: welfare before the welfare state* (ed.) D. Gladstone, 10-17. London: IEA Health and Welfare Unit.

LEWISOHN, R. 1915. A new and greatly simplified method of blood transfusion. *Medical Records* **87**, 141-2.

————— 1924. The Citrate method of blood transfusion after ten years: a retrospect. *The Boston Medical and Surgical Journal* **190**, 733-42.

MACKAY, R. 2002. *Half the battle: civilian morale in Britain during the Second World War*. Manchester: University Press.

MALUF, N. 1954. History of blood transfusion. *Journal of the History of Medicine* **9**, 59-107.

MASS OBSERVATION 1941. *Home propaganda*. London: Advertising Service Guild.

MAUSS, M. 2010 [1925]. *The gift: the form and reason for exchange in archaic societies*, trans. W.D. Halls. London: Routledge.

MIRZOEFF, N. 1999. *An introduction to visual culture*. London: Routledge.

MURRAY, T.H. 1990. The poisoned gift: AIDS and blood. *The Milbank Quarterly* **68**, 205-25.

NOAKES, L. 2006. *Women in the British Army: war and the gentle sex, 1907-1948*. London: Routledge.

OLIVER, P. 1933. The technique of blood transfusion. *Journal of State Medicine* **41**, 699-729.

O'SULLIVAN, T. 1995. Listening through: the wireless and World War Two. In *War culture: social change and changing experience in World War Two Britain* (eds) P. Kirkham & D. Thoms, 173-85. London: Lawrence & Wishart.

PARRY, J. 1986. *The gift*, the Indian gift and 'the Indian gift'. *Man* (N.S.) **21**, 453-73.

PELIS, K. 2007. 'A band of lunatics down Camberwell way': Percy Oliver and voluntary blood donation in interwar Britain. In *Medicine, madness and social history: essays in honour of Roy Porter* (eds) R. Bivins & J.V. Picktone, 148-60. London: Palgrave Macmillan.

RAVITCH, M.M. 1940. The blood bank of the Johns Hopkins hospital. *The Journal of the American Medical Association* **115: 3**, 171–8.

RICKARDS, M. 1971. *The rise and fall of the poster*. London: David & Charles.

ROGERSON, S. 1938. *Propaganda in the next war*. London. G. Bles.

ROSE, S. 2003. *Which people's war? National identity and citizenship in wartime Britain, 1939-1945*. Oxford: University Press.

SCHNEIDER, W.H. 2003. Blood transfusion between the wars. *Journal of the History of Medicine* **58**, 187-224.

SCHWARTZ, J. 1999. Blood and altruism: Richard M. Titmuss' criticism on the commercialization of blood. *The Public Interest* **36**, 30-43.

SIMMEL, G. 1950 [1908]. The stranger. In *The sociology of Georg Simmel* (ed.) K.H. Wolff, 185-9. Glencoe, Ill.: Free Press.

STARR, D. 1998. *Blood: an epic history of medicine and commerce*. New York: Knopf.

SUMMERFIELD, P. 1985. Mass Observation: social research or social movement? *Journal of Contemporary History* **20**, 439-52.

TAYLOR, J. 1991. *War photography: realism in the British press*. London: Routledge.

TAYLOR, P.M. 2003. Propaganda. In *The origins of World War Two: the debate continues* (eds) R. Boyce & J.A. Maiolom, 342-59. London: Palgrave Macmillan.

TITMUSS, R. 1997 [1970]. *The gift relationship: from human blood to social policy*. London: The New Press.

VAUGHAN, J. 1939. Blood transfusion. *British Medical Journal*, 6 May, 933-6.

————— 1942. Blood transfusion. *British Medical Journal*, 4 July, 19-21.

WAIN, S.L. 1984. The controversy of unmodified versus citrated blood transfusion in the early 20th century. *Transfusion* **24**, 404-7.

WALDBY, C. & R. MITCHELL 2006. *Tissue economies: blood, organs, and cell lines in late capitalism*. Durham, N.C.: Duke University Press.

WEBSTER, W. 2005. *Englishness and empire 1939-1965*. Oxford: University Press.

6

Bloodlines: blood types, identity, and association in twentieth-century America

Susan E. Lederer *University of Wisconsin-Madison*

In 1900 the Austrian immunologist Karl Landsteiner established that human blood was more than a simple biologically undifferentiated fluid. Through systematic mixing of the blood cells and sera of different individuals, Landsteiner discovered that human blood could be effectively divided into three distinctive groups based on the ways in which the cells reacted to the serum from other individuals. Initially labelled groups A, B, and C (the original name for the group in which red blood cells failed to clump or agglutinate to the sera of either of the first two groups), the groups later expanded to four when Landsteiner's colleagues Alfred von Decastello and Adriano Sturli repeated his experiments, expanded the pool of participants, and added the much rarer blood group AB (the group containing both A and B proteins on the surface of the red blood cell).[1] Landsteiner's discovery of ABO blood groups, for which he received the Nobel Prize in Medicine or Physiology in 1930, proved important for clinical medicine (both blood transfusion and organ transplantation), for forensic science (in criminal cases, to establish blood at a crime scene as human rather than animal and to differentiate blood of different human beings), and for legal determinations of paternity (and, in cases of 'mixed-baby mishaps' in hospitals, of maternity).

The ability to distinguish the blood of individual human beings also provided another index of individuality, a new, scientific method to separate oneself from friends and family, as well as a modern, technological means to align oneself in new ways with different people. The historical scholarship on the discovery and utility of the blood groups seldom takes up the question of what individual Americans did with the information concerning the newly acquired knowledge of blood types, and how such information influenced notions of identity and association (Schneider 1996). What did such knowledge represent to a mother, for example, who learned that she could not donate blood to her own child because they possessed different blood types? How did couples come to understand a new scientific incompatibility based on the possession of the presence and absence of Rh-factors in their blood that meant that, to some legislators and physicians, in order to prevent the birth of 'defective' offspring, they should not marry? This chapter analyses the

Blood: Will Out: Essays on Liquid Transfers and Flows, First Edition. Edited by Janet Carsten. © 2013 Royal Anthropological Institute of Great Britain & Ireland. Published 2013 by John Wiley & Sons Ltd.

dissemination of blood types into American popular discussions and popular culture through three highly publicized engagements with blood type science: hospital 'baby-switching' cases; disputes over paternity, including the sensational legal battle between Charlie Chaplin and actress Joan Berry over the paternity of Berry's daughter; and the fetishization of 'rare blood', including the advent in the early 1960s of 'rare blood clubs', for individuals whose blood types were statistically uncommon in American society. More recently, the diffusion of blood types into American culture has offered new avenues for association and identity through enthusiasm for the 'blood type diet' and through web-based affiliations based on blood type designations (D'Adamo 1996).

The idea that blood was not a simple uniform fluid identical in human beings and different species was not new in the twentieth century. When blood transfusion was first introduced in the seventeenth century, it entailed the movement of blood between animals (chiefly lambs, dogs, and calves) and from animals into humans. These seventeenth-century researchers and natural philosophers assumed that individual vital qualities could be transferred via blood from one individual to another (Samuel Pepys's famous musings about transfusing the blood of a Quaker into the Archbishop of Canterbury), and they fretted over the quantity of blood moved between bodies (they were especially concerned about plethora, or superabundance of blood). But they did not recognize material differences in the substance of blood, either human, dog, lamb, or other animal. In the early nineteenth century, when English obstetrician James Blundell first introduced the practice of using human blood for transfusion, he offered an early biological rationale for only using human blood in transfusing human beings, namely that the blood of animals differed from that of humans. Following the experiments of Barbados physician John Leacock, who found that dogs transfused with blood from lambs seldom survived, Blundell performed a series of experiments on dogs which similarly suggested the danger of crossing the species line in transfusion. Blundell did not minimize the practical reasons for using human blood to transfuse his patients. Transfusion with animal blood, he explained, necessarily entailed 'the presence of some animal in the bed-chamber'. In cases of emergency, where could such animal sources of blood be found? 'A dog', Blundell reflected, 'it is true, might have come when you whistled, but the animal is small; a calf, or sheep, might, to some, have appeared fitter for the purpose; but then, it could run not upstairs' (1834: 264). Fortunately for the physician, husbands, especially those of birthing women, were often found in close proximity to the event and could be readily tapped for as a blood source for their wives who experienced haemorrhaging during childbirth (Pelis 1999). Despite the innovative use of human blood to transfuse human patients, however, the technical problems in transfusion, especially clotting when blood was exposed to air, diminished medical interest in performing the technique.

In the first decade of the twentieth century, some of these obstacles to efficient movement of blood between human bodies were overcome through surgical innovation. In 1905, Cleveland surgeon George W. Crile adapted newly available surgical techniques for joining blood vessels end to end, enabling him to perform a series of direct transfusions between patients and donors.[2] Crile's textbook *Hemorrhage and transfusion* credited the Chicago pathologist Ludwig Hektoen with confirming the findings of Landsteiner, Decastello, and Sturli that human blood could be separated into three groups, according to the ways it reacted to the sera (Crile 1909: 318).[3] Crile did not mention the independent discovery of the four major blood groups by other researchers. Both the Czech physician Jan Jansky in 1907 and Johns Hopkins physician Henry L. Moss in 1910 separated human blood into four groups, and offered competing and conflicting nomenclature for them. The lack of consistency in referring to different blood types would continue for decades, despite efforts by expert committees, including the Society of American Bacteriologists and the National Research Council, to standardize the classification. To avoid confusions, many American hospitals continued to use all three classifications into the 1940s (Lederer 2008).[4]

The interest in the distinctive character of blood encouraged the search for other blood-borne differences in human beings, including a long-sought biological test to distinguish bloods from individuals of different races. In 1907, German physician Carl Bruck was the first to claim that he could demonstrate specific differences between human blood and that of the higher apes; he also claimed that that he could reliably distinguish the blood of a Caucasian from that of a Negro, a Malayan, a Chinese, and an Arab. Although physicians at Harvard Medical School and the Philippine Bureau of Science were unable to corroborate Bruck's findings, this did not dissuade other physicians from claiming success at determining whether a drop of dried blood came from 'the body of an Oriental, a negro, or a white man' (*New York Times* 1912: 6; see also FitzGerald 1909; Marshall & Teague 1908). Even though *Hygeia* (1926), a medical journal produced by the American Medical Association, sought to convince its intended lay readers that all human beings possessed the same four types of blood, the medical literature continued to foster enthusiasm that definitive racialized tests, including one to distinguish the blood of Gentiles from Jews, would one day be found. Even as Landsteiner challenged the numerous claims about specific racial differences in human blood, the pioneer of blood grouping reserved the possibility that such differences would be detected in the future. Despite the differences between human blood and the blood of non-human primates, Landsteiner, writing with colleague C. Philip Miller, insisted:

> [I]f serological differences do exist between the bloods of white men and American negroes – no longer a pure race – they are much smaller than those between man and the anthropoid apes. So far we have been unable to demonstrate any characteristic difference. It's not impossible, however, that slight difference might be found if individuals of several races preferably of pure blood were carefully studied by this method in all of its modifications (Landsteiner & Miller 1925: 848).

Nearly twenty years later, serologist Alexander Wiener, a co-discoverer of the Rh factor with Landsteiner, his mentor, echoed this assessment about the repeated failures to produce a serum that could distinguish blood from individuals of different races. 'By means of serological tests, the proteins and cells of animals of any species can be differentiated, as a rule, from those of animals belonging to other species', Wiener observed in 1943, but 'attempts to produce sera which would serve to differentiate bloods of different races particularly in the human species have been unsuccessful' (1943: 295).

Landsteiner's work established that human blood could be differentiated biochemically, but he did not pursue the clinical significance of this finding. As a laboratory worker, he did not treat patients. The surgeons who did transfuse blood initially played little heed to the potential adverse consequences on the red blood cell of mixing human blood containing different proteins. In 1907, Hektoen suggested that careful selection of a blood donor could avert dangerous complications in transfusion (Hektoen 1907). The same year, two Philadelphia physicians, William Pepper and Verner Nisbet, reported the death of a patient who had undergone surgical transfusion. After receiving blood from his wife and his brother-in-law, Pepper's patient soon began to experience distress. He developed jaundice, his urine became bloody, and haemorrhages appeared under his skin, suggesting that his blood had reacted badly with the blood he had received. After the patient's death, his physicians warned that the safety of moving blood from one normal individual into another could no longer be assumed; they advised caution until 'knowledge of the hemolytic action of different sera is more exact' (Pepper & Nisbet 1907: 389). In the United States this more exact knowledge of serological reactions would come in the wake of the First World War, when access to the right chemical reagents and skilled technicians made results more reliable.

Some of the increased understanding here related to the stability of the blood types. One of the most vexing issues was the compatibility of maternal and infant blood. As Henry Feinblatt noted in 1926, mistakes about blood groups and blood compatibility abounded. 'It has often been alleged', the Brooklyn clinician wrote, 'that, in the case of an infant, the mother may safely be used as the donor without preliminary compatibility tests'. However, '[r]eliance on the assumption that the mother and child are necessarily compatible may lead to disaster under certain circumstances' (1926: 31). Many physicians apparently assumed that babies did not possess a blood type, so they could in fact receive blood from any available donor. As some physicians noted, the agglutinins that determined blood group were not generally present in an infant's blood at birth or in the first month of life. Although they agreed that the percentage of children with fixed blood group increased with age, physicians disputed the age at which the blood group was established in all children. Whereas Feinblatt, among others, claimed that by age 2 all children had a fixed blood group, others insisted the question was only settled when the child turned 10 years of age. Nevertheless, despite the lack of expert consensus about the stability of the blood groups, science writers, beginning in the early 1920s, began to feature information about blood types in the lay press and other mass media.

Since Crile's pioneering efforts at surgical transfusion in the first decade of the twentieth century, reporters had followed transfusions with enthusiasm. The sacrificial nature of the blood donation (by a friend, a family member, a stranger) and the drama of the transfusion (the return of a rosy colour to a pallid, dying patient) had great appeal; thousands of short accounts of donor-recipient relations appeared in American newspapers. In the mid-1920s, these accounts first began to include reference to an individual possessing a particular type of blood. Initially, reporters mentioned that individuals shared the same blood type, without specifying which type the individual possessed. In 1926, newspapers reported how one Pennsylvania war veteran succumbed to pernicious anaemia after receiving some 107 transfusions. In his first forty transfusions, four of his brothers – 'who possessed the same blood type' – supplied the blood. When more was needed, advertisements and radio announcements brought other donors with the necessary blood type to the hospital (*New York Times* 1926). Two years later, when an article in *Popular Science Monthly* described the 'extraordinary career' of professional blood donor Thomas Kane, the author explained that transfusion required 'quality blood' from a donor whose blood had to match that of the recipient. Kane was type 2, the article noted, and his blood was 'typed up' at hospital laboratories and kept on file.

Popular attention to blood types and blood-based differences received an enormous boost from the extraordinary attention to hospital 'baby-switching' cases. In the twentieth century, as childbirth increasingly moved from the home to the hospital, one unanticipated outcome was the potential for giving the wrong baby to the wrong parents. In busy hospitals where multiple births occurred on the same day, ensuring that the right baby was delivered by nurses to the right mother confounded the staff. Hospitals attempted to develop fool-proof methods to guarantee that mothers received their own child from the nursery and not someone else's infant. 'There are bracelets around tiny wrists, adhesive labels on wee satiny backs', explained M.M. Lukes (1927). 'Babies are labeled, tagged, fingerprinted, adorned with lettered necklaces until they look more Christmas parcel post or wee criminals under surveillance than small persons designed to be mothers' darlings'. Still, mix-ups occurred, attracting intense media scrutiny. Between 1920 and 1930, when a mix-up between two infants born on the same day in the same Chicago hospital generated enormous interest in the potential utility of blood science to resolve the question of both maternity and paternity, some seventeen pairs of distraught parents had appeared in American courts to ensure that they had received the right baby.

The Bamberger-Watkins case began when, two weeks after giving birth in the hospital on 30 June 1930, Mrs William Watkins bathed her baby at home and discovered on his back a small piece of plaster on which the name Bamberger was written. Believing they had received the wrong infant, the Watkins contacted their doctor, launched an investigation, and began litigation against the Bambergers to ensure that they received the correct infant. Arnold Kegel, Health Commissioner of Chicago, convened a panel of medical and scientific experts to determine which infant boy belonged to which parents. Although Kegel identified anthropology as his 'chief hope' in resolving the parentage issue through differentiation of the dolichocephalic skulls of the Watkins from the brachycephalic skulls of the Bambergers, he also invited experts in dermatology, psychiatry, ophthalmology, and pathology to advise about the babies. According to reporters from the *Los Angeles Times* (1930), three of the four parents (both Watkins and Mrs Bamberger) possessed group IV blood, which made it difficult to resolve the parentage issue. Later reports about the baby mix-up indicated that Hamilton Fishback, the pathologist who performed the blood grouping tests on the two sets of parents and their children, found that Baby Bamberger was group IV and Baby Watkins group II. As reporter Grace Robinson explained to her readers, because Mrs Bamberger had group IV blood and Mr Bamberger group I, they could not be the parents of the infant labelled Baby Boy Bamberger: '[B]oth Watkins and Mrs Watkins were group IV, group IV people can't have anything but a group IV child. (So it begins to work out like a game of solitaire) there is no place to put the Bamberger baby except with the Watkins' (Robinson 1930: 42). Under court orders, the Bambergers and the Watkins exchanged the babies they had brought home from the hospital, but not before a number of expectant Chicago parents cancelled their plans for a hospital birth.[5] The case brought considerable attention to the existence and meaning of the blood groups and how they could be used to establish both maternity and paternity in cases of hospital errors (*New York Times* 1930).

Disputes over paternity reinforced popular knowledge of blood groups. In American courts, blood grouping to determine paternity was seldom used before 1934 (Wiener 1943). Following the failure to obtain blood in a case of disputed parentage, the New York state legislature in 1935 enacted laws to compel individuals in such disputes to furnish blood for testing. The Wisconsin legislature followed suit; by 1949, five other states had adopted similar legislation to resolve both issues of paternity and responsibility to provide financial support for the child.[6] Not all states accepted the validity of blood tests, but they none the less fostered information about different blood groups and the potential to exclude individuals as fathers. In 1946, in one of the most sensationalized cases, actress Joan Berry identified celebrity Charlie Chaplin as the father of her child. Using blood grouping evidence, Chaplin's attorneys and experts argued that the actor could not have been the father (he was group O, the mother group A, and the child group B). Despite medical consensus that Chaplin could not have fathered Berry's daughter, the California courts rejected Chaplin's claims and charged him with the responsibility to provide for the child (Regan 1949).[7]

In establishing Chaplin's non-paternity of the Berry child (on scientific if not legal grounds), physicians had more information about biochemical differences in human blood. After he took a position at the Rockefeller Institute for Medical Research, Landsteiner continued to pursue his work on the blood types. In 1927, he and physician Philip Levine described another system of blood groups, which they called the M, N, and P system. This blood group system was observed when they injected rabbits with human red blood cells and then tested the human red blood cells with the antibodies made in the rabbit's body. Chaplin's blood possessed the MN factors; Berry and her daughter possessed the N factors, offering further scientific evidence, according to blood experts, that Chaplin was not the father of Berry's child. Despite this scientific evidence, American courts preferred to operate on the earlier relational understanding of paternity rather than the biological, which ensured that children of married women would not be bastardized by the legal system (Rudavsky 1999).

Landsteiner had a long-standing interest in the evolution of blood types in the anthropoid apes and monkeys and their similarities to human blood. In 1940, working with Alexander Wiener, Landsteiner described a new blood factor created by injecting rabbits and guinea pigs with the red blood cells of rhesus monkeys. This antibody reacted strongly when mixed with the blood of most human beings. They named this the Rh factor for the Rhesus monkeys that supplied the initial bloods. Discovery of the Rh factor promised to resolve one of the ongoing mysteries in blood transfusion: why did some recipients experience distress, discomfort, and even death despite the fact that they received the 'right type' of blood?

The Rh factor proved enormously significant in resolving another clinical puzzle that confronted mothers and obstetricians. This puzzle concerned the disease known as erthyroblastosis fetalis, or haemolytic disease of the newborn. This condition occurred when a mother's blood was incompatible with the blood of her foetus. Physicians noted that women who had experienced stillbirths or with other children who developed the disease were more likely to develop the condition in subsequent pregnancies. When tested for the presence of the Rh factor, physicians learned that many of these mothers were Rh negative, their babies were Rh positive, and the mother's immune system was defending itself against this foreign presence (Lederer 2008).

How could this knowledge be mobilized to save American babies? One way to prevent Rh incompatibility in childbirth was to ensure that Rh-incompatible couples did not marry and have children. Legislators in Illinois and New York moved swiftly to act on the newly discovered Rh factor and its potential harms. In 1945, the Illinois legislature entertained a bill to require prospective marital partners to undergo a blood test to ascertain whether they had 'conflicting blood types' (Rh factor). In 1947, the New York legislature considered a bill making the test for a 'negative Rh factor in the blood mandatory of married couples' (*New York Times* 1947). Presumably armed with this knowledge, couples could decide not to marry and to seek another marital partner whose blood would be compatible. The following year, New York Republican Senator Thomas Desmond sponsored a bill to require Rh blood tests in all pregnancies. In 1949, the New York State Health Department began providing a line on all New York birth certificates to indicate that a Rh blood test had been performed. The same year the New York legislature once again considered a bill to require Rh factor blood tests in pregnancy cases (*New York Times* 1949).

Preventing the marriages of Rh-incompatible men and women was one way to avert miscarriages, stillbirths, and diseased infants. Physicians seeking to aid infertile couples via artificial insemination chose another means: explicitly selecting for Rh compatibility between donor and recipient. In the 1940s, in the first flush of artificial insemination, physicians discussed the importance of insuring Rh compatibility in order to maximize the chances for success in treating their infertile patients. By 1947, the Board of Health of the City of New York enacted regulations which required blood testing for the Rh factor before insemination, and also stipulated that physicians treating an Rh-negative woman for infertility should use only semen 'from a donor of seminal fluid whose blood is also negative for this factor' (*Journal of the American Medical Association* 1949). This information about the Rh factor was not limited to medical professionals. As science writer Hannah Lees (1946) cheerfully informed her readers in *Colliers* magazine,

> [N]ow that we have learned to test people for the Rh factor, we are beginning to learn why so many women have long records of spontaneous abortion, stillbirths and children dying in infancy. The use of artificial insemination is a pretty obvious answer for conflicting Rh couples who feel they simply must have more children.

One facet of the diffusion of biochemical differences in human blood was the recognition that some bloods were, to paraphrase George Orwell, more equal than others: that is, were more valuable in clinical settings because of their relative scarcity. By the end of the First World War, physicians Ludwik and Hanna Hirszfeld had established that the blood groups were not evenly distributed across national or ethnic groups (Hirszfeld & Balińska 2010). In the United States, for example, blood types I and II (Jansky system) were far more common than III and IV (in the ABO system, B and AB). In the 1930s, stories about people needing rare types of blood reinforced the idea that some blood groups were special. In November 1937, the *New York Times* reported how a 28-year-old Michigan man suffering from a severe streptococcal infection needed blood donors. An urgent appeal from the man's mother brought more than 2,000 potential volunteers to the hospital, but the man's doctor informed the reporter that only 'one in a thousand volunteers have the rare type of blood (type 4)' needed for the transfusion (*New York Times* 1937). A year later, the newspaper reported that a Brooklyn man died despite receiving three blood transfusions. 'Because of the difficulty in getting the right type of blood, type 4', doctors at Beth-El Hospital asked the police to broadcast an appeal for donors (*New York Times* 1938). The same year, the Baltimore Sun publicized an urgent appeal for volunteer blood donors to provide blood for a dangerously ill woman with 'the rare type', namely 'International AB, also known as Moss No. 1 and Jansky No. 4' (*Baltimore Sun* 1938).

Popular novelists, who began incorporating the knowledge about differences in human blood, encouraged the fetishization of rare blood groups. When novelist Carlton Williams invoked blood types in the plot of *Emergency nurse* (1940), blood type AB, 'the rare one', assumed prominence. A character in the novel who possesses the rare blood type desperately needs a transfusion. With no time to locate an outside donor, the surgeon is preparing to substitute a saline infusion when a young nurse volunteers that she, in fact, has blood type AB. 'Guess we all know our type these days', the nurse explains (Williams 1940: 88). (And in one of those coincidences beloved by sentimental novelists, after the patient learns that she has received the nurse's blood, she is moved to confess that she knew that it was her own daughter, not the young nurse accused of the crime, who stole money from the hospital!)

Knowing one's blood type became easier in the 1940s because of the war effort. Beginning in 1939, the United States Armed Services began including blood group information on dog tags for soldiers. As part of the American Red Cross's campaign to procure blood for the Armed Forces, civilians in cities and towns across the United States lined up to donate blood. When they did, they frequently received a wallet-sized card that identified their blood group. In 1944, for example, the Honolulu Peacetime Blood Plasma Bank issued the card shown in Figure 6.1, which identified the donor by name, address, and blood type. On the reverse side of the card, the bank explicitly insisted 'blood from all races equally good'. The Honolulu bank referred to the decision two years earlier on the part of the American Red Cross to refuse African American blood donors from the blood plasma collection efforts. The Red Cross openly acknowledged that their reasons for such refusal were 'social', not scientific. At the behest of such professional organizations as the National Association for the Advancement of Colored People, the National Medical Association, and the American Medical Association and the urging of such notable Americans as First Lady Eleanor Roosevelt, the Red Cross rescinded the decision to refuse donations from African Americans. For social reasons, the organization labelled blood from black donors N (for Negro) or AA (for African American), demonstrating that social typologies trumped scientific typologies (Lederer 1998).

In the post-war period, knowing one's blood type also reflected concerns about the possibility of an atomic attack on an American city. Following the revelation in 1949 that the Soviet Union had tested an atomic weapon, American civil defence advocates called for mass typing of the blood of civilians. In the same way that the blood type of a soldier was recorded on his dog tag, organizations such as the Public Health Service's Chronic Disease Division and civil defence planners suggested that a civilian's blood type be recorded, along with the name and address, on his dog tag. In 1950, the veterans' organization AMVETS launched a drive to distribute 150 million 'atomic radiation-resistant plastic tags' by presenting President Harry Truman (type O) with his own civilian

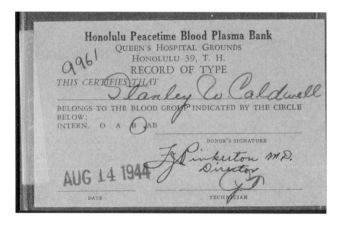

Figure 6.1. Blood donor card, with blood group identified, from the Honolulu Peacetime Blood Plasma Bank. (In author's possession. Photo by the author.)

defence tag. The organization awarded the second tag to actress Doris Day as part of its effort to persuade Americans to wear such tags in order to confront 'the tremendous needs of whole blood that would follow in the wake of atomic bombing' (*New York Times* 1950).

Individual cities and states adopted their own programmes for mass typing and identifying tags. In August 1950, officials of the Pennsylvania State Civilian Defense Office announced plans to blood-type every resident in their state. In the winter of 1950-1, the Civil Defense Office conducted a feasibility study of mass blood-typing in Jackson, Michigan, where 45 per cent of the residents were typed and given dog tags within eighty days. A survey of some 665 Jackson residents indicated that 72 per cent carried these identifications with them. By December 1952, the Civil Defense Office had blood-typed more than 1.5 million Michigan residents. Each person received a small plastic tag with blood type and Rh factor, which was also colour coded so that the blood type could be identified even if the tag was burned (Wolf & Laumann 2008).

Concern that dog tags with blood type information could be lost or separated from the body prompted a search for a more permanent recording of blood group, namely by tattooing the information on the body of the individual. Physicians from the Atomic Energy Commission, the New York State Medical Board, and the Chicago Medical Society called for mass tattooing of blood types either on the wrist or under the arm. The underarm area was chosen for the tattoo mark rather than the arms or legs, Chicago physician Andrew C. Ivy explained to a reporter from the *Chicago Tribune*, because arms and legs 'might be blown off by the atomic explosion'. Ivy's plan called for the fabrication of special steel dies approximately 3/8 inch in diameter fitted in electrically driven tattooing instruments, and for every Chicagoan to undergo the 'virtually painless procedure' at their own expense. A prominent medical educator, Ivy had served as a consultant to the American prosecutors in the Nuremberg Medical Trial in 1946, but it remains unknown whether Ivy knew that during the Second World World War members of the Waffen SS were required to have their blood type tattooed under their left arm (Gibbons 1950).

The Chicago plan was not implemented. But the project of tattooing blood types was undertaken in Indiana and Utah. In northern Indiana, Operation Tat-Type was adopted. Using a Burgess Vibratool instrument with thirty to fifty needles and an antiseptic ink, technicians tattooed the blood type and Rh factor on the chest of some 1,000 residents at the county fair. By December, 15,000 residents had been typed and 60 per cent had received tattoos. Encouraged by this response, the local medical society sponsored a tat-typing programme for all schoolchildren in Lake County, Indiana. The programme started in January 1952 with children at five elementary schools, then moved to the area high schools. In August 1950, two Utah physicians led the civil defence plan to type and tattoo residents. Speaking to Logan Rotarians, Dr Omar Budge explained the life-saving advantages of having every person's blood tested and the type of his or blood recorded on the person's skin by a simple tattooing process. He stressed the importance of a prompt and willing response on the part of every citizen to the blood-testing programme, and to every other call made by civil defence authorities, as a patriotic duty. Because tattooing represented a desecration of the human body and a violation of Mormon doctrine, creating a 'permanent imprint of blood type and factor in the skin under the left arm', it required special dispensation from Mormon leaders (Conelrad.com n.d.).

The diffusion of blood type information as part of the massive medical preparation for an atomic attack on an American city existed alongside interest in rare blood. Even as increasing numbers of Americans learned their own blood type, they learned that some types were especially rare, including the blood types AB negative and O negative. When donors of these blood types were needed, special appeals over radio and television reinforced the special status of these rare bloods. To ease the problems for people needing such blood, a new organization was founded in 1959. The National Rare Blood Club, affiliated with the fraternal order of the Knights of Pythias, involved people who mostly lacked the Rh antigen (A negative, B negative, O negative, AB negative, and AB positive). By 1961, the club boasted more than 900 members, including teachers, businessmen, machinists, clerks, housewives, editors, secretaries, physicians, and nurses. Although some of the club members supplied blood out of self-interest and self-preservation, most reported that they donated blood out of desire to help others. 'Generally they feel they own something of unusual value and "it's a crime to keep it to ourselves" ', explained journalist Theodore Irwin (1961), who also noted the pride club members experienced in being a member of 'medicine's "most exclusive" club'. Members of the Rare Blood Club did not accept money for their donations; funds from the group were available for those who lost a day's wages when they donated blood. In 1968, the club claimed more than 5,500 members aged 18-59 years with the six rare blood types, now including the addition of B positive blood. By this time, the self-styled 'raries' had donated more than 15,000 pints of their blood, buoyed by a sense of their special value to medicine (Rogers 1968).

In the first six decades of the twentieth century, scientific information about bio-chemical and immunological differences in human blood created new opportunities for differentiation and valorization. The discovery of blood types offered new ways to discriminate against others and novel means of affiliation. At first the discovery that blood of humans could be distinguished was a scientific curiosity. This information became crucial to the safe movement of blood between bodies and the success of blood transfusion in the twentieth century. But the ability to distinguish the blood of human beings also advanced other social goals, especially the desire for a definitive test of racial difference and distinction. There has been little attention to the cultural implications of scientific information about the individuality of blood. Kath Weston (2001) is exceptional for her work on the racial and class implications of sharing blood between the bodies of dissimilar people. This paper, too, aims to highlight the ways in which scientific characterization influenced identity politics and self-assessment in relation to others. By examining the trajectories of blood-inscribed identification in cases of disputed maternity, paternity, and Cold War medical preparations, it suggests that the historically contingent meaning of difference and discrimination can be rewritten, tattooed, and even forgotten.

NOTES

[1] In 1902, Decastello and Sturli identified the fourth blood group, AB, which causes agglutination of the red blood cells of both groups A and B.

[2] These direct transfusions required an incision on the donor to expose the blood vessel and a similar incision on the recipient; the exposed vessels were then sewn together for a period of time ranging from 8 to 58 minutes.

[3] Crile seemed to overlook the fact that Decastello and Sturli had identified a fourth group (what would become known as the AB group).

[4] Perhaps not surprisingly, Landsteiner, who emigrated to the United States in 1922 and joined the staff of the Rockefeller Institute, recommended that the competing systems of Roman numerals in the Jansky and Moss systems be abandoned in place of the designations A, B, AB, and O. This 'international classification' would become the standard.

[5] For other parents declining hospital birth to ensure no 'mixed baby', see *Atlanta Constitution* (1920).

[6] Wisconsin, Maine, Ohio, New Jersey, South Dakota, and Maryland (Regan 1949: 258).

[7] See *Berry* v. *Chaplin*, 74 Cal. App. 2d 652, 169 P.2d 442 (1946). Here the court held that although the scientific evidence of the blood tests conclusively established that Chaplin could not have been the father, the jury was not bound to accept this scientifically immutable fact and could find that the plaintiff had established paternity. To support the jury's fact-finding, the court noted that Chaplin had been required to stand in front of the jury next to the plaintiff and her child, so as to allow a visual comparison.

REFERENCES

ATLANTA CONSTITUTION 1920. Will scientific blood test reveal identity of baby? 12 September, 3A.

BALTIMORE SUN 1938. Red Cross seeks rare blood type for woman who is seriously ill. 9 December, 11.

BLUNDELL, J. 1834. *The principles and practice of obstetricy, as at present taught.* Washington, D.C.: D. Green.

CONELRAD.COM n.d. Atomic secrets: atomic tattoo (available on-line: *http://www.conelrad.com/atomicsecrets/secrets.php?secrets=11*, accessed 17 January 2013).

CRILE, G.W. 1909. *Hemorrhage and transfusion: an experimental and clinical research.* New York: D. Appleton and Company.

D'ADAMO, P.J. 1996. *Eat right 4 your blood type: the individualized diet solution to staying healthy, living longer and achieving your ideal weight.* New York: G.P. Putnam's Sons.

FEINBLATT, H.M. 1926. *Transfusion of blood.* New York: Macmillan.

FITZGERALD, J.G. 1909. An attempt to show specific racial differences in human blood by means of the reaction of fixation. *Journal of Medical Research* **21**, 41-5.

GIBBONS, R. 1950. O.K. blood type tattoo as aid in atom attack. *Chicago Tribune*, 1 August, 11.

HEKTOEN, L. 1907. Isoagglutination of human corpuscles. *Journal of the American Medical Association* **48**, 1739-40.

HIRSZFELD, L. & M.A. BALIŃSKA 2010. *Ludwik Hirszfeld: the story of one life.* Rochester, N.Y.: University Press.

HYGEIA 1926. Letter to the editor: blood differences of white and colored races. **4 (October)**, 607.

IRWIN, T. 1961. Medicine's 'most exclusive' club. *Today's Health* **39: 4-7**, 88.

JOURNAL OF THE AMERICAN MEDICAL ASSOCIATION 1949. Health laws governing artificial insemination. **141**, 1075.

LANDSTEINER, K. & C.P. MILLER, Jr 1925. Serological studies on blood of primates. *Journal of Experimental Medicine* **42**, 841-52.

LEDERER, S.E. 1998. Repellent subjects: Hollywood censorship and surgical images in the 1930s. *Literature and Medicine* **17**, 91-113.

——— 2008. *Flesh and blood: organ transplantation and blood transfusion in twentieth-century America.* Oxford: University Press.

LEES, H. 1946. Born to order. *Colliers*, 20 April, 20.

LOS ANGELES TIMES 1930. Babies mixed in hospital. 20 July, 1.

LUKES, M.M. 1927. Do you know your own baby? *Washington Post*, 23 October, SM3.

MARSHALL, H.T. & O. TEAGUE 1908. A study of the precipitin and complement fixation reaction. *Philippine Journal of Science* **3**, 357-77.

NEW YORK TIMES 1912. Separates blood of races. 5 December, 6.

——— 1926. 107 transfusions fail to save war veteran. 16 July, 15.

——— 1930. Chicago baby mix-up settled by exchange; Bambergers give up child on experts' ruling. 20 August, 1.

——— 1937. Gets second transfusion. 29 November, 16.

——— 1938. Infection is fatal. 12 August, 34.

——— 1947. State law asked for blood tests. 9 July, 27.

——— 1949. Safety standards for flats sought. 11 February, 14.

——— 1950. Truman gets a tag to list blood type. 22 November, 8.

PELIS, K. 1999. Transfusion, with teeth. In *Manifesting medicine: bodies and machines* (eds) R. Bud, B. Finn & H. Trischler, 1-29. Amsterdam: Harwood.

PEPPER, W. & V. NISBET 1907. A case of fatal hemolysis following direct transfusion of blood by arteriovenous anastomosis. *Journal of the American Medical Association* **49**, 385-9.

REGAN, L.J. 1949. *Doctor and patient and the law.* St Louis: The C.V. Mosby Company.

ROBINSON, G. 1930. Whose baby am I? *Liberty* **7: 41**, 36-47.

ROGERS, J. 1968. The rare ones: how they save lives. *Boston Globe*, 23 June, C12.

RUDAVSKY, S. 1999. Separating spheres: legal ideology v. paternity testing in divorces cases. *Science in Context* **12**, 123-38.

SCHNEIDER, W. 1996. The history of research on blood group genetics: initial discovery and diffusion. *History and Philosophy of the Life Sciences* **18**, 277-303.

WESTON, K. 2001. Kinship, controversy, and the sharing of substance: the race/class politics of blood transfusion. In *Relative values: reconfiguring kinship studies* (eds) S. Franklin & S. McKinnon, 147-74. Durham, N.C.: Duke University Press.

WIENER, A.S. 1943. *Blood groups and transfusion* (Third edition). Springfield, Ill.: Charles C. Thomas.

WILLIAMS, C. 1940. *Emergency nurse*. Philadelphia: Penn Publishing.

WOLF, E.K. & A.E. LAUMANN 2008. The use of blood-type tattoos during the Cold War. *Journal of the American Academy of Dermatology* **58**, 472-6.

7

'Searching for the truth': tracing the moral properties of blood in Malaysian clinical pathology labs

JANET CARSTEN *University of Edinburgh*

On Friday, 18 July 2008, the front-page headline of the *New Straits Times* (Malaysia's foremost pro-government English-language newspaper) asked rhetorically, 'What is he afraid of?' Above the headline, two red bullet points gave background to the story: 'Anwar refuses to give blood sample for DNA test' and 'Possibility of bringing in foreign medical experts to conduct tests'. Underneath, in large letters, was a quote from Datuk Seri[1] Syed Hamid Albar, Home Minister: 'If he's searching for the truth, he can get it very easily. Just give a blood sample for DNA tests ... Under our laws, we cannot force a person to give a blood sample'. On an inside page, the main news story was reported under another headline, also a quotation from the Home Minister: 'Give blood sample for the sake of truth'. Other newspapers in Malaysia ran this story with the same prominence.

These headlines came at a climactic moment in a long-running and increasingly surreal saga in Malaysian politics, in which several stories seemed somehow to converge on a DNA analysis of the blood of Datuk Seri Anwar Ibrahim, the *de facto* leader of the main opposition party, Parti Keadilan Raayat (PKR), and long-time thorn in the government's side. The many bizarre turns in this sequence of events almost defy summary, but for someone engaged at the time in research on the interface between biomedical understandings of blood and its wider symbolic resonances in Malaysia, the moment seemed almost too extraordinary to be believed. How had Anwar's blood come to be claimed by the government as an icon of truth in a tumultuous political showdown?

In brief, general elections in March 2008 had resulted in very significant gains for the opposition parties. For the first time since 1969, the ruling alliance of government parties (Barisan Nasional), headed by UMNO (United Malays National Organization), had lost its two-thirds majority in parliament – but not its overall majority – and the opposition parties had won a number of key states. This came against a background of increasing dissatisfaction among voters, particularly over what was perceived as widespread corruption in government, and stories of scandals implicating leading politicians. It seemed possible to imagine that the decades of UMNO rule might be nearing

Blood: Will Out: Essays on Liquid Transfers and Flows, First Edition. Edited by Janet Carsten. © 2013 Royal Anthropological Institute of Great Britain & Ireland. Published 2013 by John Wiley & Sons Ltd.

an end. In the weeks and months following the election, Anwar stepped up an increasingly direct attack on a faltering government, and particularly on the reputation of the Deputy Prime Minister, Datuk Seri Najib Tun Razak. This hinged on allegations about the latter's embroilment in the murder, by means of C4 explosives, of a Mongolian translator, Altantuya Shaariibuu, allegedly committed to cover up a sex and corruption scandal involving prominent government figures. This was one of several high-profile cases then being tried in the Malaysian courts.

Following the election, Anwar repeatedly boasted that, by the following September, sufficient MPs from parties in the ruling Barisan Nasional (particularly from the states of East Malaysia, Sabah and Sarawak) would have changed sides for the opposition to achieve a majority, and the government would fall. It was perhaps not surprising to observers familiar with Malaysian politics that the government would respond to such direct provocation. On 29 June, in a bizarre reprise of events ten years before, under the Mahathir government, when Anwar had been sacked as Deputy Prime Minister and arrested and jailed for sodomy, the story broke in the Malaysian press that one of Anwar's aides had lodged a report with the police alleging sodomy by the PKR leader. On the same day, amidst claims that he had received death threats, Anwar took refuge in the Turkish embassy. He emerged from there on 1 July after assurances for his personal safety had been given by the Home Minister and the Deputy Prime Minister. On the same day, the aide in question was exposed in photographs released by PKR as having links to the office of the Deputy Prime Minister. According to a report in *The Star*, at a press conference on 3 July, Anwar 'declared that evidence linking deputy Prime Minister Najib to the murdered Mongolian translator will be released in the coming days'. Describing the Altantuya case as 'like a series in a Bollywood drama', he also accused the police of suppressing evidence, and questioned 'why there was a sudden switching of the judge fixed to hear the case' (*The Star* 2008).

Following his arrest on 16 July, Anwar was taken to the main hospital in Kuala Lumpur, where, according to accounts in the Malaysian media, he was medically examined, but refused to give a blood sample for DNA testing, fearing that it might be tampered with. In a statement alleging that he had been stripped naked during this examination, which was denied by the Director of the hospital, Datuk Dr Zaininah Mohd Zain, Anwar was reported as saying,

'They measured me and examined me, front and back,' ... when meeting PKR members at party headquarters in Petaling Jaya later yesterday.
    He said the police should not ask for his DNA sample again as they had taken his blood samples many times when he was in prison for six years.
    'I had my blood tested many times for sugar level, cholesterol. But now they say those were old DNA samples,' he added (Looi 2008).

In the heightened atmosphere of the time, and amidst increasingly vitriolic accusations levelled in all directions, the role of Anwar's blood in this story was just one of many remarkable sub-themes. For not only were his previous blood samples presumably available to the police but, as at least some bloggers commented, if DNA was at issue, blood was not required. A simple mouth swab, for example, might have been easier to acquire. So, what was it about blood, as distinct, say, from saliva or hair, that had the capacity to reveal the truth? Or was it perhaps not just the blood, but also the idea of 'the sample' and its scientific testing, possibly verified by 'foreign medical experts', that would supply the desired authenticity for this rather questionable evidence?

I have begun with a vignette from a remarkable moment in contemporary Malaysian politics when a contested blood sample of the leader of the opposition alliance was claimed by some as having the capacity to reveal the truth about his character. Significantly, perhaps, what exactly the blood sample was supposed to show in this case was not explicitly spelled out in the reports in the Malaysian press. One might surmise that the authorities were perhaps either hoping to match samples produced by Anwar's political aide, or seeking a positive HIV test (which would not require DNA). This, however, was left implicit, and thus presumably all the more open to different interpretations that might cast aspersions on Anwar's character.[2] But how does blood acquire its apparent iconic status to reveal the truth about a politician's moral character? What properties and capacities of blood does this status result from? Drawing on an ethnographic project that focused on the clinical pathology labs and blood banks of two private hospitals in Penang, which aimed to trace 'the social life of blood' in Malaysia, I attempt to unpick blood's apparently over-determined capacity to accrue layers of meaning. Juxtaposing some sketches from this fieldwork, I show how the fields of biomedicine, kinship, ethnicity, and politics may become merged as blood is screened or analysed in the clinical pathology labs.

While the continuities that I trace here are in many ways specific to Malaysia, the broader significance of the discussion has parallels with ethnographic and historical research carried out elsewhere. The contested importance of this particular Malaysian blood sample, for example, can be compared to the ways in which blood-typing confirms or upsets long-held truths about the nature of religious, caste, or family ties in India (Copeman 2008: 291), or is co-opted to indicate racial characteristics or marital prospects in the twentieth-century United States (Lederer 2008; this volume; see also Haraway 1996). Discourses about 'scientific' blood testing may thus be enfolded into understandings about the ways in which blood has a particular power to reveal the truth about the person that – for all their appearance of scientific and technologically up-to-date modernity – have a very different historicity. As with the bags of sterile isotonic fluid discussed by Mayblin in this volume, new technologies may be incorporated into much older understandings. Here the truth-bearing power of blood shows striking similarities to some of the properties of medieval blood discussed by Bildhauer in this volume (see also Bildhauer 2006; Bynum 2007), as well as other cases considered in this volume, such as the Indian blood portraits described by Copeman, and the truths revealed through twentieth-century US blood-typing as examined by Lederer.

But this essay also has another aim, which is to pay close attention to the apparently rather routine, mundane, and everyday work of clinical pathology labs (see also Pfeffer & Laws 2006). One implication of the colourful newspaper reports which I have cited would seem to be that, although such labs in many respects operate in a zone that is insulated and far removed from political or familial concerns, it is possible to find the traces of such interests in laboratory life. My aim in this chapter is to show how personal, moral, and familial qualities are implicated in the social relations of the lab, and may also adhere to samples as they make their way through analysers and diagnostic machinery. Thus while the space of the lab and the more theatrical zones of Malaysian politics might seem to be 'worlds apart', we may be able to trace connections between them. Illuminating the mobility and velocity of blood as it flows between different sites and domains requires us to examine the social processes and relationships layered into such an archaeology of associations and connotations. Tracing the 'social life of blood' not only reveals its particular properties as an object, but also allows us to grasp how the separations between domains of social life, which are fundamental to an ideology of modernity (see Yanagisako & Delaney 1995), must be laboriously achieved, and can often be only precariously maintained. In the case of blood, the stakes may be unusually high when the boundaries between, for example, biomedicine and politics or kinship become over-permeable or threaten to collapse.

Lab work

The perception that a blood sample might have the capacity to reveal the truth about a prominent politician's character suggests some interesting pathways between the different kinds of knowledge generated inside and outside laboratory spaces. In the sections that follow, I show what actually happens to samples of bodily material as they pass through the labs, and illuminate the traces of personality, character, or social categories that may inhere in the sample, or may be newly attached to samples during the work processes of the lab and through the engagements of staff. How is the transition from bodies to samples, or from social relations to an object of analysis, effected? And what can it tell us about blood as a particular kind of substance or about the social relations initiated here? While Pfeffer and Laws argue that 'blood in a syringe is materially and symbolically quite different to blood circulating round the human body' (2006: 3012), my interest is in examining both how this difference is effected, and how stable and complete the separation is between the different qualities and values attached to a blood sample.

Most of the work of the clinical pathology labs is highly technical and takes the form of many small, intricate tasks. There are literally hundreds of diagnostic tests that labs may be equipped to do in their different departments on blood, sputum, urine, stool, or other samples. And diagnostic testing is only one part of the work of the labs. The medical lab technologists (MLTs) and lab technicians are also responsible for taking blood from blood donors, the screening of blood, its separation and preparation as components, their storage and refrigeration, the management of blood bank supplies, and cross-matching blood for transfusion with that of patients. The lab staff also take blood from hospital in-patients and out-patients before it is tested, and make sure the results of the diagnostic tests they carry out in the different departments of the lab are accurately recorded and speedily transmitted back to wards and out-patient clinics.

Many of the processes I observed began with the extraction of bodily fluids or tissue from patients or donors. These were then examined or analysed before results were recorded and entered into the information systems of the lab, which were in turn transmitted to doctors or nurses. The processes of extraction, analysis, storage, disposal, and data-recording are at the heart of what goes on in the labs. They involve taking what is internal to the human body and transforming it into a detached object of scientific analysis, and then into recorded information. This cannot happen without social engagement, and it is this that concerns me here. I am interested in the forms of social relations that are involved – beginning with the interactions between MLTs and patients, but also encompassing those between working colleagues, and between the staff of the labs and the samples they analyse as well as with the equipment they use.

The transformation of blood from bodily substance into laboratory object apparently involves divesting it of the social qualities it carries. This might be one effect of the work that goes on in the labs. But for many reasons, as I show below, this divestment is at best unstable; the detachment of the personal or moral attributes of blood remains partial or provisional, and it is possible for such qualities to be re-attributed or newly attributed through the engagements of social actors in the labs. In order to understand some of the ways in which such re-attributions may occur, it is necessary first to understand what kinds of spaces these laboratories constitute.

Biomedical spaces

There are different ways of entering the blood banks and clinical pathology labs. Like many houses, they have more than one point of access – front doors and back doors, as it were (see Carsten 1997: 33). And like houses too, which door one uses signifies. This is mainly a matter of distinguishing clearly areas to which members of the public are admitted from those reserved for staff who work in the labs and blood banks. One entrance might be reserved for patients having blood samples taken, another might be for blood donors. A different door (perhaps to the rear of the others) is only for staff. Visitors who belong to none of these categories seem to know which entrance is appropriate for their use. The entrances used by staff were clearly marked 'Staff only', or 'No entrance, authorized personnel only'. Other working visitors might choose between the various possible entry points, but nurses and other familiar visitors to the lab would usually use the same entrance as the lab staff.

The connections between people, the spaces they inhabit, and the processes they engage in are, in one way or another, the subject of many ethnographic studies (Carsten & Hugh-Jones 1995). While I would not wish to exaggerate the 'house-like' attributes of clinical pathology labs, it is worth noting the resonances with domestic space because of their connotations and implications for social relations between staff, some of which I pursue here. There are of course many ways to approach these sites, just as there are different categories of people who do so. Patients and blood donors may have reasons to visit these locations, but their access is restricted to specific areas, and they are not permitted to wander freely in the labs. Then there are the occasional visitors: nurses from other parts of the hospital collecting bags of blood for transfusion; engineers from medical technology firms engaged in maintenance of or repair work to the sophisticated diagnostic machinery; sales reps from such firms; computer support staff from inside the hospital, or from outside, who maintain the complex data information systems of the labs; despatch staff taking or delivering samples between different labs or between departments of the hospital; staff from the hospital stores delivering supplies; and hospital maintenance workers fixing problems with the air conditioning or other routine repairs. Some may pay more 'social' calls or combine a work task with a more sociable visit. Former colleagues as well as staff from elsewhere in the hospital may also drop by on a friendly basis.

But the main inhabitants of the blood banks and clinical pathology labs are those who actually work there. They include the receptionists and clerical staff, cleaners, despatch staff, the lab manager, and, most important of all, those responsible for running the many diagnostic tests in the labs as well as the day-to-day work of the blood banks: the medical lab technologists and lab technicians. Numerically and structurally, the MLTs are at the centre of what goes on in these spaces.

The clinical pathology labs I observed were divided into departments for different kinds of tests: biochemistry, immunology, haematology, serology, urinalysis, and bacteriology (or microbiology). Bigger sets of labs had more departments: for example, cytopathology and histopathology might be included. In most cases, these departments had two or perhaps three people working together in them. Although different departments occupied particular areas and had equipment (including some large pieces of diagnostic machinery) associated with their tests, the most striking feature of the spatial layout of these labs was that most departments were easily accessible to each other. The spaces were free-flowing, so that one could easily walk between them and see what was going on in different parts of the labs. Since the same samples or equipment might be used for different tests, and colleagues might need to consult each other over specific results, accessibility was a necessary feature of the different departments. Of course, it also had social correlates. Colleagues could easily walk over to a different part of the lab for a quick chat when there was a lull in the work. They could also help each other out at times of high pressure. People's work patterns were highly visible to their immediate colleagues and to the lab manager or others who were passing through. On the whole, these were spaces of quiet sociability and both the nature of the work and the layout favoured quite easy social interaction between colleagues working in the same or nearby departments.

While the main departments of the lab flowed into each other, and people worked at benches, sinks, centrifuges, diagnostic machinery, microscopes, and computers that were set out in these spaces in quite close proximity, some areas were more self-contained than others. The microbiology (or bacteriology) departments were in separate rooms with their own fume cupboards, sinks, and refrigerators for storing Petri dishes in which bacteriological samples were being grown on agar jelly. The doors to these departments were, for health and safety reasons, supposed to be kept shut (practices were somewhat variable), but those who were working inside were visible from other areas of the lab through windows or glassed doors. The lab managers had their own office that opened onto the main areas of the labs, but the doors to these were normally open and often the lab manager would be elsewhere – taking blood from out-patients, working in one of the other departments of the lab, or sometimes at a management meeting in the hospital.

The blood banks came under the same management as the labs, and formed part of the same spatial units. They were partially self-contained spaces within the larger clinical pathology departments. The blood banks consisted of interconnecting areas – one with seats for the reception of donors, a space for the screening of donors, and an area with several beds for donors who were giving blood. They had their own centrifuges, refrigerators, and freezers for storing blood products, as well as other equipment, and a computer for recording data on donors. Usually, two or three of the lab staff were assigned to work in the blood bank. The blood banks had their own entrances for donors and other visitors leading to a reception area, but in smaller premises this might also be the main access for visitors to the labs. Open doorways (or sometimes closed doors) for staff but not for donors or patients led between the blood bank and the main departments of the lab.

The other large working area of the clinical pathology departments was an out-patients' section where patients referred by hospital doctors came to have their blood taken. The location of these varied depending on the availability of space. But like the blood banks, they were to some degree self-contained sections that communicated with the other parts of the labs. Staff could come and go easily between these areas, but patients did not enter the main working areas of the lab. They reported to a reception desk, where a receptionist would direct them to the rows of seats in the waiting area, and would be called forward by a member of staff. MLTs and lab technicians took blood from patients in the phlebotomy area.

Apart from the main working areas of the labs, 'backroom' areas were used to house storerooms, cleaning rooms or areas, and toilets. There were also spaces for the use of staff when they were not on duty. These were clearly separated from the main working areas, screened off at one end of the labs or in a space adjacent to the main labs. They housed tables and chairs for staff to eat and drink, a fridge for food, a kettle for making drinks, perhaps simple cooking facilities, a sink, and cupboard space or shelves where staff could keep their own mugs and plates. The facilities for staff might also include an on-call room with a bed and a small shower room so that staff could stay over night or rest in a lunch hour.

The existence of these zones of non-working space, which were partly necessary because food was not allowed in the workspaces of the lab, encouraged sociability between colleagues. While there were extremely busy periods of work (usually in the mornings), often the afternoons were relatively quiet, and there was time for a pause in work and for conversation between colleagues. The nature of MLTs' work, their specific training and expertise, the fact that the labs were spatially set off from other areas of the hospital, and had their own managers (who were in turn responsible to the hospital hierarchy), all tended to encourage a spirit of internal cohesion. There was an emphasis on team-work rather than on hierarchy based on seniority. The MLTs took pride in doing their work well, which they articulated in terms of the speed and accuracy of their results, and had a strong sense of loyalty to their colleagues. They often spoke of the hospital management in somewhat wry or cynical terms, and were suspicious of attempts to increase their workloads or change their shift arrangements.

Although the labs were primarily working spaces, the rhythms of activity and the layout encouraged sociable exchange between those who worked there. Many of the lab staff had been employed there for several years or even several decades, and some had known each other from school or student days. Amongst those who knew each other less well, fleeting episodes of sociability, conversations, snacks and meals taken together could over time transform into lasting ties of friendship or kinship between colleagues. These patterns of sociability (which I do not have space here to describe more fully) had a recognizable Malaysian flavour, and also created a density of ties of kinship and friendship within and between the staff in different hospitals in Penang.

Extracting blood

The way in which sociability between colleagues left its mark on the work carried out in the labs, or attached itself to bodily samples as they made their way through the labs for analysis, was rather less obvious than the evidence of sociability itself. We could begin to consider this matter by looking at the extraction of blood from patients, both because this is generally the only contact between patients and lab staff, and because it marks the point when the sample is detached from the person in whom it originates.

Notes from my fieldwork are full of descriptions of 'blood-taking events' – some very brief, others longer and fuller, but none in themselves were quite satisfactory or complete. Each description captured part but not all of what had occured in the space of just a few minutes. Encounters between patients and MLTs varied, as did the practices of individual MLTs, and since they worked with different partners, the nature of these working relationships also marked how they carried out these tasks and their engagements with patients. In many cases, the MLTs hardly engaged with patients at all beyond asking their names. And so, the taking of blood was often a 'barely social' encounter. From the MLTs' point of view, it did not seem that chatting to or engaging with patients was required or even expected. One might contrast this with the normal behaviour of nurses towards patients. But levels of social engagement varied – and sometimes depended on the patients as much as or more than the MLTs. Some patients would recognize an MLT from a previous encounter. The patient might have been in hospital for some time or perhaps had been in before, and would strike up a conversation, or would voice a preference for which MLT should take his or her blood (generally opting for the senior one, or the one whom they knew had taken blood before least painfully). It was also striking that some of the MLTs were distinctly more chatty than others, and more likely to engage with patients when they were taking their blood. In a few cases, the MLTs showed that they knew quite a lot about a particular patient, his or her illness, and family life. Sometimes they checked on a patient's progress – either by asking the nurses on the ward before leaving or by checking the hospital information system later from the lab computers.

Quite often, particular patients whom they had seen on the wards were discussed later among the MLTs in the labs. One morning, an elderly patient whose blood had been taken the previous day died on the wards. I was surprised at how much the two MLTs I spoke to knew about him. They were able to tell me that the patient was an 88-year-old man whom they thought was from the United Kingdom. One of them explained that she had had to source rhesus negative blood for him on the previous day. He had had a stroke and multiple fractures, and had been living in a hotel for the last twelve years with no family, she said, and had been brought to the hospital by a friend. Another MLT went to find the urine test request form for the same patient, while another who joined the conversation mentioned that the lab would need to ask the hospital to cancel the charges as the test wouldn't now be run. By this time several MLTs were visibly upset, and this was compounded when they noticed a form in the blood bank from another hospital stating that one unit of O negative had been 'borrowed from [X hospital] to return 2 units O type whole blood'. The first MLT explained that this had been used on the previous day: 'I think [he had] internal bleeding'. Because of the nature of their work, as this example shows, more sociable exchanges with patients or knowledge about their backgrounds intermingled with items of medical knowledge.

There were differences too between how the MLTs took blood: for example, in how they observed hygiene procedures. Some always wore latex gloves on both hands when they took blood; others sometimes did, or usually wore gloves on one hand but not both. Some always washed their hands before leaving each ward; sometimes this was done after taking blood from a particular patient. The variations were partly idiosyncratic, and the MLTs were not necessarily consistent in when and how they applied the standard procedures. Occasionally, it was obvious that they were being particularly careful – disposing of a tourniquet they had tied around a patient's arm as well as their gloves, and washing their hands after taking blood from a particular patient. Usually, this was a patient whose blood was being tested for HIV. And once again, there might be discussion back in the labs that revealed how social understandings could become entangled with the process of getting lab results: Was the patient Indonesian? Did he have bruising or other marks on his skin? Was he good-looking? Did he seem young? These kinds of questions or comments, which suggested that HIV status went together with other attributes, were likely to circulate in the lab together with a blood sample in a Vacutainer (see below) with a red sticker to indicate that special caution should be observed. If the patient in question was female, it seemed to be assumed that she had been infected by her husband. The questions then were more likely to concern her familial status, and comments by staff to indicate that they felt sorry for her.

When I asked different MLTs to talk me through what was involved in taking blood, I was interested to find that there were often quite small differences between them. Some of these were technical matters to do with accessing a vein, or avoiding getting an air bubble into the syringe. MLTs emphasized that competence in this part of their job involved a combination of skill, experience, and luck (see also Pfeffer & Laws 2006: 3015). There were some MLTs who took special pride in being able to take blood without causing the patients pain. It was indicative that when I asked different people in the labs about their techniques for taking blood, not only did variations between them emerge, but also their awareness of these was demonstrated in their frequent references to the preferred techniques of colleagues. And so, personal preferences and idiosyncracies, skill, experience, and a little luck, as well as different degrees of social engagement with patients, entered into this single routine procedure of the lab. We might say then that, in these various ways I have described, the samples that are obtained in these procedures are never fully detached but carry traces of social engagement with them as they make their way through the labs.

Samples, testing, and screening

When I asked one of the lab managers for a list of the tests performed in the lab, he kindly printed one off for me – it covered thirty-one A4 pages with perhaps an average of twenty-five tests on each. Some of these came in groups or 'packages' for particular types of patients (those being tested for heart disease or diabetes, for example), or a category of corporate insurance cover which came with standard routine tests. Some were performed for many patients each day; some were requested relatively rarely. Different kinds of tests were automated to different degrees, and this partly depended on the lab size and level of equipment. The standard tests on blood chemistry and immunology were very highly automated with batches of Vacutainers arranged in racks to pass through a sophisticated blood analyser. Within a few hours, several hundred analyses of blood chemistry and immunology could be performed which could test levels of, for example, blood sugar, cholesterol, different hormones, lipids, proteins, or enzymes, or for the presence or absence of drugs, or of specific cancer markers, as well as screening of donated blood or that of patients for syphilis, Hepatitis B surface antigens, Hepatitis C antibodies, and HIV antibodies. Other kinds of tests, such as some immunological and other tests – those for dengue fever, lupus, lactose intolerance, or further confirmatory tests for HIV – were performed individually or in very small numbers by MLTs using kits that required careful and precise measurement. On a few occasions I followed senior members of staff when they conducted less routine procedures: preparation of a sample for a fertility procedure such as IUI (intra-uterine insemination), or genetic testing of tissue for breast cancer.

The blood counts for haemoglobin and different white and red cells, as well as platelets in the blood, and ESR (erythrocyte sedimentation rate), which were performed in the haematology departments, were also performed in batches mechanically. But when the analyser showed abnormal results, further examination was conducted by staining and fixing a slide, which was then examined by the MLT under a microscope. Standard operating procedures were subject to change as new machinery or diagnostic tools became available. Blood grouping was done manually in both the labs I observed, but when I visited one lab after an absence of some months, a new machine had been acquired for blood grouping and cross-matching. Tests in the urinalysis and bacteriology departments required more manual intervention, and some of the analysis also involved visual examination – for example, to report on the colour or cloudiness of urine, or checking cultures of bacterial growth in Petri dishes. Some tests were newly introduced while I was in the labs, and this might coincide with the introduction of new equipment or the arrival of a new consultant at the hospital who specialized in a particular branch of medicine.

Several of the older staff in the lab spontaneously spoke of how the work of the labs had altered during their employment through increasing technologization. Some could remember when almost all tests were done manually and far fewer tests were carried out in the labs – many were sent out – and this was part of the shared history of relations between colleagues. But it was clear from the work preferences of MLTs that increasing automation was not necessarily seen as a good thing. Reducing their own intervention also made the work more routine. Several told me that they preferrred working in the parts of the lab that were less automated, such as microbiology, even though one might have expected growing bacterial cultures from stool, sputum, or other samples to be a less favoured work task. It was clear that, for most MLTs, the aspects of the work which gave satisfaction were those that involved making their own judgements based on experience and knowledge, especially when these led to a tricky or unexpected diagnosis.

The day-to-day maintenance of complex machinery took up a considerable amount of staff time. The more sophisticated and elaborate machines which were heavily used (such as the blood chemistry and immunology analysers) had daily maintenance programmes that were run early each morning. Depending on how the work rotas of the lab were organized, this could mean staff on duty in that department having to come on duty an hour or more before their colleagues. Machinery was also liable to break down, and thus hold up the work of the lab and the reporting of results. Such events generated stress as doctors and nurses trying to chase results would soon start to phone the labs. When new diagnostic machines were introduced in the labs, some MLTs were specifically trained in their routine maintenance, but engineers from the medical tehnology companies were also regular visitors to the labs and part of their extended social relations. On one occasion, when the main blood chemistry and immunology analyser in one lab had broken down and the two MLTs who were most expert in its operation were absent, there was a certain amount of banter among colleagues, which I recorded in my notes:

> Kamariah is trying to get recalcitrant Architect machine to work. She says, 'Big brother not there; Mama not there' [referring to the members of staff who were normally responsible]. Shanthi comes to help but clearly it needs lots of coaxing. Kamariah says normally they start running at about 9.15 or 9.30, so by now it's getting a bit late. Later in the morning, Siu Meng also says, 'Architect's mother not there'. Later she explains, 'Apparently, they filled the reagent bottles but didn't reset the machine. Now [it] won't work. Lots of tests [are] waiting'.[3]

Such humorous use of kin terms gives a flavour of the working atmosphere of the labs, and of the ways in which machines could be lightheartedly anthropomorphized. The humour turned in very Malaysian fashion on the particular kin relations imagined between the machines and their more senior relatives among the lab staff who operated them – a mother and a big brother. Kinship terms were also sometimes used between colleagues. One older male lab technician was referred to and addressed as 'Uncle' (in English) as a prefix to his name, and two of the MLTs who were married women with children were often addressed by name after a Malay kinship prefix, '*Mak*' or '*Kak*' (auntie or older sister), depending on who was speaking. The terms were partly ways of marking age or other difference when it did not necessarily correlate with seniority of position in the lab. Hierarchical relations could also be humorously exaggerated by terms of address as a way of marking, but at the same time dissipating, their connotations – another familiar Malaysian device. One of the lab managers who was on good terms with his staff was thus sometimes addressed in a friendly joking way by the latter as 'Boss' (using the English term) or '*Towkay*', a Chinese term with wide resonance in Malaysia, which is usually used for a boss or middleman in more commercial contexts. But such humour also shows how it was possible to draw the inanimate equipment of the lab into the social world of the staff. This of course raises the question of whether something similar could also happen to samples or to the recorded information derived from them.

The label as mediating artefact

Once they reached the lab, blood and other samples were literally disembodied substances. Blood samples were enclosed in sealed test tubes, Vacutainers – a widely used brand of test tubes with many different coloured stoppers to indicate which additives are present in the tubes for different kinds of laboratory analysis.[4] Urine and stool samples came in small, transparent, lidded plastic pots. All samples would first be labelled in the wards when MLTs took blood or when urine or other samples were given by patients or in the out-patients section. The labelling systems were the basis for recording test results manually or digitally. To outward appearances, the rows of identical-looking test tubes, with their sticky labels affixed, set out on racks on lab benches or arranged ready for the blood chemistry or immunology analyser in batches with the same coloured stoppers to indicate a particular kind of test, seemed more or less indistinguishable – except by looking closely at the labels, which had the patient's name and an individual barcode. A combination of manual and mechanized procedures was in use, but in the end results were recorded in the information system that was accessed from the computers in the lab. In the most obvious way, samples and recorded information could be seen as objects or as objectified information, divorced from the bodies or persons from which they were derived.

The idea of lab work producing masses of objectified data that were recorded in information systems was materialized in several ways. Samples labelled with barcodes going through various analysers in the lab might be one. Another was the lab statistics displayed on notice-boards in the form of tables, graphs, or coloured pie charts to demonstrate monthly variation in numbers of tests carried out over the year by different departments, numbers of units of blood collected, numbers of reactive screening results for donors, units of different blood components supplied by the blood bank, or the year-on-year increases in numbers of tests carried out over a period of several years by the lab. These were important indicators of the productivity of staff, and essential tools in discussions with a hospital management that seemed always anxious to improve efficiency and increase profits derived from the lab.

But things were more complicated since, for obvious reasons, as they left the lab or even before this, test results or items of recorded information were reconnected to patients. And blood products too, stored in their sealed plastic bags and stacked on the shelves of the blood bank refrigerators, might need to be traced back to their source. Labels can be seen as key to social engagements because they mediated between, on the one hand, detached samples or products as they moved through the lab or blood bank and, on the other, their sources of origin in particular people (see also Bowker & Starr 1999).

Just occasionally, a lapse in procedures meant that samples came to the lab unlabelled or wrongly labelled. Because the consequences were potentially very serious, lab staff took great care to avoid such mistakes. When one of the MLTs found a sample tube in a bag with no label on it, she explained to me that there was no way to know whether it was actually from the same patient designated on the request form that accompanied it. She told me they might have to call patient back, and both the doctor and the patient would be angry. On a different day, I observed as one of the MLTs phoned out-patients about blood that had been wrongly labelled. The phlebotomist hadn't checked the identity of the patient, and so would have to take the blood again. The MLT told me that she got very upset about this kind of thing because there was 'no need to make the patient suffer twice'. On another occasion, I found one of the MLTs working in urinalysis trying to sort out a stool sample that had not been barcoded. She told me it was 'probably because some people don't want to handle a stool sample jar'.

It was not just identifying information, or the test required, that was indicated by labels. One morning while I accompanied an MLT as she was collecting blood from patients on the wards, she showed me a red sticker on the request form to indicate an infectious disease. Sometimes they forget to put a red label on, she told me. Then, if the MLT needed to use a small needle to take blood, she might not be wearing gloves. But they haven't had any serious accidents, she added. In this instance, then, a label communicated special information about precautions to be observed – although all the lab staff were aware that, potentially, any sample might carry risks for the staff who handled them.

It would be impossible to give an exhaustive account of all the systems of labelling of blood samples and products here, but I want to highlight the quite elaborate procedures in place to ensure that, however disembodied or anonymous samples or blood components might appear, they remained connected to their particular source. This was of course necessary so that test results or screening procedures could eventually be re-attached to patients or donors, or for the source of donated blood to be verified at any point from when it had been extracted to after it had been used in transfusion. Disembodied samples moving through the lab in containers or bags of blood components, with their labels affixed to them, are thus a particular class of object – detached from persons but also indirectly attached or re-attachable. In outward form they might be almost indistinguishable from each other but they remain closely identifiable (unless a mix-up in the labelling procedures or recording of information disrupts these connections), and this opens up a space for the re-attribution of personal or moral qualities. This suggests that we might modify or elaborate on Pfeffer and Laws' (2006) argument cited above that sample blood is perceived by medical and lab staff, as well as by patients, as a quite different kind of substance from blood in the body.[5] It also indicates that the world of the lab is not necessarily radically separated from the public discourse in which Anwar Ibrahim's blood sample could be vaguely imputed to somehow have the power to reaveal his moral status.

Getting results; pursuing information

I have mentioned that when results were delayed (or even when they were not), it was usual for doctors or nurses to phone the lab to try to get lab results quickly over the phone. It was a simple matter for MLTs to go into the computer system using either the name of a patient or his or her hospital number and look up the results. This was part of the routine work that went on in the labs. That it might potentially be problematic was brought home to me one day when I witnessed a trainee pick up a phone that was ringing in the blood bank when no one from the permanent staff was available. When the MLT in charge of the blood bank returned to her post she immediately scolded the trainee. Telling him that he should not under any circumstances answer the phone, she explained that the person phoning would not necessarily realize that he was speaking to a trainee (phones in the lab were usually answered by giving the name of the department rather than the person speaking). If it was a doctor calling, or there was an emergency and instructions were rapidly conveyed without waiting for a response, the fact that a trainee was answering could lead to a misunderstanding with potentially serious consequences.

I have described how MLTs often knew quite a lot of information about patients from whom they had taken blood on the wards. And sometimes they checked on a particular patient's progress or history out of concern or just curiosity. Thus when I was invited to witness surgery, the MLTs in the lab were able to tell me something about the patient beforehand, and how he progressed after surgery, by checking the hospital information system connected to the lab computers. But it was not just in answer to queries from me that such information might be pursued. On one occasion, while I was observing some routine tests in the urinalysis department, the MLT working there expressed surprise as she was recording the negative results of a urine pregnancy test and noticed that the patient was 66 years old. Referring to the patient as 'Auntie, aged 66', she said that no other tests had been requested, and added that this didn't happen very often. This initiated some joking with the two trainees who were working with her. When they asked her what the result of the test was and she told them, one of them suggested perhaps the patient should try again. After scolding him for his levity, the MLT told the trainees that having many children could cause late menopause. I was impressed by the way in which, although none of those involved had actually met the patient, a quite detailed discussion with imagined scenarios had been extrapolated from a urine sample bottle and a request form. On the following day, I asked the MLT whether she had discovered anything further about the patient. She told me she had asked around, but that it had been quite difficult to find someone who knew anything. It had turned out that the patient was part of a new research treatment using heavy radiation. For this reason, she said, they had to do a pregnancy test and pap smear. She had found this out from a nurse on a third-class ward, she added. But what was striking to me was the way that this MLT had of her own accord followed up her curiosity and had gone to considerable trouble out of interest derived from what she perceived as an anomaly on the request form.

There were many other instances when I heard lab staff speculate about particular patients or watched as they pursued test results on the lab computers. Tracking information in this way might sometimes be initiated by something unusual that had struck them on the request form or a test result, but it could also be a particular interest in a patient whom they had encountered on the wards or among the out-patients. Sometimes a desire to get to the bottom of something could also be instrumental in achieving a diagnostic result. When I asked MLTs about what gave them most satisfaction in their work, several mentioned cases of illness that had been particularly difficult to diagnose. In one such interview an MLT recounted a case from about two years before:

> When I [did] my afternoon shift one time, had [a] child's test. [The] child was transferred from Alor Setar. Don't know [the] cause of high fever. [I] noticed a malarial parasite in blood. [I] checked red cells – haema slide. [I] informed [the] ward nurse. [The] doctor phoned back. [He] was very pleased to know cause. Called me, [to] ask for confirmation, quickly. [I] asked for other test – [can get] haemolysis with drug for malarial parasite. Some doctors [are] very ego[tistical] – [they] don't listen to MLTs. Next day, [he] came to lab. Normally consultants don't come to lab. [She explained that she was worried as to why he had come; she thought she might be in trouble.] [He brought] commendation letter – one for me, one for lab manager.

In this case, it seemed that the fact that the patient was a child who was seriously ill had heightened the MLT's desire to do her work as well as possible to achieve a rapid and accurate result. In this and many other instances, MLTs' efforts to re-humanize their work by paying attention to the source of the blood sample contribute to their engagement and satisfaction, and also improve the quality of their work.[6]

Sometimes there was a more direct connection between the results that were being pursued and lab staff. Partly because family members of hospital employees were eligible for treatment at reduced costs, lab staff quite often ran tests on the samples of their relatives. In such cases, and particularly for elderly parents or grandparents, they would try to expedite matters as simply as possible. This could mean MLTs taking the sample at home before coming to work in order to save elderly parents having to come to the out-patients department, or getting them registered early so that they would not have to spend too long waiting. Because, as I described above, many of the lab staff had worked together for a long time, they were often familiar with each other's family members, and would chat to them when they met them in the hospital or if they came to the labs. It was therefore not just one of the lab staff who might be aware of their own relative's blood or other sample being tested; this knowledge would usually be shared among quite a lot of people. In fact, it was because I was frequently told about somebody's mother or grandmother being unwell or coming for tests that I learned about these connections between colleagues. Staff would also help each other by looking up the results quickly. I became particularly aware of this when my daughter was sent for blood tests at the hospital and, in order to reassure me that nothing was seriously amiss, the lab staff kindly looked up her results as they became available.

Blood tests and the screening of donated blood, as well as tests on other bodily material, might also be necessary for members of the lab staff themselves if they donated blood, when they were unwell, as a routine health test, or after an accident in the labs. This of course meant that colleagues could easily be in possession of confidential information about each other as well as about each other's family members. In my conversations with staff, I was told several times by MLTs of occasions when they had had an accident in the lab in the past that had required testing for infectious diseases. And there were of course cases of illness that were unrelated to work in the labs that arose while I was there. My sense was that staff accepted this level of shared information among their colleagues as an unavoidable feature of working life and a by-product of the relations they had with each other, and that this further strengthened their sense of loyalty to each other.

Qualities of blood

Although I was intrigued by the question of whether patients or members of their families voiced preferences for receiving blood from particular sources, since I did not conduct research with patients, I did not directly pursue this question. I touch on these matters here only insofar as they affected lab staff. Blood bank staff did tell me about patients who had explicitly requested that they only receive the blood of family members. I was also told by one MLT about a patient who had actually spotted from the label on a blood bag that was ready to be used for his transfusion that this was not the blood of the family member that had been donated specifically for his use. MLTs, however, were aware that blood from family members was not necessarily likely to be more safe than that of others. As one MLT told me, 'the only really safe blood is your own'.

There were other accounts too which touched on the idea that specific qualities might be transferred with transfused blood. One MLT told me that patients sometimes commented on their skin getting darker after transfusion. She mentioned the case of a Chinese woman who was transfused after childbirth, and who had said the blood she received must have come from a Malay or Indian because her skin got darker after the transfusion. These ideas bring into play a highly sensitive discourse in Malaysia relating to inter-ethnic transfers of blood (or organs), specifically about whether Muslim patients are happy to receive blood from non-Muslim donors. In other words, it raises questions about the halal status of blood (see also Peletz 2002).

One member of the lab staff told me that some people requested family blood because they knew about the 'window period' when HIV infection couldn't be detected by routine screening procedures. Some people prefer autologous transfusion, she said (in other words, using blood donated by the patient prior to surgery). She noted that Malays donated mainly to the public hospital, and less to private ones. They request Malay blood, she said, because of the prohibition on eating pork. The same MLT told me about a patient who had a low haemaglobin level. A family member had insisted on the patient getting Malay blood, and the patient had a rare blood group. 'Very difficult', she commented, adding that 'Chinese people mostly want family blood – fathers want sons' blood'. As we spoke, I spotted a note above the reception desk in the blood bank concerning a patient for transfusion, which stated 'to use own family blood'. But she was clearly uneasy discussing these matters: 'especially about the Malay patient – very sensitive in Malaysia'.

It is indicative that preferences for blood from Malay donors were only ever alluded to in rather hushed tones and in a manner which made clear its sensitivity by staff of the blood banks and labs.[7] But here, as in other operations of the lab, we can perceive the different meanings of blood more or less visibly seeping into each other. And here I return to Anwar Ibrahim's blood sample with which I began this essay. In that controversial and high-profile case, the blood sample was apparently supposed to reveal whether Anwar had or had not had sex with one of his aides – in other words his moral status. The sample's power resided in its capacity to verify a matter that was ultimately only knowable by the two protagonists. The potential instability of the meanings of this particular blood sample inhered in layers of history – not just a general history of the manner in which Malaysian politics had been conducted over several decades, but also a very particular history relating to Anwar's previous arrest and imprisonment (and subsequent release) on the very same charge under the Mahathir government. While for the government it might be obvious that Anwar's moral corruption would emerge in unanswerable terms from the analysis of a sample, for a substantial part of the Malaysian public the story as presented simply lacked credibility. The blood sample, in other words, might reveal truths quite unintended by the government.

Rather than clarifying Anwar's moral status, what emerged from this sample was the excess of meanings pertaining to blood, also demonstrated by other contributions to this volume, and the resultant impossibility of containing these within any of the fields of social relations in which they arose. The polyvalent meanings of blood itself, and the resonances between its material, medical, and moral connotations, readily become self-evident as they flow between the multiple fields and discourses in which blood participates.

Conclusion

I began this chapter with the iconicity of blood itself. Something about Anwar's blood sample, it was claimed, might encapsulate the truth about his moral character. The truth that would emerge was, however, left remarkably unspecified in these reports – it is not at all clear what could be ascertained through the sample or the tests to which it might be subjected. In the context of widespread incredulity, it seemed that the government sought to lend legitimacy to Anwar's surprising arrest through scientific tests. Or perhaps what was being sought was a vivid reminder to opponents of the government of Anwar's previous imprisonment under the same charge, and the power of the state that could be brought to bear.

The world of the clinical pathology labs where such samples are analysed seems a long way from the heightened rhetoric of Malaysian politics. To gain some sense of how moral attributes may be attributed to or shed from a sample, and the multiplicity of layered resonances at play, I have paid close attention to the work surrounding blood and other bodily materials in clinical pathology labs, and to conversations that accompany such work. Although the work of the lab mainly involves tasks that are standardized, mechanized, and routine, we have seen that there is also a space for variation, skill, experience, and luck. Social engagement can intervene in some of the least expected processes. Even the sophisticated medical technology that is used in the labs can sometimes be drawn into the sphere of social relations – vividly materializing Bruno Latour's (1993) notion of hybrids. And test tubes of samples or bags of blood components that seem outwardly indistinguishable necessarily retain connections to their sources in particular patients or donors. Here labels and forms have a special role to play in enabling these connections to be made. When a urine sample can trigger a possible story about an unknown '66-six year old auntie', or when Vacutainers contain the blood of a relative, friend, or colleague, we can see how attributes of social relations – along with their 'everyday truths' – permeate the space of the labs. The qualities that adhere to samples, or are newly attached to them, do so through the socially embedded engagements of staff, through the samples themselves and the connections the latter retain (or are perceived to retain) to the persons from whom they derive, and through the mediating objects of forms and labels that are attached to samples.

But why do these processes matter? What can they tell us about the properties of blood itself? The many possibilities that exist for inserting blood or other tissues into discourses which are politically or morally charged are suggestive of the capacities these bodily materials have for metaphorical extension. Even when it is apparently detached from its source, and contained in sample tubes or blood bags, blood nevertheless retains a symbolic potential. Rather than closing off a field of 'objective' scientific investigation, the interventions of medical science embed samples in further networks of relations, apparently multiplying the capacities of blood for symbolic elaboration (see also Hugh-Jones 2011). Just as Anwar Ibrahim's blood sample was required in order to reveal his moral character, Thai demonstrators in 2010 co-opted the language of the blood donation campaign to express their political disaffection (see Introduction and Weston, this volume), while in India, as Copeman (2008; 2009) has shown, the continuities between blood donation and wider political and sacrificial meanings of blood suffuse the space of the blood donation camp. As the sites of scientific procedures and analysis, the spaces of blood donation or testing are required to be insulated from the kind of interests expressed in electoral politics. This is one import of the clearly marked boundaries of the lab that exclude members of the public. The notices on doors that state 'staff only' indicate that work undertaken within is isolated from possible interference. One might think of such marked boundaries as the material expression of the domaining that underwrites the integrity of scientific procedures.

That 'foreign experts' were invoked by politicians as necessary to uphold the trustworthiness of test results suggests, however, that such boundaries are difficult to safeguard. Anwar Ibrahim's reported resistance to supplying the required blood sample was equally telling. One might conclude that the purpose of obtaining this sample had deliberately been left unclear to encourage different kinds of speculation about his moral probity. And this relates to the excess of meanings and associations of blood, which render its capacity to encapsulate the truth unstable and contested. Many different truths may be revealed by a blood sample, but these may go beyond the health, identity, or moral status of the person from whom it derives. When the objectivity of scientific analysis cannot be guaranteed, or the safety of donated blood for transfusion is compromised, it is not only the health of individual patients that may be at risk. We have seen that the test result that lacks credibility has the potential to expose the vulnerability of the body politic – sometimes with dramatic consequences.

NOTES

The research on which this chapter is based was funded by a Leverhulme Major Research Fellowship and a British Academy Small Research Grant. I am very grateful to the Leverhulme Trust and to the British Academy for making this work possible, to the staff of the hospitals in Penang where this research was carried out, and to the participants at the workshop where this material was first presented, especially to Jacob Copeman and Sophie Day and to the anonymous readers for *JRAI* for their helpful comments on previous drafts. The names of all research participants and some identifying information have been changed to protect the confidentiality of participants.

[1] 'Datuk' and 'Seri' are Malaysian honorific titles.

[2] What was at stake here seems somewhat different from the use of DNA in paternity testing, which in France, India, and elsewhere has also jeopardized the moral standing of politicians.

[3] Direct quotations were noted down at the time. English was the *lingua franca* in the hospitals, and was spoken fluently by most members of the lab staff. I have tried to retain the characteristic rhythms and diction of Malaysian English, which tends to be somewhat staccato with articles often omitted and preponderant use of the present tense.

[4] For example, lavender capped tubes contain EDTA, a strong anticoagulant used in full blood counts; red capped tubes contain no additives and are used in antibody and drug tests.

[5] The difference between these studies may partly have to do with methodology. Pfeffer and Laws (2006: 3012-14) explain that they worked through interviews and focus groups as well as observation. Whereas the data

discussed in their article are mainly drawn from the interviews and focus group discussions, the data I collected in Malaysia relied heavily on the observation of staff in laboratory settings. However, Pfeffer and Laws also note how blood tests 'can also provide incriminating information about people as moral agents' (2006: 3015).

[6] I am grateful to Ian Harper for underlining this point, and suggesting the term 're-humanizing'.

[7] The relevant Muslim authorities had made clear that, from an Islamic standpoint, there was no problem with such transfers.

REFERENCES

Bildhauer, B. 2006. *Medieval blood*. Cardiff: University of Wales Press.

Bowker, G.C. & S.L. Starr 1999. *Sorting things out: classification and its consequences*. Cambridge, Mass.: MIT Press.

Bynum, C.W. 2007. *Wonderful blood: theology and practice in late medieval northern Germany and beyond*. Philadelphia: University of Pennsylvania Press.

Carsten, J. 1997. *The heat of the hearth: the process of kinship in a Malay fishing community*. Oxford: Clarendon Press.

——— & S. Hugh-Jones 1995. *About the house: Lévi-Strauss and beyond*. Cambridge: University Press.

Copeman, J. 2008. Violence, non-violence, and blood donation in India. *Journal of the Royal Anthropological Institute* (N.S.) **14**, 278-96.

——— 2009. *Veins of devotion: blood donation and religious experience in India*. New Brunswick, N.J.: Rutgers University Press.

Haraway, D.J. 1996. Universal donors in a vampire culture: it's all in the family: biological kinship categories in the twentieth-century United States. In *Uncommon ground: rethinking the human place in nature* (ed.) W.M. Cronon, 321-66. New York: Norton.

Hugh-Jones, S. 2011. Analyses du sang. *Terrain* **56**, 4-21.

Latour, B. 1993. *We have never been modern*. New York: Harvester Wheatsheaf.

Lederer, S.E. 2008. *Flesh and blood: organ transplantation and blood transfusion in twentieth-century America*. Oxford: University Press.

Looi, E. 2008. 'Anwar was not stripped naked' HKL director: his decency was not violated. *The Star*, 20 July (available on-line: *http://thestar.com.my/news/story.asp?file=/2008/7/20/nation/21873962&sec=nation*, accessed 24 January 2013).

Peletz, M.G. 2002. *Islamic modern: religious courts and cultural politics in Malaysia*. Princeton: University Press.

Pfeffer, N. & S. Laws 2006. 'It's only a blood test': what people know and think they know about venepuncture and blood. *Social Science and Medicine* **62**, 3011-23.

The Star 2008. Anwar: proof on Najib soon. 4 July (available on-line: *http://thestar.com.my/news/story.asp?file=/2008/7/4/nation/21738312&sec=nation*, accessed 24 January 2013).

Yanagisako, S. & C. Delaney 1995. Naturalizing power. In *Naturalizing power: essays in feminist cultural analysis* (eds) S. Yanagisako & C. Delaney, 1-22. New York: Routledge.

8

The art of bleeding: memory, martyrdom, and portraits in blood

JACOB COPEMAN *University of Edinburgh*

'Tum mujhe khun do, main tumhen aazadi doonga' – 'Give me your blood, and I will give you freedom'. These words, spoken by Subhas Chandra Bose (1897-1945; popularly known as Netaji) at a political rally in Burma in 1944, are some of the most quoted in India's modern history.[1] Their immediate purpose was to stimulate a willingness on the part of 'the Indian masses', contra Mahatma Gandhi's message of non-violence, to engage in armed struggle in order to bring to an end long-standing British colonial rule. To assert that it is an iconic phrase hardly does it justice. Its applicability – the different sorts of occasion on which it is uttered – appears to know no bounds. My interest here is in the sanguinary extractions it appears to precipitate in contexts of political practice. A quotation, states Barber, 'is only a quotation when it is inserted into a new context'; it involves both detachment and recontextualization (2005: 274). Inserted into present-day political contexts, Bose's words 'precipitate' (or constitute the rhetorical occasion for) various sorts of 'shedding'. Petitions formed of the blood of political campaigners, medical blood donation on Bose's birth and death anniversaries, portraits in blood of various political figures – all fairly common occurrences within a variety of mass political Indian milieus – are frequently framed as responses to Bose's exhortation, which, re-embedded into a multitude of new contexts, continues to draw its power from an acute recognition of its pre-existence as a call to shed blood in order to be rid of a foreign colonial power. The (sanguinary) nationalist exchange relation invoked by Bose has indeed enjoyed a rich and diverse career.

   My particular interest here is in a recontextualization of Bose's iconic refrain that sees it deployed as inspiration for the use of human blood for painting purposes. Whilst seeking to explore in quite general terms the propensity in Indian political culture towards sanguinary forms of communication and expression, my principal ethnographic examples here concern the blood portrait as a kind of sub-style or technique within the larger milieu of sanguinary political expressionism in the country. I focus on an example of blood portraiture that was directly inspired by Bose's utterance – an exhibition of blood portraits that I visited on numerous occasions in Delhi in 2009. The subjects of the portraits, including Bose among them, were 'freedom fighter' martyrs – sacrificial heroes of the Independence struggle. The following details concerning the

Blood: Will Out: Essays on Liquid Transfers and Flows, First Edition. Edited by Janet Carsten. © 2013 Royal Anthropological Institute of Great Britain & Ireland. Published 2013 by John Wiley & Sons Ltd.

exhibition and the processes involved in commissioning and maintaining the paintings derive from my visits to the exhibition, where I spoke at length with its organizer and visitors, but also from newspaper accounts and the visitors' book, with its thousands of entries, to which I was kindly given access.

Given that South Asia is a region justly famed for restrictions placed on flows of substance (especially those substances considered most defiling, such as blood), the use of human blood for purposes of 'art', and mass political communication more generally, may evoke some surprise.[2] This essay will suggest that it is in part *because* of such restrictions that the genre possesses a marked expressive force. Fears concerning blood loss and anxieties about the mixing of substances can cause instances of precisely those things to form powerful statements – about a differentially composed but none the less singular nation, for example (Copeman 2009a: chap. 7). Artworks have long formed an integral feature of nationalist narratives. Idols and images from India's ancient past 'continue their lives resituated as art objects in Indian museums', playing a key part in 'the colonial and postcolonial project of constructing an Indian national identity' (Davis 1993: 45). There is also a well-established tradition of explicitly patriotic art, insightfully documented by Pinney (2004) and Ramaswamy (2008). Such art often depicts nationalist heroes having spilled, or in the act of spilling, their blood. The patriotic art that I explore here likewise depicts martyrs revered for having shed their blood, but differs in also being composed *of* human blood; moreover, these portraits speak to a very contemporary set of concerns to do with memory and forgetting. I examine the role of these paintings as defences of a particular (nationalist) 'body of [treasured] remembrances' (Halbwachs 1950: 22), which is experienced by their creators as under threat.

If these literally bloody patriotic works differ from mainstream Indian patriotic art, they also differ from the use of blood in Western art.[3] Discussions of the use of body substances (particularly blood) in Western art typically argue that it marks a return to primitive ritual (e.g. Siebers 2003), and/or that it results 'naturally' from the trauma consequent on the cataclysmically bloody events of the twentieth century. The flow of the blood of performance artists such as Marina Abramović is often analysed according to its 'shock value' (Weiermair 2001), while, more recently, 'bioart' – a 'field which is now emerging at the intersection of the creative arts and the bio-medical sciences' (Palladino 2010: 96, see also Anker & Franklin 2011), and which frequently employs as media human (and animal) substances, sometimes in bio-molecular or diseased form – has been considered to offer the potential to reconfigure, even to subvert, the constraints of 'bio-political governmentality' (Palladino 2010: 106). There are no doubt points of connection between these genres and Indian blood portraiture – all of them, for instance, raise questions concerning distinctions between presence and representation, while questions of loss, ritual, and 'shock value' are certainly raised in the Indian case. This essay will suggest, however, that unlike the forms of body art described above, the Indian case presents us with a direct political intervention (if bioart *does* provide radical political commentary, it does so only obliquely). The Indian case also speaks to a very specific political history and present-day situation and possesses its own unique set of representational and mnemonic complexities – complexities that this essay seeks to unpack.

Inside the Red Fort

The sign outside the tin-roofed exhibition hall, situated within Delhi's Red Fort (Lal Quila) complex and framed by an elongated Indian tricolour, stated in Hindi and in

English: 'Exhibition of Blood Paintings of Young Martyrs' (Fig. 8.1). The exhibition ran from October 2009 until spring of the following year, and the number of visitors it received was in the hundreds of thousands (3-4,000 per day, according to official figures). Few of these visitors, however, entered the complex with the express intention of visiting the exhibition or in the knowledge that it even existed. The primary purpose of nearly all the visitors was to inspect the richly symbolic historical buildings of the Red Fort. Past the fort's famous Lahore Gate and a row of stalls selling tourist memorabilia, however, just prior to the main set of buildings, lies the exhibition hall, conveniently enough located for a large proportion of tourists to make the impromptu decision to pay it a visit (there was no additional cost). Most visitors were Indian; a good proportion of them had arrived on coach trips from the provinces, visiting the Red Fort as part of a nationalist itinerary that included other notable sights in the capital such as Mahatma Gandhi's memorial and former Prime Minister Indira Gandhi's house. I estimate that between 5 and 10 per cent of visitors were foreign tourists. Despite the location of the exhibition at an international tourist site, however, the primary intended audience was an Indian one, as we shall see.

A great Mughal structure, the fort possesses dense nationalist associations: for instance, the Prime Minister addresses the nation and raises the Indian flag at the Red Fort each year on Indian Independence Day, and it houses a chair said to have been used by Subhas Chandra Bose during his days in Burma at the helm of his self-styled Provisional Government of Independent India (Azad Hind). And it is Bose's famous utterance, 'Give me your blood, and I will give you freedom', from which the organizer of the exhibition, Ravi Chander Gupta, took his original inspiration (*prerna*). Indeed, the very first portrait he gave his blood for – painted by his friend and colleague the artist Gurdarshan Singh Binkal – was of and for Bose, painted as it was

Figure 8.1. Outside the exhibition. (All photos by the author.)

in 1997, Bose's centenary year (Fig. 8.2). Significantly, the painting was made in front of Delhi schoolchildren. For Gupta, a retired schoolteacher, the children's dispiriting ignorance of former patriotic sacrifices was one of the motivating factors behind the portraits: 'The biographies of martyrs should be included in course curriculum. Paintings, posters and calendars of freedom fighters should be promoted so that more and more people know them and read about them'. As one news report puts it: 'Gupta feels that very few people are aware about our freedom fighters and especially the youth'.[4] Another reports that Gupta's organization hopes to 'take the 150-portrait "Shaheed" exhibition across the country "since it is the only way of creating aware-ness about the sacrifice of the martyrs. Those born in the post-Independence era cannot feel the struggle of freedom fighters," Ravi Chander Gupta ... said'.[5] A selection of the eighteen books Gupta has written on the martyrs, several of which were pub-lished by the Indian government, were on display at the entrance to the exhibition alongside the visitors' book (Fig. 8.3). Gupta has been particularly concerned to high-light the role played by child martyrs in the Independence struggle, most of whom barely register in official accounts. He lives alone; as he put it to me: 'the martyrs are my family'.

At the entrance to the hall was positioned the very first blood portrait made: that depicting Bose in his classic military pose. Beside the portrait of Bose, the exhibition's rubric was displayed:

Figure 8.2. Subhas Chandra Bose (Gupta's first painting).

Figure 8.3. Ravi Chander Gupta with books he has written on the martyrs.

> Why use blood as ink? (*Rakt ki syahi se hi kyun?*). Those martyrs could have supported their old parents. They could have led a life of luxury with their families, could have become high-level writers, industrialists, businessmen, or leaders and earned money and fame. But they chose something else ... the path of sacrifice. They loved their country more than their families. They wanted to see the future generations as citizens of a free and prosperous nation. We heard that the history of the sacrifice made by the martyrs would be written in gold letters.[6] But where has it been written? I thought, if not in gold letters, it can be written in blood letters ... and the process started. This exhibition is a humble tribute to the martyrs.

The lament 'But where has it been written?' takes us to the heart of Gupta's project – his fear that knowledge of the noble sacrifices of the many citizens who died fighting for freedom is fading away:

> I am spreading awareness through this exhibition. This is to remind the people who are forgetting. The [sacrifices of the] *shaheed* (martyrs) are not taught on the curriculum. It is the need of the time to bring these stories onto [school] courses so that children may gain inspiration from them. The government is sleeping on this.

Another of Gupta's concerns is the impression he has of youthful martyrs as having been scripted out of the nationalist narrative, so he undertook twelve years of research on their histories, documenting more than 500 children and young adults (from the ages of 6 to 20 years) who died in the freedom struggle. Many, though not all, of the portraits in the exhibition depict these hitherto neglected child martyrs.

Speaking of the very first portrait for which he provided blood, that of Subhas Chandra Bose, Gupta told me: 'I wanted to use my dearest thing (*sab se priya vastu*) – to offer it to Neta Ji. The dearest particle of my life – this is blood only. I can do this for him'. As an offering to Bose, it seems almost like a last-ditch attempt on the part of Gupta to respond to Bose's exhortation that he be given the blood of the citizenry. Too young at the time, decades later Gupta is perhaps finally able to participate in a glorious cause. This is, then, a sacrificial portraiture: for the martyrs and for the nation. But the use of blood is also understood to be efficacious in respect of Gupta's larger concern to remember the martyrs:

> The public is attracted to portraits of blood. I started this to attract the public and get their attention. People are more interested if the portraits are in blood; they are more motivated, more curious if blood is used rather than paint. Blood creates sentiments; sentiment (*bhavna*) is attached to blood. It acquires social value and importance if done in blood.

Of further note are the patriotic songs, mainly from Hindi films of the 1950s, which played continuously in the hall and that added to the multisensory nature of the exhibition. I asked Gupta about his choice of music: 'I am playing these songs to inculcate love for the country, to create an atmosphere. When you enter a *mandir* (temple) you light incense and transform the atmosphere. Like that, these songs create an atmosphere of patriotism'. A song I heard numerous times during my visits is the classic 'Ai mere watan ke logo' ('O! People of my country!'), sung by Lata Mangeshkar, which commemorates Indian soldiers who died during the 1962 Sino-Indian War, and which was famously performed before India's first Prime Minister Jawaharlal Nehru on the country's 1963 Republic Day. Its themes correspond closely to those emphasized by Gupta, centring as they do on blood and memory:

> O! People of my country! Keep on chanting the slogans [the slogans praising India]. This is an auspicious day for all of us. Unfurl our beloved tricolour, but don't forget that at the borders brave people have lost their lives. Remember those who never returned home ... When the Himalayas were wounded [by Chinese forces], when our freedom was in peril, as long as they had any breath left in them, they fought ... When it was [the festival] of Holi they played [it] with their blood. When we were sitting in our homes they were being pierced by bullets ... Some were Sikh, some were Jat [a cultivating caste] and some Maratha [hailing from Maharashtra], some were Gurkha and some from Madras. Whosoever died at the border, every such warrior was an Indian. The blood that fell on the hills of the Himalayas – that blood was Indian ... Lest you forget them this story has been recounted ... Victory to India, Victory to the Indian Armed Forces ...

Holi is a spring festival celebrated in honour of the god Krishna in which playful reversals of gender, generation, class, and caste are enacted in a variety of ways (Cohen 1995: 401). It usually involves the throwing of various brightly coloured substances – vividly re-imagined in 'Ai mere watan ke logo' as bright red blood. Usually considered particularly pleasurable, or *masti*, the festival is here melded with the high seriousness of national sacrifice. Of further note is the song's integrative aesthetic, with its references to different religious, caste and regional 'types' of fallen hero – Sikh, Jat, and so on. The song thus introduces and enfolds themes of memory and integrated difference (by way of an idiom of blood) that are critical to the analysis below. In referring explicitly to the Sino-Indian War of 1962 it also underlines the important point that, though Gupta is principally concerned to remember those who fought and died in the fight against colonial rule, in addition his portraits memorialize Indians who have died in subsequent conflicts – the most recent of his portraits depict martyrs of the 1999 Kargil conflict between India and Pakistan.

Martyrs and memory

Mazzarella has recently referred to the way in which the achievement of Indian Independence in 1947 was not only a moment of victory but also 'in a very important sense a moment of loss' – a 'loss of the loss', as he puts it (2010: 1-2). This is useful in helping us to understand the predicament of Gupta and other members of the organization he has formed to produce and look after the paintings. Scholars have been active in emphasizing various sorts of alienation and loss consequent upon colonial rule (e.g. Nandy 1983); at the same time, however, it can be argued that 'colonization enabled a fullness of nationalist subjectivity ... In this paradoxical sense, British colonial rule was for India the loss that made possible the affective plenitude of mass nationalism' (Mazzarella 2010: 2). Gupta and his colleagues seek to revivify this affective plenitude in a kind of delayed challenge to, and contemporary variant of, the 'loss of the loss'. Of particular concern is the popular and bureaucratic failure to remember past sacrifices considered to be the occluded condition of the present relentlessly future-orientated national situation. To paraphrase Engelke (2007), Gupta's blood portraits speak to a problem of nationalist presence.

Recall now the lines from Gupta's exhibition rubric: 'We heard that the history of the sacrifice made by the martyrs would be written in gold letters. But where has it been written? I thought, if not in gold letters, it can be written in blood letters'. The portraits are thus objects in the service of memorialization – a subject that a number of sophisticated anthropological studies have tackled in recent years (e.g. Carsten 2007; Kuchler & Melion 1991; Miller & Parrott 2009). The memorializing thrust of the portraits is necessary because existing memorialization processes are experienced as inadequate or tokenistic.[7] Their purpose is to invoke a memory that is not passive but active, as the stimulus of a revivified sacrificial spirit. This is memorialization as a call to action.

Gupta recalled to me his days as a schoolteacher in a government school in east Delhi: 'I felt the children knew nothing. They thought we achieved freedom without lifting a finger. They sang popular songs about Gandhi and *ahimsa* (non-violence). They thought we got freedom without picking up a weapon! And so I said, well, I need to tell the children it's not true'. This is, then, an explicitly anti-Gandhian project of re-education. Nationalist historiography – at least in terms of its manifestation in school curricula – thus hinges on what Gupta sees as a Gandhian perversion; a perversion to be corrected, in part, by the exhibitions he stages.

I mentioned earlier the 'relentless' future orientation of a present moment that seems to form, for Gupta and his organization, yet another 'loss of the loss' insofar as it further eviscerates the affective plenitude of mass nationalism and its manifold sacrifices. The problem is that the new neoliberal consumerist order, inaugurated in the early 1990s, seems to possess a finite and shallow national memory akin, so to speak, to 'a glass, which when it becomes full, begins to shed its old content as the new is poured in' (Macfarlane 1997: 23). It is no accident, I suggest, that Gupta's painting project was begun at this time of expedited social and economic transformation.

Connerton discusses the intimate linkages between the valorization of memory and processes of cultural forgetting. Memorials exemplify this inverse relation, 'for the desire to memorialize is precipitated by a fear, a threat, of cultural amnesia' (Connerton 2009: 27). He offers the example of museums: 'It was when the age of mechanical reproduction caused objects to become obsolete at an ever accumulating speed that many Europeans devoted their energy to a cult of monuments without earlier parallel and founded public museums on an unprecedented scale' (2009: 27). Particularly pertinent for the present discussion is Connerton's claim that 'when a nation feels itself to be no longer a place where history on a grand, a truly memorable, scale is being made, it turns inward to cultivate its memorials' (2009: 28).

The Indian case both reflects and inverts this scenario. The post-1990s dismantlement of the Nehruvian planned economy – the withdrawal of the state from its role as principal overseer of production – has led to the increasing integration of India into the world economy and the consequent dramatic emergence of a middle-class consumerist ideology. Now an assertively modern aspiring global power, Indian metropolitan newsstands and bookshops are full of '2020 Vision Documents' (manifestos spelling out just how – and certainly not *if* – India will shake off the embarrassing impertinence of its 'developing country' status by that magic date). Truly, in Connerton's terms – and so far as its metropolitan elite is concerned – this is a country in the business of making history, and of gaining its rightful inheritance, and as such it is precisely *not* turning inward to cultivate its memorials. The energies of its political and media class all seem directed towards a glorious future. An urgent need to remember is thus precipitated by the insistent future-orientated impulse of the present moment.

It is not only Gupta and his organization who are alarmed by this future-fixated impulse. In 2009 a blood donation camp was staged in a spatio-temporal conjunction saturated with nationalist significance: the place was Jalianwala Bagh in Punjab, scene of one of the colonial government's most notorious atrocities when in 1919 General Dyer ordered his soldiers to fire indiscriminately upon the peaceful protesters in the park; the time was Mahatma's Gandhi's birthday (Gandhi Jayanti). The camp's organizers stated that its aim was 'to awake the government from deep slumber to grant the status of freedom fighter to the martyrs killed during the massacre of 13 April 1919'. Perhaps, then, this event, as well as Gupta's own efforts, is indicative of the intimate link 'between memorialization and the moment of felt transience' (Connerton 2009: 28). The association surfaces with particular acuity, says Connerton, at times when soon there will no longer be left any first-hand witnesses of the remembered events – as with the current urge to build memorials to the Holocaust. The observation perhaps holds for the case of the Indian nationalist movement, too. Maybe this, as much as the present future orientation of metropolitan India, explains the current acute presence of a counter-tendency – an urgent will to remember.

It is a sociological truism that 'people constantly transform the recollections that they produce' (Zelizer 1995: 216). For Gupta's organization, such transformation is precisely the problem – it aims to intervene in the negotiation process of collective memory in order to revivify and stabilize a particular body of remembrances. But the project is not only one of restoration. Gupta counters transformation with transformation, for in foregrounding those who died fighting colonial rule – that is, by highlighting the active role of *violent revolutionaries* in overthrowing the imperial yoke – the very narrative that India achieved Independence non-violently is called into question. In this sense Gupta's project is anything but conservative.

Coming together to bleed
By the mid-2000s more than a hundred portraits had been completed, with Gupta busying himself exhibiting them in schools and elsewhere. By this time he had also formed an organization, the Shaheed Smriti Chetna Samiti (Society to Awaken

Remembrance of the Martyrs; henceforth 'the *samiti*'), in order that the paintings would be cared for after his passing. Tellingly, the Sanskrit word *smriti* is literally 'that which is remembered'. Until 2004, all the paintings were formed of Gupta's blood. However, after two bypass surgeries (Gupta is now 73), doctors forbade him to provide any more of his own blood, so the artist Binkal now uses his own blood to paint the martyrs. But there arose a problem – the paintings were fading, and the artist could hardly be expected to provide *all* the necessary blood for their re-touching.

So there is a telling irony here: blood is the ink with which to redeem the promise of gold letters for the immortalization of the freedom fighters, but blood as artistic material is inconstant and ephemeral, partaking of the flux that is the hallmark of materials (Ingold 2007). Analogous with the faded memories the paintings are supposed to enliven, blood, too, fades. Ssorin-Chaikov has explored the material and temporal fragility of timelessness in respect of an exhibition of gifts given to Stalin on his birthday in 1949. Presented to an 'immortal' leader in the context of a 'timeless' socialist present, many of the gifts were broken in the rush of constructing the exhibition, and the exhibition itself, created 'for good', existed only until Stalin's death a few years later (Ssorin-Chaikov 2006: 358). Such entropy at the heart of the timeless memorial was potentially dangerous: 'A special sub-committee was set up at the Communist Party Central Committee Administration to observe the decay of numerous food items and the condition of breakables such as china. It was to document that there was no *intention* involved in the decomposition of gifts to Stalin' (2006: 370, original emphasis). However, in the case of the *samiti*'s decaying portraits, the potential danger of simply *re-presenting* the fragility of memories of the martyrs' timeless sacrifices in material form was turned into an opportunity.

In 2008 in Ghaziabad, a district of Uttar Pradesh state adjacent to Delhi, a special 'blood camp' was staged in order to collect blood for use in re-touching the portraits. The blood of 125 people was collected. The portraits' decay was thus turned into an opportunity for co-re-creation: that is, for the artworks' re-creation according to a template of national participation. 'Difference' (e.g. of caste, religion, or geographic provenance) among blood contributors was actively encouraged, with the portraits – now composed of multiple mingled bloods – becoming sanguinary microcosms of the national *unitas multiplex*.

As Gupta noted to me:

> There were a lot more people but we didn't need more. It was organized for making national sentiments. We used bottles – only 20 ml each. We put an anti-clotting chemical into it; there was just that, and the blood. We mixed the blood together and directly used it. First of all you sketch on the paper with a pencil and then you paint over it with [regular] paint so that there is only a very faint outline, and then you paint over the faint outline with the blood.

Depicted on the banners adorning the Ghaziabad event were the words: 'Shahido keliye rakt sangrah shivir' ('Blood collection for the martyrs'). 'People came running to contribute for the martyrs', says Gupta. Blood was donated, then, *for* the martyrs. Despite an effort to distinguish between blood collection and medically useful blood donation, this was indeed, in a sense, a blood *donation* camp, but with recipients who were dead rather than living. More specifically, the donation was to their memories – the call was for donations that would keep the dead (rather than the precariously living) alive (in people's memories). The element of exchange is fairly explicit: the martyrs gave their blood for the nation; contemporary Indians are exhorted to give them their blood to keep their memory alive.

I focus for a moment on the mixing mentioned by Gupta. Of course, in many situations in the subcontinent bodily mixing is anathema – strict corporeal separations are enforced in order to maintain caste purity; indeed, all sorts of restrictions adhere in the flow of substance (see, e.g., Lambert 2000). However, partly because of this very negative power attributed to the mixing of substances, there inheres within the 'politics of substance' a strong utopian potential (Alter 1992: 258). Mixing in the form of, say, an inter-caste marriage or a transfusion sourced from different religious 'types' (see Cohen 2001) can carry powerful messages about nationhood, reason, and civic-mindedness. The Nehruvian integrative nationalist or rationalist activist can gain great satisfaction from transgressing restrictions in flows of substance; but in 'constructively' inverting the typical pattern of restrictions, the pattern can, paradoxically, be reproduced – it is simply the valuation of the transgression that is altered. Perhaps, therefore, what Gupta sees when he looks at the (re-touched) paintings is an exemplary saturation, a concentration of the differential blood of the nation that speaks an answer to the heroes it depicts: a contemporary response to a bygone exhortation (to shed one's blood for the nation), a vital instantiation of the very sentiment (willingness to shed one's blood) that the portraits seek to inspire.

Also of interest was the use of 20 ml collection bottles – far smaller than the medical limit. As Gupta explained to me: 'We collected 20 ml only [from each person] so that many people could be involved. Only one syringe each'. Gupta is clear, then, that multiple sources of blood, though not strictly necessary, were nevertheless desired (and facilitated). He also explains that women, Muslims, and children all contributed. (The backgrounds of the contributors were *alag-alag*, 'different-different', as he put it.) This was thus an example of the spatial concentration of difference that is characteristic of the Indian nationalist ideology of national integration more generally (Copeman 2009a: chap. 7). As Hugh-Jones (2011) has observed, '[B]lood-brotherhood [may be] produced not only by mixing blood together but also by mixing together to give blood'. This was, then, an Arendtian coming together of diverse individuals for a shared purpose – the enactment of a belated response to Bose's exhortation in the form of extractive artistic participation (Arendt 1994). Present-day bleeding under the sign of Bose's refrain is a way of sustaining the vitality of this refrain, with all its connotations of affective nationalist plenitude.

Consider now the question of repeatability raised by Bynum in respect of Christ's 'once for all' blood sacrifice: '[I]f Christian sacrifice is once for all, how are the sanctifying effects maintained in a temporal world? If Christ is not sacrificed anew on the altar, how do Christians plug into, or keep afresh, a moment of erupting holiness that is anything but momentary?' (2007: 245). Gupta and his *samiti* are similarly concerned with keeping afresh and plugging into the 'original' nationalist sacrifices that took place in the struggle for Independence. Rather like the blood donation events staged on Bose's birth and death anniversaries, the sanguinary nature of the portraiture they produce is a means of continually responding to, and keeping fresh, the nationalist exhortation to sacrifice (one's blood). As Bynum summarizes the problem of Christ's bleeding sacrifice: '[H]ow could it be momentary yet eternal?' (2007: 245). For the medieval German blood cults she analyses, the immediacy, but also the participatory nature, of 'blood miracles' alongside the Mass formed a kind of solution. With the crucifixion multiply re-enacted by way of miraculous bloodshed events, Christ was kept bleeding multi-locally and trans-historically. Taking blood from a national 'congregation' for mixing into the martyrs' portraits denotes a similarly participatory solution to the problem of maintaining nationalist plenitude as an ongoing 'eruption'. Re-touching will presumably be required again, along with a renewed call to a differentially imagined citizenry to give its blood for the martyrs. When the time comes, what will be demonstrated, once more, is how the generative flux of the world of materials (Ingold 2007: 12) may yield rich nationalist dividends.

Traces

But what sort of representation is achieved through use of the blood medium? For Gupta, as was noted above, the use of blood is important for gaining people's interest – it is, in this sense, a tactical usage. But it is also significant because, in being formed through acts of bleeding, there is an important sense in which the portraits constitute themselves the emulation they call for – adding to their hoped-for precipitative force. There is a venerable tradition of patriotic Indian portraiture, a genre that gathered in intensity during the struggle for Independence, and which made similar demands on the contemporary viewer, who was encouraged to make sacrifices of a comparable nature to those depicted (particularly iconic are those depicting Bhagat Singh offering his own bloody head to Bharat Mata [India as mother goddess] [see Pinney 2004; Ramaswamy 2008]). While Gupta's paintings certainly connect to this lineage of didactic portraiture, they also obviously differ: first, in being of far more recent provenance, speaking to a present-day situation understood to be marked by accelerated forgetting; and, second, in being literally composed of the blood they seek to elicit from others. Moreover, these are metonymic extractions: a small part of one's blood is indicative of the larger deficits the giver is willing to offer in the future if necessary. This is a kind of memorialization that, as I have noted, is also a call to action. In terms of 'aesthetics', this emphasis on efficacy – the intention that the blood portraits should cause things to happen – appears congruent with Gell's (1998: 97) observation that representational art in India is a unity of form and function (see also Pinney 2004: 190).[8] Whether or not the portraits are in fact successful in this respect is a point I address below, though the following example provides part of the answer.

Leafing through the visitors' book with Gupta – a favourite occupation of his during the long days of the exhibition, at which he was always present – I asked him which, of the thousands of comments, he found most gratifying. He guided me unhesitatingly to the words of an 8-year-old schoolboy from Delhi: 'These paintings are from the heart. When the time comes to sacrifice my blood for the protection of my country I will sacrifice my whole life'. As Gupta put it to me: 'This exhibition is to inspire the people to make sacrifices. Sacrifices are not all over now. You can still do it; you *should* still do it. The sacrifices are not only in the past; even in the future there is a time for sacrifice for the country'. In other words, Gupta is calling for the re-temporalization of sacrifice.

The paintings are thus a form of enactive remembering – depictions of blood sacrifice that perform the bleeding they represent and seek to inspire. I have referred to the hoped-for precipitative force of the portraits, so it is important to consider where such a force might come from. As was noted above, the portraits are (amongst other things) a retort to 'weak' Gandhian nationalism. And the retort appears to 'work', in part, through their being imitative of the bleeding they seek to inspire (see Bynum [2007: 4] on imitations of Christ's bleeding). This, then, is a kind of mimetic bleeding art – 'mimetic' insofar as 'originary' blood sacrificers are paid homage to by bleeding in turn, but mimetic also in terms of the willingness to sacrifice one's blood that it is supposed to incite in the viewer. The paintings call for emulation as models of and models for sacrificial bleeding.

That this is imitative art, which in turn (it is hoped) will be imitated, is suggestive of a kind of sympathetic magic; for that which is desired (patriotic bleeding, or at least *willingness* to bleed) is imitated in order to make it happen in the future ('[T]he magician infers that he can produce any effect he desires merely by imitating it' [Frazer quoted in Taussig 1993: 47]). Moreover, as the portraits perform the bleeding they both represent and seek to inspire, complexity is 'added in' to the idea that this is representational art at all: that is to say, the distinction between representation and presence is problematized, a blurring that is quite common in 'body art' (Jay 2002: 65). Certainly, blood is the medium through which the fallen freedom fighters are represented, but it is also a literal corporeal trace of the artist's presence. This has interesting consequences, as we shall see.

Consider Gell's famous delineation of the aniconic symbol, which he compares to the foreign diplomat: 'The Chinese ambassador in London ... does not look like China, but in London, China looks like him' (1998: 98). Similar to the ambassador, who is a 'spatio-temporally detached fragment of his nation' (1998: 98), aniconic works of art, such as religious idols, make gods present in visual form. One can 'represent' in the manner of a painting (iconically), but one can also 'represent' in the manner of an ambassador (aniconically). Blood portraits are both iconic *and* aniconic: iconic because they visually depict fallen martyrs; aniconic because the artist is *present* in the painting not only in terms of conceptualization and technique, but also, critically, as physical residue. That the corporeal self of the artist is mixed with the primary subject of the portrait, thereby 'entering into' the subject of representation, suggests that what results, paradoxically, may be considered a kind of self-portrait.

We can discern here a quite familiar South Asian template. Hindu rituals contain identification between worshipper and deity as a central theme and objective (in *puja*), with identification reinforced subsequently through the offering of substances such as food and flowers (*prasad*). *Puja* (worship) aims to 'create a unity between deity and worshipper that dissolves the difference between them' (Fuller 2004: 57). There is, I suggest, a *puja* element to the portraits, with the blood of which they are composed a kind of offering to the depictions it comprises. In this sense, the sign and the flesh are one; or one might say that the iconic and aniconic elements lose their separate identities in the space of the portrait-as-*puja*. Recall that the sense of an offering was explicit at the special re-touching event discussed above, with the public asked to give blood for the martyrs in return for the blood they sacrificed in the work of securing national Independence. That the wider Indian genre of patriotic art, of which Gupta's works constitute a subspecies, incorporates nationalist heroes into the Hindu pantheon substantiates the argument that a *puja* element inheres within the portraits. Ramaswamy refers to a portrait in blood depicting Mahatma Gandhi exhibited in the National Gandhi Museum in New Delhi. The 'literally bloody painting shows Gandhi with not one but three heads (two of them painted in the colours of the national flag), signifying his apotheosis into the Hindu pantheon with its many multiheaded and multilimbed gods' (Ramaswamy 2008: 838). While it is rare for such patriotic portraiture to use blood as its representational medium, it is not unusual for the martyrs depicted to appear transfigured into Hindu gods. It is therefore not outlandish to suggest that Gupta's blood portraiture, as offering, connotes a form of communion analogous with that of *puja* and its transfer of substances. Like the idols of gods discussed by Gell, the portraits are not only depictions. There is an aniconic element, too, for the portraits index, quite literally, the artist's spatio-temporal presence as substantive offerings to the icons they comprise. The painting itself is transactional in this sense; it enframes *puja*.

Recall also Gupta's comparison, referred to above, between exhibition hall and temple space, with the music of *desh-bhakti* (patriotism) considered to be analogous to the way incense helps create a mood of devotional communion.

What is more, Guha (2007) has suggested that Bose's exhortation – specifically its call for blood sacrifice – derived from the traditions of bloodthirsty Kali worship so popular in Bose's native province of Bengal. If this is correct, then the refrain to which the *samiti* responds had its origins in a similar set of sacrificial logics to those that the paintings now enframe. And of course, it is no longer only the artist's blood that communes with the images it is used to depict. The need for re-touching resulted in collection of blood from several hundred others. That there are multiple bloods mixed into the image collectivizes the *puja* that is enframed in the space of the portrait.

But this is not all that the 'literalism' of the artist's presence achieves. I turn now to the affective dimension of the portraits, focusing on visitor responses to them. Are the portraits efficacious in the manner intended by Gupta and his *samiti*?

Affective literalism

The responses I obtained at the exhibition at the Red Fort do not provide a clear-cut answer to the above question. A good portion of the visitors I spoke with were not aware, despite the information displayed, that human blood had been used for the portraits. However, to some degree the exhibition I attended was not typical of the other occasions in which the paintings have been displayed (school classrooms, stand-alone exhibitions, etc.). Attendance, this time round, tended to be an epiphenomenon of the primary purpose of the tourist's visit (i.e. to see the main Red Fort buildings). Many attendees, then, could hardly be said to have been stimulated to attend by the novel prospect of a sanguinary mode of portraiture, though that is not to say that others have not been so at other perhaps less atypical display venues (Fig. 8.4).

Figure 8.4. A visitor at the exhibition before a portrait depicting Raja Nahar Singh of Ballabhgargh and Seth Ramji Das Gur Wale, both of whom were involved in the Indian Uprising of 1857.

Responses gained from discussion but also in (mainly Hindi) written form in the visitors' book, though diverging little from what is a quite familiar nationalist 'script' that emphasizes the requirement to honour and remember the country's fallen heroes, were mainly of a manner that Gupta would find gratifying: that is, they offered evidence that the 'correct' nationalist interpretations and sentiments had duly been stimulated by the works on display. One visitor, Brijmohan Prasad from Punjab, stated: 'Old memories are being refreshed'. Meghnaath Rai from Bihar stated similarly: 'These people gave their lives to liberate the country – we should take inspiration (*prerna*)'. Even more pleasing for Gupta: 'I wish that my name was also included among these *shahids*, then I could have called myself a true child of Mother India'. Another comment, this time in English: 'I am proud to be an Indian and also proud of those persons who forgot about themselves and gave their whole blood for our motherland. *Jai Hind* (Hail India)'. A further observation, from Manoj Mishra of Faizabad, reflected similar sentiments to those of Gupta concerning memory and willingness to sacrifice: 'This exhibition is in the blood of the artist! It is inspiring for the new generations. If any other country raises its evil eye (*buri nazar*) towards India the entire young generation will be prepared to hang'. Other visitors made similar comments concerning a present situation characterized by forgetfulness and consequent lessening of willingness to sacrifice: 'These portraits in blood are inspiring. It is important that these ideas reach the new generation as it is straying (*binak*) from its path'. In respect of the precipitative aim of the exhibition, comments such as 'I want to be like them and give my life for the country' are strongly indicative of the kind of positive response Gupta was looking for.

A noteworthy aspect of the responses offered by those who were explicitly aware that the paintings were composed of blood is their emphasis on sentiment and, in particular, the heart. For instance, one Sajid Ali, who attended the exhibition with his two toddler-age children in order to further their knowledge of the freedom struggle, stated: 'This exhibition makes one feel proud to be Indian. Being in blood, the sentiments come straight from the heart (*jazbaat dil se nikle hain*)'. A Mr Rampal, from Uttar Pradesh, told me: 'I have a high respect for the persons who gave blood for these paintings. It touches my heart'. Rabiya Muhammed from Orissa noted in the visitors' book: 'The paintings are from the heart and now patriotic feeling (*desh ke prati prem*) is increased in my heart also'. Many more such examples could be given. And as Gupta himself told me: 'Some say that blood should not be used for this purpose.[9] But I say, it is the most special substance for [the promotion of] national sentiments because it comes literally from the heart (*sidha dil se*)'.

In Western contexts, in order to insist upon the sincerity of a particular feeling, it is a commonplace to assert that such a sentiment 'comes from the heart'. Though many non-South Asians would surely maintain that the heart is the seat of the emotions, such understandings are nevertheless premised more on metaphorical than on physiological ideas about the provenance of 'sentiments' (see Bildhauer [this volume] on the association of blood with emotions in medieval Europe, and Alberti [2010] on connections between the heart and affective states). In Schneider's (1980) famous analysis, Americans view love as consequent on blood ties, without these things necessarily being identical to one another. What is interesting about the visitor responses recorded above is the sense that, because the medium of the portraits has literally passed through the human hearts of those from whom it has been extracted, the sentiments of the works are more forcefully conveyed and authentic. Indeed, there is the suggestion that the blood medium does not merely connote the nationalist sentiment that incited its extraction but that it *is*, quite literally, that sentiment as unmediated affect. Sentiment thus appears as a kind of material.

If, following Mazzarella, 'any social project that is not imposed by force alone must be affective in order to be effective' (2009: 299), then strikingly visible blood-as-affect appears to be a key source of the required affective efficacy in the case of Gupta's project. None of this will be particularly surprising for South Asianist scholars familiar with the potential for the particulate transmissibility of personhood in the region, and indeed I have shown elsewhere how certain categories of blood donor in the subcontinent see their blood as being made up largely of spirit, love, knowledge, and intentions (Copeman 2009a: 91). What is, however, worthy of consideration is that the understanding here of sentiment as a kind of material appears consequent on the role of the heart as source of that material.

The presupposition that the heart is the seat of genuine feeling seemingly causes the blood that has flowed from it literally to embody the sentiments that gave rise to its extraction. The comments above appear to indicate that it is this derivation of the medium that makes the portraits largely 'effective' in the manner desired by Gupta insofar as congruent sentiments are in turn produced in their viewers.

In a study of 'sinking heart' syndrome among Punjabi people living in England, Krause (1989) notes the literal nature of understandings of the condition, referring to Ayurvedic conceptions of the heart as a reservoir for emotional processes (1989: 568). From love and pride to shame and fear, feelings 'belong to the body and they flow [literally] from the heart'. As Krause also notes, the word for heart, *dil*, is frequently used for 'I' in Punjabi. For the village Muslims in Chitral, Pakistan, studied by Marsden, 'the most important source of a person's genuine thought is the heart (*hardi*)' (2005: 88), while for Mauritian Muslims of Indian origin, the ability to listen in a sensitive way to devotional poetry in honour of the Prophet Muhammad is described as 'hearing with the heart' (*dil se*) (Eisenlohr 2010: 320). In the *Upanishads*, the heart is the central spiritual power in the body; moreover, 'Supreme heaven shines in the lotus of the heart'. It is reported that 'the literality of this image caused beautiful, poetic confusions in anatomical beliefs' (Young 2007: 16). Finally, the example *par excellence* of the heart as the literal repository of genuine feeling: the story of Hanuman, the Hindu monkey deity and ardent devotee of the gods Ram and Sita, who, when his devotion is mocked, rips open his chest to reveal Ram and Sita literally ensconced in his heart (see Gell 1998: 143; Young 2007: 16).

It is clearly beyond the scope of this essay to provide a comprehensive cultural history of the heart in South Asia, suffice it to say that in the cases under consideration the portraits' material composition from a substance delivered, literally, from the heart, and partaking of the sentiment it embodies and produces, appears to lend force to their affective efficacy. Such a finding is congruent with understandings elsewhere in South Asia that see the heart as the literal repository of genuine sentiment. Blood-as-affect thus possesses both an indicative function (in regard to the sentiment of the artist/ blood-giver) and a precipitative function (in regard to congruent sentiments provoked in the viewer), as is indicated by the aforementioned reflection that, since 'the paintings are from the heart ... patriotic feeling is increased in my heart also'.

Sanguinary politics

So where does such portraiture fit into the larger sanguinary politics referred to at the beginning of this essay?

Blood extraction in political contexts (principally for purposes of medical donation, petitions, or paintings) may be considered, following Bairy (2009), a key present-day form of political enunciation, for such extractions – speaking as and on behalf of a subject position (Bairy 2009: 112) – are intensely communicative. Somewhat akin to the transformative fasts undertaken by Gandhi, they seek to persuade from the moral high ground of political asceticism. They are a means of presentation and public positioning of self and cause. Such an observation does not, however, explain how or why these extractions have become such a means. I return to these points in a moment after providing a sense of the wider sanguinary milieu.

Gupta's *samiti* is joined in particular by Hindu nationalist organizations in its proclivity for portraits in blood. In each case blood extraction seems to communicate metonymic intentions, by which I mean that the portion extracted is an indication of the whole the agent is willing to give if called upon. It is a demonstration of intent. Consider here a newspaper article from 2007 headlined 'Hindu activists paint Lord Rama with blood to protest against Sethu Samundram project' (*Hindustan Times* 2007). What the headline refers to is a chain of limestone shoals which featured prominently in the famous Hindu mythological text the *Ramayana* and are thought to be threatened by a government project to dredge a channel between India and Sri Lanka in order to cut costs for freight shipping. I quote from the report: 'The painting using blood as a medium is intended to show the anguish of the Hindu community. "We have expressed the pain we have felt regarding Ram Sethu. If one can give blood (for the cause) he can shed it as well" '. In addition to being an ascetic demonstration of bodily commitment, there is also a threat of further bloodshed.

'This is a message to those who are opposed to [the Hindu god and king] Ram and the ones concerned with the project that they should relinquish the idea of destructing the bridge or they will have to face the consequences,' said a leader of [Hindu right formation] the Bajrang Dal.

The blood portrait was thus a kind of premonitory bloodshed, a sanguinary forewarning. Also of interest is that the god Rama formed the subject of the painting, suggesting a further point of connection with the *samiti*'s portraits: that is, the painting becomes the site of an offering of substance according to a logic of enframed *puja* in which devotees 'mix into' the deity. Further examples of Hindu nationalist blood portraiture could be readily provided.

That activists of the Hindu right employ blood in such a way is not particularly surprising. Whilst it is important not to impute internal consistency to a highly differentiated set of groups and pragmatic alliances, Hindu nationalist activists have, broadly speaking, been at the forefront of developing a political aesthetics of blood 'speech'. A protest rally against Islamic terrorism organized by the Bharatiya Janata Party (BJP) and Rashtriya Swayamsevak Sangh (RSS) in 2001 featured the

collecting [of] signatures in blood on huge banners proclaiming the 'death of terrorism'. ... A three-wheeler equipped with loudspeaker and manned by a BJP worker did the rounds of colonies around [politician] Khurana's constituency, inviting people to sign their names in blood. "Campaigners first allowed blood to be drawn, saw it being put in a test tube and then dipped cotton padded needles to sign on the banner. And as they did so they were drowned in a chorus of nationalistic slogans", while the wasted blood was poured down the drain... Even school children were included in the "sacrifice" of blood – and all this in a city where the government has been repeatedly announcing a shortage of blood for accident victims (Taneja 2001).[10]

During political demonstrations in 1992 that led to the destruction of the Babri Masjid mosque in Ayodhya, the Hindu nationalist youth group the Bajrang Dal, referred to above, welcomed BJP party leader L.K. Advani to the city by applying a ritual mark (*tilak*) of blood on his forehead (Fuller 2004: 272).[11] On other occasions they have offered him cups of blood. Many activists of the Hindu right, then, see themselves as 'people of blood' (Heuze 1992: 2261), and employ human blood for a wide variety of enunciative purposes. What I am simply seeking to show here is that the *samiti*'s use of blood has its place in a network of political extractions: the transactional enframement of the blood painting, and its metonymic 'threat', are both also features of the wider Indian sanguinary politics and can be used in order to articulate far narrower political visions than that of the *samiti*'s broadly inclusive and 'secular' nationalism.

Yet perhaps such shared features should cause us to reconsider whether the *samiti* is in fact as broadly inclusive as has been suggested. Gupta informed me that he has recently received the promise of a permanent home for his portraits in Vrindavan at the ashram of female Hindu ascetic Sadhvi Rithambara. Not only would the location she has offered place the portraits firmly under a Hindu sign, Sadhvi Rithambara is a Vishwa Hindu Parishad activist of particular notoriety – noted for her anti-Muslim rhetoric and widely regarded to have been instrumental in fuelling the tensions that resulted in the afore-mentioned destruction of the Babri Masjid. For Gupta, who intends to take the *sadhvi* up on her offer, this is a welcome solution to a practical problem:

> Very few people come forward with money. I have to spend Rs 400 a day [roughly £6]. We found it very difficult to get land for [a dedicated] museum in Delhi. But we will go to Vrindavan ... Sadhvi Rithambara, who has an ashram there, has spent 30 lakhs [£40,000] [on housing the portraits and contributing to their upkeep]. She is protecting this heritage for the coming generations.

To quote Sadhvi Rithambara herself upon inaugurating an earlier exhibition of the paintings in Vrindavan: 'It is a rare work. The atrocities of past rulers have been exposed through portraits prepared in blood and it is praiseworthy. It is a symbol of committed patriotism'.[12]

The symmetry with the case of Bose is remarkable. Having earlier been President of the Indian National Congress and a colleague of Gandhi, Bose later formed alliances with Nazi Germany and Fascist Italy in order to fight against the British. Although Bose was a 'stoutly secular' figure (Guha 2007), Hindu right formations such as the BJP nevertheless seek on occasion to claim Bose as their own. Now the *samiti*'s nationalism is not reducible to that of the Hindu right (just as Bose's is not, despite the BJP's claim), even if in some ways it allies with it in order to perpetuate Gupta's larger vision (as, arguably, did Bose in respect of European fascism). It is, in any case, rarely the case that a neatly demarcated Nehruvian or Gandhian nationalism stands diametrically opposed to a neatly demarcated nationalism of the Hindu right (or any other variety of Indian nationalism). Rather, all sorts of dialectical combinations of nationalist sensibility can and do arise (Cohen 2008). What the *samiti* and the Hindu right do share, of course, is a commitment to the principle of bloodshed (of one's own and of others) as a prere-quisite for national integrity. In other words, in each case the brand of nationalism espoused is resolutely non-Gandhian. If the *samiti* is broadly inclusivist and the Hindu right broadly exclusivist, the third feature of their common non-Gandhianism (or propensity towards the sanguinary) seems to be the enabling factor in respect of the alliance formed by Gupta and Sadhvi Rithambara.

Quite apart from proponents of non-Gandhianism, blood extractions (particularly medical donations) have been held up across the political spectrum as a medium of promise for purposes of political expression. There is even a sense in which blood donation has promised a purification of the political. Bildhauer (this volume) notes that in late medieval Germany blood was considered 'something that gives immediate access to the truth, that cannot be faked, and that, as pure matter, is beyond discourse and symbolism' (p. S61). Blood can therefore produce 'authenticity effects' (see also Carsten, this volume). The affective literalism suggested by the *samiti*'s use of a medium deriving from the heart might be considered an example of this.

Also noteworthy here is the widespread understanding in the subcontinent that blood loss leads to permanent volumetric deficit and consequent depletion of strength, an understanding that seriously hinders blood donation in the subcontinent (see Copeman 2009a: chap.1). This is frequently expressed in the formulation: 'If I donate blood, I will need a transfusion, so why should I give?' If someone, in the possession of such an understanding, nevertheless donates his or her blood, then one might be more willing to acknowledge that that person's enunciation is sincere (and less a matter of 'a politics of pure calculative instrumentality' [Spencer 1997: 15]). The newsmagazine *Tehelka* stated of Gupta's Red Fort exhibition: 'His tribute may be sincere, but his manner of expressing it is odd'.[13] What the article doubted was not his sincerity but the artistic value of the portraits (which in any case was to miss the point – it was their efficacy, not their status as fine art, that was at stake for the *samiti*). To adapt Bildhauer's formulation, the donation of blood as enunciative act promised to provide immediate access to the truth of the donor's convictions. Given the widespread fears mentioned above, willingness to shed blood demonstrates commitment 'that cannot be faked'. Amidst the acute awareness that political commitments can be – and are – faked, the shedding of blood promised 'unsymbolization', physical proof of sincerity and commitment. This argument is congruent with van de Port's observation about the critical role of the body in seeming to 'precede' all opinionating and therefore in 'upgrading the reality calibre of social and cultural classificatory systems' (2011: 86). This promise of im-mediated political enunciation hinged on anxieties about depletion. We might put it thus: since enunciative bloodshed transcends my own willingness to do likewise, I am forced to construe it as compelling.[14]

Blood donation at political rallies or on the birthdays of politicians is performed not only as an act of devotion to the leader in question, but also as *the truth* of party members' commitment to the medical well-being of constituents. The 'transparency' of blood donation as a mode of enunciation has also found it used in conjunction with anti-corruption campaigns. A blood donation event I attended in Delhi was advertised thus: 'Let's join together and finish corruption. We will begin a new, fresh India. 9 December is the birthday of Sonia Gandhi*ji*. Let all Congress people come and donate their blood at 10 am, Talkatora Road'. Staged by the Youth Congress on the Congress leader's birthday, blood donors signed anti-corruption pledges as they chanted 'Long live Sonia Gandhi'. The donation of blood added an authenticity effect to the signing of the pledge (to be truthful, to not be corrupt like other political parties) in addition to its being, undoubtedly, an expression of devotion to Sonia Gandhi. Political blood donation events, to borrow Power's (1997) phrasing, may be thought of as rituals of verification (of commitment, or of the 'truth' of one's enunciation).

One can begin to gain a sense of the way in which blood donation has provided a promise of im-mediated political enunciation. But the 'promise' I have referred to has remained somewhat enigmatic. Indeed, blood donation might be said to have become a technique of political ellipsis (or compromised enunciation) as much as truth-telling that results in paradoxical double-movements of reform and reversion. This is the irony of India's sanguinary politics: it is precisely because it has developed into such a consummate sign of worthy political asceticism and enunciation that blood donation has become ripe for appropriation for purposes of obscuration. For example, in 2002 a controversy arose when Hindi film icon Amitabh Bachhan inaugurated a series of blood donation camps for the Uttar Pradesh-based political outfit the Samajwadi Party (SP). They were staged during a state assembly election campaign, a time when the Election Commission's model code comes into force, which is meant to prohibit 'vote buying' by candidates eager to hand out 'electoral freebies' (frequently saris, cooking vessels, alcohol, and cash [see Roberts 2010]). The SP's rival, the Congress Party, lodged a complaint with the commission, alleging that 'Mr Bachhan and the SP leaders were using the blood donation camps to gain political mileage. "These camps are being synchronized with the election campaign and they amount to an offer of allurement to the voters" '.[15]

The complaint was that blood donation was being deployed in order to legitimate otherwise forbidden political bribes. One implication was that since the event was associated with the SP, the blood collected might be viewed as a 'gift' to the public from whom it seeks votes. Probably more pertinent, however, is the way in which the 'token of regard' which is by law quite acceptable for blood donation event organizers to offer to blood donors on completion of their donation can be used to set up an exchange that otherwise would be obstructed. This is where blood donation as a technique of political ellipsis comes into its own. At a time when gifts to voters are explicitly forbidden, and this indeed being the only time that political functionaries would want to make them, the exchange is performed obliquely in the guise of another exchange (that which legitimately inheres in the set-up of blood donation events). That is, taking the donor-voter's blood allows the party in turn to offer back that which they would not be allowed to give if there wasn't a blood donation event acting as 'exchange cover' whilst also making visible an electorally useful association between the party and social service.

Further, a news article headlined 'After the bloodletting, the blood donation' reports on a blood donation camp organized by the notorious Mumbai 'don of Dagdi Chawl', Arun Gawli. It speculates dryly that his own blood donation may have been an attempt to 'atone for his sins'. In fact, the blood donation camp formed part of a publicity drive for his newly constituted political party, the Akhil Bharatiya Sena, through which Gawli seems to have been trying to demonstrate his 'reformed' character (Indian Express 1997). Just as the SP is likely to have convinced few people that it was not engaged in 'vote buying' by other means, the tone of the news article documenting Arun Gawli's blood donation evinces marked scepticism about the party leader's supposed reform. Nevertheless, the very attempt to employ blood donation as a means to attain easy political virtue seem to bring blood donation as a mode of political enunciation into disrepute. It is because blood donation is such a readily available (and deployable) sign of political asceticism and 'truth-telling' that its enactment now gives rise to high levels of distrust and scepticism. A practice associated with discipline and social improvement, it is also used to 'legitimate' bribes and engage in political and religious spectacles of excess in which political parties and religious movements vie to collect the most blood (see Copeman 2009a: chap. 5) *precisely because* of the aforementioned association. In this sense it enables the fruition of the phenomena to which its sign is opposed – hence my suggestion that public blood donation embodies a double-movement of reform and reversion.

Conclusion

This essay has offered a consideration of India's sanguinary politics through focusing principally on its artistic aspects. As I have tried to show, the portraits in blood produced by the Shaheed Smriti Chetna Samiti share features with the wider sanguinary politics concerning substantive identification between artist and icon and metonymy. Carsten (2011) has recently called attention to the unbounded properties of blood as a liquid form (both corporeally and conceptually). Employing this suggestive terminology, we might say that these portraits provide 'intimations of unboundedness'. The part given is an indication of the whole that is not given but which one is nevertheless willing to give if called upon.

Far less common than blood donation conducted on mass political occasions, blood portraiture does not partake of the competitive duelling between political parties (and indeed devotional movements) that has come to compromise perceptions of the sincerity of this latter mode of sanguinary political enunciation. For Gupta and his *samiti*, the promise that the names of the martyrs would be written in gold and eternally glorified has gone unfulfilled. The portraits were borne of this painful realization. A means of reviving faded memories, the portraits, too, began to fade, thus forming a kind of meditation on impermanence; the re-touching of the portraits also a re-touching of memory.

No doubt the use of blood as a medium *was* a tactical means of rousing interest and generating footfall. I have argued, however, that the significance of the medium extends well beyond mere calculative deployment. This is because, in being formed through acts of bleeding, the portraits constitute themselves the emulation they call for, indicating that it is not passive but active memory that the *samiti* hopes the portraits will inspire as both mnemonic devices *and* templates for action. The portraits may be considered a contemporary analogue of the call made by Bose for the citizenry to shed its blood. However, they are more 'representationally complex' than Bose's refrain – for they seek to stimulate willingness to shed one's blood in part through the use of blood to make that exhortation. Such bleeding is thus mimetic in two senses: in imitating the bleeding of one's sacrificial forebears, but also in terms of the willingness to sacrifice one's blood that it is supposed to incite in the viewer.

Moreover, the presence of the blood provider as physical residue within the painted image constitutes that image as enframed communion. The nationalist exchange relation invoked by Bose thereby becomes a form of patriotic *puja*. The literal nature of the affect the portraits embody – direct and unmediated from the heart, so to speak – lends further force to their function as not only models of but also models for sanguinary commitment. The larger Indian sanguinary politics, dominated by blood donation, seemed at one stage to promise a comparably 'transparent' mode of political enunciation. While it would be too simple to assert that blood donation has been recast as a dissembling political form – its continued enactment in a large variety of mass political and devotional settings suggests it continues to possess communicative efficacy of some kind – its political career nevertheless seems to exemplify 'the paradoxical tendency of transparency measures to yield, in practice, new opacities' (Mazzarella 2006: 476).

NOTES

Special thanks are due to Janet Carsten for the invitation to contribute to this book, and for her editorial care and attention. I am indebted to the other participants in the 2010 Edinburgh workshop out of which the present book arose. A draft was also presented at the University of Sussex, and I am grateful to audience members for their critical engagement and to Alice Street for the invitation.

[1] Revered in West Bengal and elsewhere in India, Subhas Chandra Bose is nevertheless a controversial figure as a result of opposing Mahatma Gandhi's non-violent method of overcoming colonial rule. This led Bose, during the Second World War, to ally with Nazi Germany and Fascist Italy. Though, as we shall see below, Bose was 'stoutly secular' (Guha 2007), this has not stopped the Hindu right (as well as the Communist Party) seeking to appropriate his legacy at various times.

[2] This is frequently in order to maintain caste distinctions based upon relative purity.

[3] Famously, Marc Quinn's *Self*, a frozen sculpture of the artist's head made from his own blood.

[4] *Mid-Day*, 25 January 2008.

[5] *http://www.rediff.com/news/2006/jan/03martyrs.htm* (accessed 21 January 2013).

[6] Bose himself is reported to have declared to his fellow revolutionaries: 'Our names will be written in gold letters in the history of free India; every martyr in this holy war will have a monument there'.

[7] Simpson and Corbridge have made a similar observation: 'Visitors to [India's] capital city, New Delhi, might be surprised to find so few memorials to Gandhi, Nehru, and other heroes of the Freedom Movement, although they will find faded photographs of the two men ... in the Block and District offices of the Indian state' (2006: 570).

[8] However, see Rampley (1993: 275) who notes that much Western art has also frequently been valued for its efficacy (ability to produce particular effects).

[9] See Copeman (2009*b*: 19-20) and Hugh-Jones (2011) on the common criticism that the use of excorporated human blood for purposes of political expressionism or art, if not ultimately donated for medical purposes, is wasteful of a potentially valuable resource.

[10] Quotations from *Indian Express*, 3 October 2001.

[11] 'A mosque built in Ayodhya by the Muslim Emperor Babar in the sixteenth century is believed by militant Hindus to have displaced a temple to Lord Rama, the God-king hero of the Ramayana, at the very site of his birth. In December 1992 [Hindu supremacist activists] demolished the mosque over the course of two days. Hindu-Muslim rioting then broke out in towns across north India' (Simpson & Corbridge 2006: 570).

[12] See note 5 above.

[13] *Tehelka*, 9 October 2009.

[14] See Gell (1999), on whose formulation I draw on here (which in turn draws on Simmel's theory of value).

[15] *The Hindu*, 2 February 2002.

REFERENCES

ALBERTI, F.B. 2010. *Matters of the heart: history, medicine, and emotion*. Oxford: University Press.

ALTER, J. 1992. *The wrestler's body: identity and ideology in North India*. Berkeley: University of California Press.

ANKER, S. & S. FRANKLIN 2011. Specimens as spectacles: reframing fetal remains. *Social Text* **29**, 103-25.

ARENDT, H. 1994. *Essays in understanding: uncollected and unpublished works by Hannah Arendt* (ed.) J. Kohn. New York: Harcourt Brace & Company.

BAIRY, T.S.R. 2009. Brahmins in the modern world: association as enunciation. *Contributions to Indian Sociology* **43**, 89-120.

BARBER, K. 2005. Text and performance in Africa. *Oral Tradition* **20**, 264-77.

BYNUM, C.W. 2007. *Wonderful blood: theology and practice in late medieval northern Germany and beyond*. Philadelphia: University of Pennsylvania Press.

CARSTEN, J. (ed.) 2007. *Ghosts of memory: essays on remembrance and relatedness*. Oxford: Blackwell.

——— 2011. Substance and relationality: blood in contexts. *Annual Review of Anthropology* **40**, 1-17.

COHEN, L. 1995. Holi in Banaras and the Mahaland of modernity. *GLQ* **2**, 399-424.

——— 2001. The other kidney: biopolitics beyond recognition. *Body & Society* **7**, **2–3**, 9–29.

——— 2008. Science, politics and dancing boys: propositions and accounts. *Parallax* **14**, 35-47.

CONNERTON, P. 2009. *How modernity forgets*. Cambridge: University Press.

COPEMAN, J. 2009*a*. *Veins of devotion: blood donation and religious experience in North India*. New Brunswick, N.J.: Rutgers University Press.

——— 2009*b*. Introduction: blood donation, bioeconomy, culture. *Body & Society* Special Issue: Blood donation, bioeconomy, culture (ed.) J. Copeman **15**: **2**, 1-28.

DAVIS, R.H. 1993. Indian art objects as loot. *Journal of Asian Studies* **52**, 22-48.

EISENLOHR, P. 2010. Materialities of entextualization: the domestication of sound reproduction in Mauritian Muslim devotional practices. *Journal of Linguistic Anthropology* **20**, 314-33.

ENGELKE, M. 2007. *A problem of presence: beyond scripture in an African Christian church*. Berkeley: University of California Press.

FULLER, C.J. 2004. *The camphor flame: popular Hinduism and society in India*. Princeton: University Press.

GELL, A. 1998. *Art and agency: an anthropological theory*. Oxford: Clarendon Press.

———— 1999. The technology of enchantment and the enchantment of technology. In *The art of anthropology: essays and diagrams* (eds) A. Gell & E. Hirsch, 159-86. London: Athlone Press.

GUHA, R. 2007. Our violent streak. *The Hindustan Times*, 5 September (available on-line: *http://www.hindustantimes.com/editorial-views-on/BigIdea/Our-violent-streak/Article1-246523.aspx*, accessed 22 January 2013).

HALBWACHS, M. 1950. *The collective memory*. Paris: Presses Universitaires de France.

HEUZE, G. 1992. Shiv Sena and 'national' Hinduism. *Economic and Political Weekly* **27**, 2189-95, 2253-63.

HINDUSTAN TIMES 2007. Hindu activists paint Lord Rama with blood to protest against Sethu Samundram project. 16 December (available on-line: *http://www.highbeam.com/doc/1P3-1399423571.html*, accessed 22 January 2013).

HUGH-JONES, S. 2011. Analyses de sang. *Terrain* **56**, 4-21.

INDIAN EXPRESS 1997. After the bloodletting, the blood donation. 22 May (available on-line: *http://www.financialexpress.com/old/ie/daily/19970522/14250753.html*, accessed 22 January 2013).

INGOLD, T. 2007. Materials against materiality. *Archaeological Dialogues* **14**, 1-16.

JAY, M. 2002. Somaesthetics and democracy: Dewey and contemporary body art. *Journal of Aesthetic Education* **36**: **4**, 55-69.

KRAUSE, I.B. 1989. Sinking heart: a Punjabi communication of distress. *Social Science & Medicine* **29**, 563-75.

KUCHLER, S. & H. MELION (eds) 1991. *Images of memory: on remembering and representation*. Washington, D.C.: Smithsonian Institution Press.

LAMBERT, H. 2000. Sentiment and substance in North Indian forms of relatedness. In *Cultures of relatedness* (ed.) J. Carsten, 73-89. Cambridge: University Press.

MACFARLANE, A. 1997. On creative and analytical methods (available on-line: *http://www.alanmacfarlane.com/TEXTS/holmes.pdf*, accessed 21 January 2013).

MARSDEN, M. 2005. *Living Islam: Muslim religious experience in Pakistan's north-west frontier*. Cambridge: University Press.

MAZZARELLA, W. 2006. Internet x-ray: e-governance, transparency, and the politics of immediation in India. *Public Culture* **18**, 473-505.

———— 2009. Affect: what is it good for? In *Enchantments of modernity: empire, nation, globalization* (ed.) S. Dube, 291-309. London: Routledge.

———— 2010. A torn performative dispensation: the affective politics of British World War II propaganda in India and the problem of legitimation in an age of mass publics. *South Asian History and Culture* **1**, 1-24.

MILLER, D. & F. PARROTT 2009. Loss and material culture in south London. *Journal of the Royal Anthropological Institute* (N.S.) **15**, 502-19.

NANDY, A. 1983. *The intimate enemy: loss and recovery of self under colonialism*. Delhi: Oxford University Press.

PALLADINO, P. 2010. Picturing the messianic: Agamben and Titian's *The Nymph* and *The Shepherd*. *Theory, Culture & Society* **27**: **1**, 94-109.

PINNEY, C. 2004. *Photos of the gods: the printed image and political struggle in India*. Delhi: Oxford University Press.

POWER, M. 1997. *The audit society: rituals of verification*. Oxford: University Press.

RAMASWAMY, S. 2008. Maps, mother/goddesses and martyrdom in modern India. *Journal of Asian Studies* **67**, 819-53.

RAMPLEY, M. 1993. Physiology as art: Nietzsche on form. *British Journal of Aesthetics* **33**, 271-80.

ROBERTS, N. 2010. Puzzles of representation: vote buying and 'fraudulent' conversion in a Chennai slum. Paper presented to the Association of Asian Studies Annual Meeting, Philadelphia, 27 March.

SCHNEIDER, D. 1980. *American kinship: a cultural account*. Chicago: University Press.

SIEBERS, T. 2003. The return to ritual: violence and art in the media age. *Journal for Cultural and Religious Theory* **5**: **1**, 9-32.

SIMPSON, E. & S. CORBRIDGE 2006. The geography of things that may become memories: the 2001 earthquake in Kachchh-Gujarat and the politics of rehabilitation in the pre-memorial era. *Annals of the Association of American Geographers* **96**, 566-85.

SPENCER, J. 1997. Post-colonialism and the political imagination. *Journal of the Royal Anthropological Institute* (N.S.) **3**, 1-19.

SSORIN-CHAIKOV, N. 2006. On heterochrony: birthday gifts to Stalin, 1949. *Journal of the Royal Anthropological Institute* (N.S.) **12**, 355-75.

TANEJA, N. 2001. Blood and saffron: the gory rituals of the Sangh Parivar. *People's Democracy* [Weekly Organ of the Communist Party of India (Marxist)] **XXV**: **41**, 14 October (available on-line: *http://pd.cpim.org/2001/oct14/2001_oct14_uswar_bjp.htm*, accessed 23 January 2012).

TAUSSIG, M. 1993. *Mimesis and alterity: a particular history of the senses.* New York: Routledge.

VAN DE PORT, M. 2011. (Not) made by the human hand: media consciousness and immediacy in the cultural production of the real. *Social Anthropology* **19**, 74-89.

WEIERMAIR, P. 2001. Reflections on blood in contemporary art. In *Blood: art, power, politics and pathology* (ed.) J.M. Bradburne, 205-15. Munich: Prestel.

YOUNG, L. 2007. The human heart: an overview. In *The heart* (ed.) J. Peto, 1-30. New Haven: Yale University Press.

ZELIZER, B. 1995. Reading the past against the grain. *Critical Studies in Mass Communication* **12**, 214-39.

9

Blood and the brain

Emily Martin *New York University*

The multiple meanings and symbolic resonance of blood: the missing blood

What is the relationship between the blood and the brain of the human body according to contemporary neuroscience and neuroanatomy? In a class on advanced cognitive neuroscience that I attended as an initial part of an ethnographic project on experimental psychology, I was struck by the absence of any mention of blood in relation to the brain in my assigned class texts, discussions, and lectures.[1] In the long sections on brain anatomy throughout our textbook there was no mention of blood vessels, and in the substantial chapter on cognitive deficits there was no mention of the role of blood in causing brain deficits (Ward 2006). My interest was piqued. I looked at many other popular representations of neuroscientific research – both texts and images – and found the same striking absence of any mention or depiction of blood in relation to the brain. Typical popular neuroscience images and drawings show and describe the anatomy of the brain devoid of the blood vessels that surround and permeate it. For example, of the fifteen illustrations of the brain in the entry 'The human brain' in Wikipedia, none show any trace of blood vessels.[2] Some images on the Wikipedia site show brain structures: the gray matter made up of neurones, which is anatomically divided into different parts that are known to have different functions (Fig. 9.1). But there are no blood vessels in the images. A profusely illustrated popular book, *Images of mind*, contains a historical discussion of how changes in blood flow to the brain were linked to specific forms of brain activity (Posner, Raichle & Goldman-Rakic 1997: 54-7). But none of the many anatomical or brain imaging illustrations in the book depict the vessels that bring blood to the brain. Another popular illustrated book, *Mapping the mind*, contains scanning or anatomical images of the brain on nearly every page. But the only mention of the brain's blood supply occurs in a brief case study of a person with a vascular abnormality (Carter 1999: 74-5). Why has the blood gone missing?

This question takes on more than casual interest because of the strikingly central symbolic roles blood has played historically in Euro-American ideas and practices about the body and soul. As Bettina Bildhauer shows in this volume, in late medieval thought blood served to define the outlines of the person, to hold body and soul

Blood: Will Out: Essays on Liquid Transfers and Flows, First Edition. Edited by Janet Carsten. © 2013 Royal Anthropological Institute of Great Britain & Ireland. Published 2013 by John Wiley & Sons Ltd.

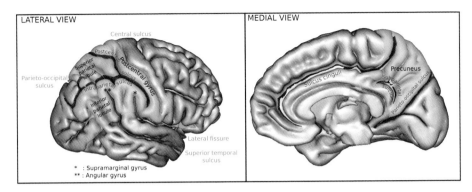

Figure 9.1. Parietal lobe, gyri and sulci of brain. Credit: Sebastiano23 (Own work) [CC-BY-SA-3.0 (http://creativecommons.org/licenses/by-sa/3.0)], via Wikimedia Commons. *http://commons.wikimedia.org/wiki/File%3AParietCapts.png*

together, and to grant access to the truth. 'That which was suffused with blood was the person' (p. S65). In many contemporary contexts blood can express complex messages about religious mysteries, as Fenella Cannell (this volume) shows for American Latter-day Saints, and blood can enliven the language used to describe financial markets and transactions, as Kath Weston (also this volume) shows for the symbolism of financial analysis.

In some of these contexts, it is not unusual for blood to be ranked hierarchically with other vital substances. If in medieval times blood was superior and miraculous, in descriptions of recent financial markets, 'blood' vies for importance with older metaphors based on physical force and energy. In my own earlier work on reproductive biology (Martin 1992 [1987]), I found hierarchies among types of blood in the human body. The lowest kind of blood was menstrual blood, conceived as a waste product, merely the result of a failed conception. So crucial was the reproductive purpose of the female body and so debasing was its failure that one biology textbook could describe menstruation as 'the uterus crying for want of a baby' (Ganong 1985: 63). Menstrual blood was the sign that a woman's body had failed in its proper purpose.

Given the strong symbolic associations commonly present in understandings of blood, its absence from contemporary depictions of the brain calls for investigation. Has the blood of the body been demoted to a lower realm, and therefore come to be depicted as separated from the higher realm of pure thought: that is, the neural tissue? If so, is this demotion connected to a widespread tendency to privilege the neural matter of the brain as the source of more and more kinds of human activity, from neuro-aesthetics and neuro-culture to neuro-economics and neuro-psychology, a trend Fernando Vidal (2011) has called 'neuro-x'?

To begin exploration of this question, I went in search of more specialized literature where the blood in the brain might be mentioned. To find descriptions and images of brain vasculature in contemporary scientific or popular science materials, I had to go to children's science literature (Chudler 2011), to neuroanatomy textbooks (Fix 2007: 40; Snell 2009: 474; Waxman 2003: 92), or to medical literature focused on pathological conditions such as aneurysm or stroke. These images make it clear that the brain is perfused with blood vessels and suggest that the absence of blood in at least some cognitive neuroscience texts and mainstream popular media is nothing minor.

Ghostly blood

Despite the lack of illustrations of blood vessels in cognitive neuroscience texts, blood does have a kind of ghostly presence there. The primary tool for visualizing cognitive functions today is functional magnetic resource imaging (fMRI). fMRI scanning (like its predecessor, positron emission tomography [PET] scanning) detects variable blood flow to the capillaries that pervade every part of the brain (Fig. 9.2).

Greater blood flow in particular parts of the brain is taken to indicate greater neuronal activity there. Subjects inside fMRI machines are given tasks that carefully pinpoint different cognitive functions like memory or attention. As the subject performs these tasks, the fMRI scans the brain and produces images of where there is the most blood flow. So all fMRI images are actually pictures of blood flow within the brain. But in this narrative from an educational television video, it is apparent how quickly the blood's function is glossed over:

> When a particular area of my brain is working hard, extra blood flows there [images of blood flowing into capillaries in neural tissue] through my arteries to provide energy for the active nerve cells. The scanner can detect these changes in blood flow, giving us a completely new window into the fascinating world of the mind. [At this point the audio changes to classical music, and the video to images of grey matter with highlighted coloured sections showing extra blood flow linked to neural activity – no more blood activity is shown directly for the remainder of the video]. Using this technique we can actually watch the brain work.[3]

The video then shows the brain's grey matter turning on its axis, with different parts highlighted in colour, while the narrator says 'this part of the brain is where we process all sounds, and this is where we appreciate music. Amazingly, there are even separate

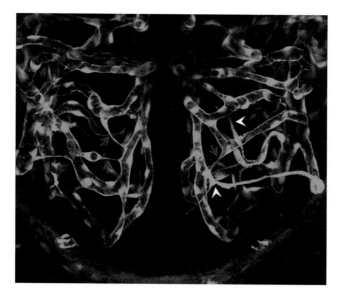

Figure 9.2. Brain blood vasculature as a function of blood flow. (Arrows indicate the relatively few sites, compared to other tissues, where capillaries in the brain are shut off.) Credit: Caitlin Sedwick [CC-BY-2.5 (http://creativecommons.org/licenses/by/2.5)], via Wikimedia Commons. *http://commons. wikimedia.org/wiki/File%3ABrain_blood_vasculature_as_a_function_of_blood_flow_-_journal.pbio. 1001375.g001.png*

bits for melody, for rhythm and for pitch'. What we are watching are pictures of increased blood flow, but the blood has been left behind and the neural processing – for which the blood is a sign – has taken its place.

Finding the blood

Since I had learned little in my cognitive neuroscience class about how blood interacts with the brain, I set out to get some answers. The key concept, not surprisingly, is the blood-brain barrier. The concept is usually attributed to Paul Ehrlich, who in 1885 injected Trypan blue dye into the circulatory system of animals and noted that the dye stained all the animal's organs but did not appear in the brain or other nervous tissue (Ehrlich 1885).[4]

Ehrlich thought that the dye was not taken up by the nervous system because it lacked 'affinity' with the dye, the way some cloth resists taking up dye. Subsequently in 1909, Ehrlich's student, Edwin Goldmann, did the reverse experiment and injected dye into the cerebral spinal fluid (CSF) of animals. The animals died, but not before Goldmann could see that the dye stained the brain and spinal cord but did not circulate to the rest of the body (Goldmann 1909). At this point it was something of a puzzle how the brain received nourishment and discarded waste, since blood was somehow being kept from circulating to the brain. One special kind of tissue in the brain, the choroid plexuses, did stain blue: these are capillary rich tissues that line part of the ventricles of the brain. Reasonably, Goldmann hypothesized that the brain gained nourishment and discarded waste through the CSF, via the choroid plexuses (Goldmann 1912). Perhaps reluctant to discard the conviction of his mentor, Ehrlich, that lesser affinity explained why the brain did not take up dye, Goldmann did not promote the idea of a barrier between blood and brain. Goldmann could have done so, because the term 'blood-brain barrier' (BBB) had been introduced in 1900 by Lewandowsky. Lewandowsky observed that certain pharmacological substances produced no neurological effect when injected intravenously but produced neurological symptoms when injected into the CSF (Lewandowsky 1900; see also Bradbury 1979; Clarke & O'Malley 1968; Mott 1913).

Anatomical understanding of the BBB awaited the greater resolution of images provided by the electron microscope in the late 1960s. The contemporary view of the anatomy of the BBB was explained to me by a biology professor experienced in teaching premedical undergraduates:

> I'll start with our circulatory system. We have what is called a closed circulatory system ... the blood leaves the heart and comes all the way back to the heart so all that's happening in closed tubes. That poses a problem – so how is it going to deliver the nutrients, hormones, or whatever, or pick up waste products because it's always inside these tubes? Suppose you wanted to water the lawn and the water stays inside the hose? ... You realize pretty quickly they can't be completely closed, they must let some things out and others back in. So where our blood vessels become permeable – allow things to come out and go back in – happens in the capillaries. Capillaries in different parts of our body are more or less tightly sealed so what can get into the brain and come out of it is very tightly regulated ... a capillary is formed by a cell, one cell, when its nucleus sends out a sort of tongue, called a philopodium, this big flat thing that wraps around and forms a tube. So individual cells from the blood vessel form the capillary. Endothelial cells form the surface facing the blood. Where it comes back and connects to itself it doesn't fuse, it can connect tightly or loosely. In most parts of the body, capillaries are relatively leaky so that molecules can be delivered to or taken up from the tissues. But with the tight junctions in the brain, most things can't leak out.
>
> The astrocytes [Fig. 9.3] make the blood-brain barrier even tighter. Astrocytes are neural cells, but not neurones, and they are thought of as support cells for the super-magisterial neurones that do the work. They wrap around the capillaries: don't you dare let anything out into my brain! They make a double layer ... a continuous layer around the capillary ... They cover the entire surface of the capillary

Figure 9.3. The blood-brain barrier and astrocytes type 1. Credit: Ben Brahim Mohammed (Own work) [CC-BY-3.0 (http://creativecommons.org/licenses/by/3.0)], via Wikimedia Commons. *http://commons.wikimedia.org/wiki/File%3ABlood_Brain_Barriere.jpg*

with what are called 'feet'. They have pumps or pores that will let only the right things through: glucose, hormones, salt ions, water, oxygen.

These capillaries are all over the brain – you can't see them in the illustrations that show the major blood vessels in the brain because they are so small, but they are embedded everywhere. Each one of them is covered in its own BBB. Every neurone is within millionths of a meter of a capillary.

The brain also has another circulatory system – the cerebral spinal fluid – but it is nowhere near adequate to provide full circulatory support.

In sum, the brain has two circulatory fluids: the CSF, which is manufactured inside the brain itself, and blood, which is elaborately purified by the BBB before it reaches any neural cells.

Controlling the blood

In 1987 when I published *The woman in the body*, I used an illustration from a pre-medical textbook current at the time to demonstrate the controlling functions of the human body that were assumed to lie within the brain. In the illustration, the brain and spinal cord are visible within the body of a man playing chess to illustrate that they integrate and control all bodily functions. At the time, I was interested in the assumptions that would make it seem logical to describe menopause as a chaotic loss of centralized control over hormone production. As I learn about the blood-brain barrier twenty years later, it seems to me that the brain is still envisioned as the controller of the rest of the body. But blood, rather than a sign of regular or irregular hormonal production as in menstruation and menopause, appears here in a maternal guise. The brain needs blood. It relies on blood for nourishment and for removal of waste. The pure cognition produced by the brain's neurones, surrounded by clear cerebral spinal fluid, still relies on lower-level functions provided by the body's blood. The body's blood is purified by the tight junctions and the astrocytes, to be sure, but it still serves lower functions compared to neurones. Here is an excerpt from further conversation with the biologist quoted earlier, with my remarks in brackets:

[Why is it that 999 out of 1,000 pictures of the brain don't show anything about the blood?]
Neuroscientists couldn't care less about the blood.
[Why not?]

If you were to show pictures of a city and all of the things taking place – the mayor's office, the policemen's office, the schools, all the activities everybody is doing that make up the sort of neural network of the city – would you show the water supply and the sewer supply?

[Probably not, no, that's how they think about it?]

Right, it's just supporting all of those activities, it's not directing them, not engaging in neural processing.

[So it provides nourishment and takes away the waste, and it's red and the colour of earth – so it's female. And brain is clear, white, fluid – pure thought – and in charge of everything and so it's male?]

Well, I wouldn't have gone there but I do see what you are saying. It's actually the grey matter of the brain where most of the processing takes place ...

[No, I meant that the clear, pure, ethereal spirit fluid of the cerebral spinal fluid contrasts to the red, vital, but frightening and dangerous blood. What do women do? They nourish and they clean up. What do men do? They think and direct everything and they are served.]

CSF is more ethereal, right.

[Do you think all this is crazy?]

I don't think it's the dominant reason for ignoring blood, nobody wants to think about that because, first of all it's another level, removed from ... here are the neurones doing all this high-speed processing, with incredible complexity. Differences in blood flow can perturb this processing but nobody wants to think about that. If you are a neuroscientist, you are not interested in strokes, embolism, clots, because those just degrade what wonderful things the brain can do.

[So it's dangerous, blood, the whole system that brings blood to the brain?]

One third of us die because of strokes.

This conversation made me curious about whether CSF might be considered more ethereal than blood, but compared to neural tissue – the stuff of thought – it could still appear relatively primitive, perhaps like the 'blood' of the brain. Historically, CSF has attracted the gamut of descriptions: from 'water' surrounding the brain (Hippocrates), or 'excremental liquid' eventually to be purged into the nose (Galen), to 'spirituous lymph' or 'highly gifted juice' (Swedenborg), or fluid in which the brain is suspended like the foetus is suspended in the womb (Magendie) (Hajdu 2003: 334-5).

Some of these historical associations are retained in the terminology of brain anatomy. In my course on cognitive neuroscience, I learned that the many sections and sub-sections of neural tissue are named with terms that refer to their topological position (front, back, top, bottom, middle) together with Latin or Greek terms that describe function or shape: insula (island), lobe (roundish projecting part), cortex (outer shell), gyrus (circle). In contrast, compare the terminology we learned for the anatomy of the base of the brain, the site where CSF originates. We learned that the CSF is produced primarily by a structure known as the choroid plexus in the lateral, third, and fourth ventricles. CSF flows from the lateral ventricle to the third ventricle through the interventricular foramen (also called the foramen of Monro). The third ventricle and fourth ventricle are connected to each other by the cerebral aqueduct (also called the aqueduct of Sylvius). CSF then flows into the subarachnoid space through the foramina of Luschka (there are two of these) and the foramen of Magendie.

Monro, Sylvius, Luschka, and Magendie were all scholars from seventeenth-/ eighteenth-century Europe who discovered these structures through dissection. In classical and early modern times, most interest lay in the ventricles, where mental experience was thought to reside. Accordingly, drawings presented the ventricles in exacting detail, whereas the cortex was often undifferentiated, and sometimes drawn to resemble intestines (Gross 1999: 24-5, 120; Ward 2006: 6).

To contemporary ears these names are archaic, to be sure, historically specific, owned even: these structures and their names remain tied to their origins and the individual scientist who discovered them. By contrast, the grey matter sections of the brain, which (with some exceptions) only began to be differentiated by function in the nineteenth century, have modern technical names like frontal cortex, cingulate gyrus, or medial temporal gyrus (Gross 1999: 130).

Just why the blood of the body and the 'blood' of the brain might be relegated to the primitive and female corner of this cosmology would require further anthropological and historical exploration. Anthropologists have explored the cultural significance of blood as a marker of certain kinds of moral relationships, especially those that extend across generations (Cannell, this volume; Carsten 2000; Weston 1997). Attached to historically embedded and culturally specific meanings, blood might seem the opposite of pure, abstract cognitive mental operations. In the logic of the classical and Galenic systems, the heart and the blood with which it was associated were seen as connected to the emotions: '[T]he heart warmed the blood in order to generate and sustain particular emotional states; it moved in response to the sensations of anger, love, and fear; it was affected by the operation of the soul, with its links to mind and body' (Alberti 2010: 4; see also Bildhauer, this volume). Influenced by Aristotle, Renaissance physicians pictured the blood, sent round the body by the heart, as involved with the desires of the soul: 'The humours were concocted in the heart, and the spirits produced were sent around the body to effect the soul's desires' (Alberti 2010: 21). The heart relied on 'melancholy blood to produce pain and sadness; blood and choler for anger' (Alberti 2010: 21). The brain, in contrast, was seen as cold and wet; hence it could provide a counterbalance to the heat of the heart (Gross 1999: 20).

Historians have also found rich layers of meaning attached to religious uses of blood in medieval times. According to Caroline Bynum's research, blood in ritual images and tokens of faith had a dense web of symbols attached to it and was, by turns, 'life and death, continuity and separation, immutability and violation. It is both a protest against change and a breaching or pouring forth. It is spilled out and lifted up' (2007: 136). It would over-simplify this complex account to single out any theme, but Bynum is at pains to stress that in medieval theories of physiology, the 'fetus is formed from maternal uterine blood, animated by the blood or seed of the father and is fed by blood, both in the womb and from the breast' (2007: 158). Hence 'in a startling sense, the blood from which the individual is constituted is gendered female; the body *is* the mother's blood' (2007: 158, emphasis in original). In medieval times, menstrual blood was the substance of generation rather than, as now, the sign of degeneration.

With William Harvey's mechanistic metaphors in the seventeenth century, the way was paved for the heart to change from a living thing to a pump. In short order, Descartes's dualism of mind and body fully replaced humoral understandings with mechanical understandings of both mind and body. In the eighteenth century, emotions became understood as primarily physical phenomena, a product of interaction among the ideas transmitted by the external senses (sight, smell, etc.) to the mind, which aroused nervous power and led to the actions of the passions. 'Lively and exhilarating' passions were associated with the influx of blood, and 'languid and depressing' ones with the outflow of blood (Alberti 2010: 31).

But the passions themselves were on the road to being displaced in importance by the mind and brain.

It was the brain that would be prioritized in discussions of emotions and the self. Since the nineteenth century and the segregation of the body and the mind into a series of disparate parts, it has become commonplace for the brain to be considered the organ most associated with life (indeed 'brain death' has succeeded 'heart death' as the number one criterion for determining life cessation) (Alberti 2010: 7; see also Gross 1999: 7).

In his late nineteenth-century work on psychology, William James summarized his view of the primacy of brain activity, which relegated the brain's circulatory system to dependent status. Describing experiments on three persons whose brains were exposed by an injury to the skull, which allowed the experimenter, Angelo Mosso, to take tracings of the blood pulse to those areas, James reports:

> The intra-cranial blood-pressure rose immediately whenever the subject was spoken to, or when he began to think actively, as in solving a problem in mental arithmetic. Mosso gives in his work a large number of reproductions of tracings which show the instantaneity of the change of blood-supply, whenever the mental activity was quickened by any cause whatever, intellectual or emotional (James 1950 [1890]: 98-9).

Although James is clear about the primacy of mental activity causing increased blood supply, he is also clear that the brain is full of blood: '[T]he brain itself is an excessively vascular organ, a sponge full of blood, in fact' (1950 [1890]: 98).

Over the centuries, the brain replaced the heart as the primary site for locating the emotions. Along the way it became plausible to simply omit the heart's blood from the brain, to elide James's image of the brain as a 'sponge full of blood'.

Vessels of the blood

Scientific papers specifically on the significance of the blood-brain barrier sometimes explicitly call attention to the elision of the BBB from most accounts of the brain. One describes the omission of the BBB as a

> vexing impediment. Neuroscience textbooks bury it in the appendix, Ph.D. programs give it a cursory treatment, and pharmaceutical companies have tried to ignore it. But the blood-brain barrier is a stubbornly real obstacle for potential drugs against many disorders of the central nervous system (Miller 2002: 1116).

The BBB, as this writer indicates, is of intense contemporary interest for some because it seems to hold the key to enabling psychotropic drugs, among others, to enter the brain. So BBB research with the goal of drug transport is one area where blood-brain interactions are treated directly. The other such area concerns pathological events when blood breaks its bonds and causes a stroke or other cerebral vascular accident. Although this area is too large for me to discuss here, I can make one observation, which relates to the importance of control in standard Euro-American views of the human body. This is the obvious point that blood is imagined as contained – flowing in tubes called blood vessels. In the educational video I mentioned earlier, a 3D angiogram is used to visualize an aneurysm in a woman's brain, accompanied by a drawing of the blood flowing in a hose-like tube. The aneurysm is pictured as a bulge in the wall of the 'hose'. The first-line remedy was to fill the bulge with metal coils, to prevent too much pressure on the weakened walls of the bulge, but when the coils began to slip out, a second remedy was applied: a stent, which was intended to replace the walls of the tube.[5]

No one could dispute that the bursting of an aneurysm would be a catastrophic event. But the way Western medicine views the blood as safe only when contained within the walls of its vessels is worth looking into more closely. In *The expressiveness of the body*, Shigehisa

Kuriyama makes the compelling point that the separation of the nerves from the arteries and the connection of the arteries to the pulse of the blood happened very early in Greek medicine. He summarizes: '[P]icturing the tubular artery remained throughout the enduring basis of Western pulse analysis' (Kuriyama 2002: 3). Arteries and veins were depicted as 'tubular conduits walling in vital fluids' (Kuriyama 2002: 47). Eventually, physicians connected these early notions to the idea that the heart was the pump responsible for the movement of blood and the beat of the pulse. These notions were also behind Western medical practitioners' preoccupation with blood-letting, a remedy for the fearful excess of blood that could impair health (Kuriyama 2002: 207-8).

Unavoidable as these ideas might seem, Kuriyama argues that quite different pictures guided Chinese medicine from its inception. Instead of conduits, there were rivers that spread and wandered; instead of blood, there was vital energy that moved through the body like a wave (Kuriyama 2002: 52).

Facing blood in the brain

People who have had strokes or aneurysms provide a fruitful way to understand how the logic of anatomy is experienced in daily life. An Internet site with narratives written by people with aneurysms shows the dominance of the idea that blood needs to be confined in 'tubular conduits'.

Leaking:
- The aneurysm didn't leak, rather it burst the artery.
- No medical person can explain why in most cases the aneurysm will burst but in my case it was a slow leak. As one nurse in the local hospital claimed, there was an angel on my shoulder for the duration.
- They noticed a leak in one of my repaired aneurysms.
- I have an active leak.
- My low blood pressure had saved my life, allowing the aneurysm only to leak blood instead of a full blowout and death or disability.
- When they found I had a leak they transported me the next day to another city and hospital. I had laid from Saturday night till Thursday with a leak going on inside my brain and no one knew.

Too much blood:
- There was too much blood on my brain to find the aneurysm.
- There was so much blood in my head that the blood was moving my brain to the right side. Unbelievable!
- My brain was called an angry brain it was so red. My head had so much blood in it they did not know what they were dealing with. They sent it to pathology.
- When they opened me up the aneurysm ruptured and spewed blood all over the operating room. The doctor started suctioning as quickly as possible to prevent any damage to my brain or spine.

Bursting, rupturing, blowing out:
- The people there did a CAT scan, and they saw the vast AVM (Arteriovenous Malformation). It's a tangle of blood vessels that forms before you're born. It can be in your head or along your spine. If it ruptures, it can kill you instantaneously.
- You may wonder how I can live just sitting around waiting to 'blow a gasket' (as my husband calls it).
- They thought the aneurysm was ready to blow.
- The Day My Brain Exploded: Though my subarachnoid aneurysm burst on Dec. 19, 2002, the reality of the whole situation is just now settling in.
- As I waited I felt like a time bomb – tick, tick, tick – there is no choice than they would go in but I would have more problems. So you know that I feel that time bomb will never stop ticking.
- Then one of the medics was checking my eyes and I 'blew a fuse.'[6]

Even with only this brief glance into how people talk about blood in the brain, it is clear that there are no ideas about waves of vital force or meandering, spreading rivers of energy, but rather consistent notions of pipes under pressure in a closed system. Any break or leak, not to mention too great an increase of pressure, threatens the pristine and bloodless brain above all.

It would be instructive to explore what would happen if we imagined the brain differently: as suffused with the blood it actually does contain, blood that might be given a more elevated status than a 'ladies' auxiliary' to the neurones. I would be interested in whether such a change could modify popular conceptions of how the brain/mind relates to the body and perhaps even how patients experience the trauma of a stroke or aneurysm. Images that depict the capillaries in the human brain are rare. One that can be found on the Internet is an electron micrograph of a male brain post-mortem.[7] The capillaries have been injected with a polymer to make them visible, and they are pictured as a dense mat of white lines around and in every part of the neural matter. The photograph is of a section of the brain only about 1 mm wide, which gives an idea of the great number of capillaries that pervade the brain. Some researchers are already anticipating a larger role for the circulation of blood in the brain. In some corners of medical imaging research and cognitive neuroscience itself, the role of the heart and the respiratory system on the images of the brain made by means of fMRI is already being investigated (Chen & Calhoun 2011). Although these explorations are now in their infancy, it is certain that the relationships between the heart-blood and brain systems will be understood better as time goes on. It is less certain whether the blood will remain the 'female' half of the brain, dangerous and powerful in its vitality, and subordinate to the cognitive domain of the brain's neurones. Whatever new visions of the blood in the brain emerge, it is certain that cultural factors, involving ideas about gender or other distinctions, are likely to play a part. When scientists, like anyone else, pay attention to an object in the world, they inevitably foreground selective aspects of the object for the purpose of explaining or understanding what they are interested in. As Kath Weston argues (this volume), when metaphors or other figurative devices appeal to the nature of biological processes, they carry the implication that what they describe is part of the nature of things, rather than a contingent, culturally inflected choice. When a view of the brain and its blood, carrying implications for a gendered division of labour, seems to become part of the nature of things, alternative accounts seem less possible. As Weston points out so vividly in the case of the circulation of the economy's lifeblood, such images 'pre-empt debate', render opposed views invisible, and make it seem fruitless to imagine the world could be otherwise.

In neuroscience more broadly, there has recently been a 'revolution in our conception of the plasticity of the adult mammalian brain' (Gross 2000: 72). This revolution has surprisingly brought blood in the brain to the fore in new ways. In the early 1990s, when the dogma that no new neurones are added to the adult mammalian brain began to be seriously challenged, Isaacs and colleagues showed that vigorous exercise increased blood flow to the cerebellum in adult rats (Isaacs, Anderson, Alcantara, Black & Greenough 1992). The increased blood flow is thought to be one possible reason for the link between exercise and the genesis of new neurones (neurogenesis) (Gross 2000: 70). By the end of the 1990s, neurogenesis was firmly established in adult primates (marmoset and macaque) (Gould *et al.* 1999) and humans (Eriksson *et al.* 1998). There was an efflorescence of research to follow up the implications of this momentous paradigm shift (Gross 2000: 72; Rubin 2009). But it was not until ten years later that radically new data emerged about the role of the blood vessels perfusing particular niches in the subventricular zone (SVZ) of the rat brain (Tavazoie *et al.* 2008).

Specialized capillary cells penetrate the BBB allowing small blood-borne molecules into the brain, a finding that not only changes the concept of the BBB, but also suggests that blood-borne messengers are involved somehow in the generation of neurones from the stem cells now known to exist in this region (Tavazoie *et al.* 2008: 285-6).

It would be foolhardy to predict how the metaphors I have traced in this essay will sort out in the face of this dramatic upheaval. Will the blood that makes its way into the SVZ be seen as of old: a maternal, nourishing helper subordinate to the main players, the neural stem cells, now in possession of the power to regenerate themselves? Or will the flow of blood in the brain act as a guide for exploring brain function, perhaps linking neurones to the rest of the body through the circulation of blood? This would be a further paradigm shift, replacing the established hierarchical gendered set of metaphors with another set – a complex, whole organism-interacting system. Such a system could embrace emotions, perceptions, sociality, and all other experiences that are part of human life.

Concluding remarks

My ethnographic project on experimental psychology is only at its beginnings, and hence my conclusions must be tentative. However, my preliminary exploration indicates that the absence of blood from many contemporary depictions of the brain does not mean that blood has lost its symbolic salience. Even if future understandings continue to relegate blood to the lower, 'female' portions of the human body, we will have to wrestle with the danger the sequestered blood poses to the pure neural realm of cognition. The concept of the blood-brain barrier can lead us to think of blood and brain as separate, as if blood were for the body but not the brain. In fact, via the selective regulation of the BBB, the brain is perfused with capillaries, James' 'sponge full of blood'. The 'super-magisterial neurones' require a constant supply of blood to do whatever work they do. As we have seen, the ubiquitous use of fMRI is dependent on blood flow in the brain, while relegating it to a ghostly invisibility. My initial question was whether picturing the brain as made up solely of neural tissue (and its fluid, the CSF) plays into the increasing tendency to see neural processing as the source of most human activities. Given the preliminary nature of my research, this must remain an open question. But at the least I can say that if we listen to either those who live with the results of a brain aneurysm or those who develop ways to deliver drugs to the brain through the BBB, we can see that the idea of a brain without blood is a mirage. The brain without blood is not merely a metaphor, it is a brain that cannot support life fully. None the less this powerful mirage may be playing a role in entrenching the believability of a purely cognitive view of human capacities: as if the 'incredible complex' work of neurones were only carried out in the brain; and as if any neurones could do their work without the nourishment of blood.

NOTES

I thank the conference participants and especially Janet Carsten for all of their valuable editorial insights. Much appreciation goes to the anonymous *JRAI* reviewers for their suggestions, to Beatrix Rubin for holding a conference on 'The Plastic Brain', and Richard Cone for checking my facts about neurogenesis.

[1] This is a project on the history of scientific research on 'attention' and on the constitution of the human as an experimental subject. In addition to taking classes in cognitive neuroscience, I am volunteering as a subject in psychological experiments on cognition and emotion.

[2] *http://en.wikipedia.org/wiki/Human_brain* (accessed 24 January 2013).

³ 'The mysteries of human brain' (video, available on-line: *http://www.youtube.com/watch?v=gLxU8oge7vg*, accessed 24 January 2013).

⁴ The dye was called a 'vital' dye because it did not kill the animal. The dye was produced by the German textile industry, which is no doubt an interesting story in itself.

⁵ As note 3.

⁶ Aneurysm & AVM Support website (*http://stu.westga.edu/~wmaples/brain*, accessed 28 January 2013).

⁷ *http://www.envinfo.org* (accessed 28 January 2013).

REFERENCES

ALBERTI, F.B. 2010. *Matters of the heart: history, medicine, and emotion.* Oxford: University Press.

BRADBURY, M.W.B. 1979. *The concept of a blood-brain barrier.* Chichester: Wiley.

BYNUM, C.W. 2007. *Wonderful blood: theology and practice in late medieval northern Germany and beyond.* Philadelphia: University of Pennsylvania Press.

CARSTEN, J. 2000. *Cultures of relatedness: new approaches to the study of kinship.* Cambridge: University Press.

CARTER, R. 1999. *Mapping the mind.* Berkeley: University of California Press.

CHEN, Z. & V. CALHOUN 2011. The impact of respiratory and cardiac effects on the phase and magnitude of resting-state fMRI signal (Proceedings Paper). In *Medical imaging 2011: biomedical applications in molecular, structural, and functional imaging* (eds) J.B. Weaver & R.C. Molthen, Proc. SPIE 7965, 79652A.1-79652A.10.

CHUDLER, E. 2011. Neuroscience for kids: the blood supply of the brain (available on-line: *faculty.washington.edu/chudler/vessel.html*, accessed 22 January 2013).

CLARKE, E. & C.D. O'MALLEY 1968. *The human brain and spinal cord: a historical study illustrated by writings from antiquity to the twentieth century.* Berkeley: University of California Press.

EHRLICH, P. 1885. *Das Sauerstoff-Bedürfniss des Organismus: Eine farbenanalytische Studie.* Berlin: August Hirschwald.

ERIKSSON, P.S., E. PERFILIEVA, T. BJÖRK-ERIKSSON, A.M. ALBORN, C. NORDBORG, D.A. PETERSON & F.H. GAGE 1998. Neurogenesis in the adult human hippocampus. *Nature Medicine* 4, 1313-17.

FIX, J.D. 2007. *Neuroanatomy.* Philadelphia: Lippincott Williams & Wilkins.

GANONG, W.F. (ed.) 1985. *Review of medical physiology* (Twelfth edition). Los Altos, Calif.: Lange Medical Publishers.

GOLDMANN, E. 1909. *Die äussere und innere Sekretion des gesunden Organismus im Lichte der 'Vitalen Färbung'.* Tübingen: H. Laupp'schen Buchhandlung.

——— 1912. On a new method of examining normal and diseased tissues by means of intra-vitam staining. *Proceedings of the Royal Society of London. Series B, Containing Papers of a Biological Character* 85: 577, 146-56.

GOULD, E., A.J. REEVES, M. FALLAH, P. TANAPAT, C.G. GROSS & E. FUCHS 1999. Hippocampal neurogenesis in adult Old World primates. *Proceedings of the National Academy of Sciences* 96, 5263-7.

GROSS, C.G. 1999. *Brain, vision, memory: tales in the history of neuroscience.* Cambridge, Mass.: MIT Press.

——— 2000. Neurogenesis in the adult brain: death of a dogma. *Nature Reviews Neuroscience* 1, 67-73.

HAJDU, S.I. 2003. Discovery of the cerebrospinal fluid. *Annals of Clinical & Laboratory Science* 33, 334-6.

ISAACS, K.R., B.J. ANDERSON, A.A. ALCANTARA, J.E. BLACK & W.T. GREENOUGH 1992. Exercise and the brain: angiogenesis in the adult rat cerebellum after vigorous physical activity and motor skill learning. *Journal of Cerebral Blood Flow & Metabolism* 12, 110-19.

JAMES, W. 1950 [1890]. *The principles of psychology.* New York: Dover.

KURIYAMA, S. 2002. *The expressiveness of the body and the divergence of Greek and Chinese medicine.* New York: Zone.

LEWANDOWSKY, M. 1900. Zur Lehre der Zerebrospinalflussigkeit. *Zeitschrift für Klinischer Medizin* 40, 480-4.

MARTIN, E. 1992 [1987]. *The woman in the body: a cultural analysis of reproduction.* Boston: Beacon.

MILLER, G. 2002. Drug targeting: breaking down barriers. *Science* 297: 5584, 1116-18.

MOTT, F.W. 1913. The late professor Edwin Goldmann's investigations on the central nervous system by vital staining. *The British Medical Journal* 2: 2753, 871-3.

POSNER, M.I., M.E. RAICHLE & P. GOLDMAN-RAKIC 1997. *Images of mind.* New York: Scientific American Library.

RUBIN, B.P. 2009. Changing brains: the emergence of the field of adult neurogenesis. *BioSocieties* 4, 407-24.

SNELL, R.S. 2009. *Clinical neuroanatomy.* Philadelphia: Lippincott Williams & Wilkins.

Tavazoie, M., L. van der Veken, V. Silva-Vargas, M. Louissaint, L. Colonna, B. Zaidi, J.M. Garcia-Verdugo & F. Doetsch 2008. A specialized vascular niche for adult neural stem cells. *Cell Stem Cell* **3**, 279-88.

Vidal, F. 2011. The cerebral subject. Lecture given for The Psyences Project, New York University, 11 February.

Ward, J. 2006. *The student's guide to cognitive neuroscience*. New York: Psychology Press.

Waxman, S.G. 2003. *Clinical neuroanatomy*. New York: Lange Medical Books/McGraw-Hill, Medical Pub. Division.

Weston, K. 1997. *Families we choose: lesbians, gays, kinship*. New York: Columbia University Press.

Index